Principled Agents?

Principled Agents?

The Political Economy of Good Government

Timothy Besley

OXFORD
UNIVERSITY PRESS

OXFORD
UNIVERSITY PRESS

Great Clarendon Street, Oxford OX2 6DP

Oxford University Press is a department of the University of Oxford.
It furthers the University's objective of excellence in research, scholarship,
and education by publishing worldwide in

Oxford New York

Auckland Cape Town Dar es Salaam Hong Kong Karachi
Kuala Lumpur Madrid Melbourne Mexico City Nairobi
New Delhi Shanghai Taipei Toronto

With offices in

Argentina Austria Brazil Chile Czech Republic France Greece
Guatemala Hungary Italy Japan Poland Portugal Singapore
South Korea Switzerland Thailand Turkey Ukraine Vietnam

Oxford is a registered trade mark of Oxford University Press
in the UK and in certain other countries

Published in the United States
by Oxford University Press Inc., New York

British Library Cataloguing in Publication Data
Data available

Library of Congress Cataloging in Publication Data
Data available

Typeset by SPI Publisher Services, Pondicherry, India
Printed in Great Britain
on acid-free paper by
Clays Ltd., St Ives plc., Suffolk

ISBN 978-0-19-927150-4 (Hbk.)
ISBN 978-0-19-928391-0 (Pbk.)

1

For my parents

Contents

Preface to Paperback Edition   x

Preface   xi

Acknowledgements   xiv

1   **Competing views of government**   1
     1.1   The issues   1
     1.2   This book   2
     1.3   Background   4
            1.3.1   The size of government   4
            1.3.2   Corruption   10
            1.3.3   Property rights   14
            1.3.4   Trust and turnout   17
     1.4   Economic policy making   20
            1.4.1   Foundations   21
            1.4.2   Good policies   23
            1.4.3   The public choice critique of welfare
                     economics   25
     1.5   Political economy   27
     1.6   Incentives and selection in politics   36
     1.7   Concluding comments   43

2   **The anatomy of government failure**   45
     2.1   Introduction   45
     2.2   Three notions of government failure   48
            2.2.1   Pareto inefficiency   48
            2.2.2   Distributional failures   49
            2.2.3   Wicksellian failures   52
            2.2.4   Comparisons   53
     2.3   An example: financing a public project   55
            2.3.1   Private provision   56
            2.3.2   Government provision   57

Contents

2.4 Sources of government failure   59
    2.4.1 Ignorance   59
    2.4.2 Influence   61
    2.4.3 The quality of leadership   68
2.5 Sources of political failure   70
    2.5.1 Voting   71
    2.5.2 Log-rolling and legislative behavior   74
2.6 Dynamics   77
    2.6.1 Investment linkages   78
    2.6.2 Political and policy linkages   82
    2.6.3 Investment and politics   89
2.7 Implications   93
2.8 Concluding comments   97

3 Political agency and accountability   98
3.1 Introduction   98
3.2 Elements of political agency models   102
    3.2.1 The nature of the uncertainty   103
    3.2.2 The motives for holding office   104
    3.2.3 The nature of accountability   105
    3.2.4 Retrospective voting   105
    3.2.5 Model types   106
3.3 The baseline model   108
    3.3.1 The environment   108
    3.3.2 Equilibrium   110
    3.3.3 Implications   111
3.4 Extensions   123
    3.4.1 Polarization and competition   124
    3.4.2 Information and accountability   128
    3.4.3 The nature of the distortion   136
    3.4.4 Within-term cycles   141
    3.4.5 Multiple issues   144
    3.4.6 Multiple two-period terms   148
    3.4.7 Indefinite terms   154
    3.4.8 Multiple agents   157
3.5 Discussion   165
    3.5.1 Civic virtue and the quality of
        government   165
    3.5.2 Decentralization versus centralization   166
    3.5.3 Autocracy versus democracy   169

	3.5.4	Accountability to whom?	169
	3.5.5	Wage policies for politicians	170
	3.5.6	Behavioral versus rational choice models	172
3.6	Concluding comments		172

4 Political agency and public finance
(with Michael Smart) — 174
4.1	Introduction		174
4.2	The model		177
4.3	Three scenarios		180
	4.3.1	Pure adverse selection	180
	4.3.2	Pure moral hazard	182
	4.3.3	Combining moral hazard and adverse selection	185
4.4	Implications		188
	4.4.1	Equilibrium voter welfare	189
	4.4.2	Are good politicians necessarily good for voters?	191
	4.4.3	Turnover of politicians	193
	4.4.4	The spending cycle	194
4.5	Restraining government		195
	4.5.1	A direct restraint on the size of government	199
	4.5.2	Indirect restraints	200
	4.5.3	Summary	209
4.6	Debt and deficits		210
4.7	Governments versus NGOs		214
	4.7.1	Framework	216
	4.7.2	Aid to the government	219
	4.7.3	Comparisons	220
	4.7.4	Further issues	222
4.8	Competence		223
4.9	Conclusions		225
	Appendix		226

5 Final Comments — 228

References — 234

Index — 249

Preface to Paperback Edition

This edition of this book contains only very minor changes from the hardback. There are a number of new papers that use the agency approach that have come to my attention since I completed the initial manuscript. There are also some older references that I missed. In either case, I have not tried to incorporate them here. Equally, I have not been able to respond to the feedback that I have received on the book from colleagues who have been kind enough to pass along their views. I have, however, corrected a few typos and updated some of the existing references where appropriate. I am grateful to Hannes Mueller for assisting me in this task.

London, March 2007

Preface

This book began life as the Lindahl Lectures which I delivered at the University of Uppsala in October 2002. I remain honored to have been asked to deliver these lectures. Erik Lindahl developed some powerful ideas in public economics and political economy. He represents the spirit in which this book is written—using ideas in political economy and public economics to understand how to make the world a better place. I am particularly grateful to Soren Blomquist and Bertil Holmlund for their hospitality during my visit and their patience and understanding for the delay in writing up these ideas. I am also grateful to the faculty and students at Uppsala who made my visit such a stimulating one.

The main reason for the delay in writing up the lectures has been a creeping ambition to develop some of the ideas more deeply and systematically. For example, it became clear to me that the agency model of politics was less well understood than I had previously thought and the opportunity to develop a more systematic exposition of its potential was too tempting. The manuscript also presents an opportunity to make a statement on the divide between the so-called benevolent dictator view of the government and the public choice view. Having been schooled in one as a graduate student, I have since been on a journey which has tried to square my belief in the importance of sound (and not necessarily minimal) government with the self-evident proposition that government office is frequently abused. It has become clear to me that incentives in government are first order and should be taught as part of any course in public economics. To the original lectures, I also added a more refined chapter on the idea of government failure.

This book is intended as a contribution to the burgeoning field of political economy—combining ideas from economics and political science. I have tried to keep technicalities to a minimum. But some familiarity with the basic tools of micro-economics is necessary to appreciate some of the arguments. The coverage is far from definitive. The field is still evolving fast. The treatment here focuses mainly on the agency approach to politics which takes asymmetric information in politics seriously. It pays much less attention to spatial models.

I was supremely fortunate in having the opportunity to present some of the ideas in this book to the Encounters with Authors series organized by the Harvard Center for Basic Research in the Social Sciences (CBRSS). I am particularly grateful to Jim Alt and Ken Shepsle for their invitation and hospitality. I also benefited from their numerous insights on this project that they offered while I was there. The participants in that workshop were extremely supportive, giving me countless ideas and helping me to avoid infelicities. I am especially grateful for the feedback that I received at the workshop from Daron Acemoglu, Alberto Alesina, Abhijit Banerjee, John Londregan, Arthur (Skip) Lupia, Adam Meirowitz, Sharun Mukand, Jim Snyder, and Enrico Spolaore.

Many people have influenced my thinking on the topics of this book. Throughout my career I have enjoyed the counsel and, above all, friendship of Steve Coate. He and I have collaborated on a large number of projects and many ideas developed here (especially the good ones!) are probably his. However, they have been etched into my mind by years of discussion with Steve so that I no longer recognize this. Anne Case collaborated with me in my first efforts in political economy when we stumbled on the agency approach while trying to understand determinants of re-election rates among US governors. Anne has taught me many things which are relevant to the ideas in this book and the part of Chapter 3 on US governors is based on our joint work. Michael Smart has also collaborated with me in understanding the agency model in public finance settings. Chapter 4 of this book reports mostly on joint work with him. His work with Daniel Sturm also greatly influenced the formulation of the agency problem that I use in Chapter 3.

The LSE is a unique place and I have been privileged to serve as a member of the economics department and of the Suntory and Toyota International Centres for Economics and Related Disciplines (STICERD) since 1995. It has provided me with colleagues whose curiosity, integrity, and energy are second to none. I especially thank my STICERD-based colleagues Oriana Bandiera, Robin Burgess, Maitreesh Ghatak, Markus Goldstein, and Andrea Prat with whom I have had many helpful conversations relevant to this book as well as receiving comments on parts of it.

There are many others whose comments and encouragement have helped to improve my understanding of the issues dealt with here. I particularly thank Daron Acemoglu, Bruno Frey, Jim Hines, Clare Leaver, Gilat Levy, Stephen Morris, Roger Myerson, Torsten Persson, Jim Robinson, Paul Seabright, Andrei Shleifer, Daniel Sturm, and Guido Tabellini. Konrad Burchardi, Marieke Huysenstruyt, Masa Kudamatsu, Marit Rehavi and Silvia Pezzini provided excellent research assistance at various points. Masa deserves special mention: he read the entire manuscript carefully and made a host of important comments which lead to substantial improvements.

Last, but not least, I thank my wife, Gillian, and my sons, Thomas and Oliver, for their forbearance and support.

Acknowledgements

The Lindahl Lectures are sponsored by Uppsala University and given every two years in honour of Erik Lindahl, a distinguished Swedish economist (1891–1960), Professor of Economics at Uppsala University (1942–58). In 1986 Uppsala University established the lectures in honour of Lindahl's contributions to monetary theory and public finance. Previous lecturers include:

1987 Professor Dale W. Jorgenson: *Tax Policy and US Economic Growth*
1989 Professor Anthony B. Atkinson: *The Design of Taxation and Social Security*
1991 Professor Joseph E. Stiglitz: *The New Welfare Economics: Public Policy in the Presence of Asymmetric Information*
1993 Professor Mervyn King: *Financial Markets and Economic Policy*
1996 Professor Agnar Sandmo: *The Public Economics of the Environment*
1999 Professor Peter A. Diamond: *Social Security Reform*
2002 Professor Timothy Besley: *Principled Agents? Motivation and Incentives in Government*
2004 Professor Edward L. Glaeser: *The Economics of Cities*

1

Competing views of government

The aim of every political Constitution, is or ought to be, first
to obtain for rulers men who possess most wisdom to discern,
and most virtue to pursue, the common good of society; and
in the next place, to take the most effectual precautions for
keeping them virtuous whilst they continue to hold their public trust.

Madison (1788[1961])

1.1 The issues

Economic analyses of government divide into two broad camps. One
emphasizes government in the public interest. It outlines the range
of activities that government can undertake to improve the lives of
its citizens. Government provides the underpinnings of the market
system by establishing property rights and a means of adjudication
through the courts. Government can regulate externalities which
private actions fail to internalize. Government can provide public
goods which the market will tend to underprovide. Government can
regulate abuses of market power in cases where competition is limited. Finally, government can distribute resources towards socially
favored groups. The logic behind this has been developed at length
and provides the modern theory of the state from a welfare economic
point of view.[1]

At the other extreme are accounts of government seen mainly as a
private interest. Government can be a focus for rent seeking in which
the power to tax results in private, wasteful efforts to capture the state

---

[1] See, for example, Atkinson and Stiglitz (1980).

which then rewards the powerful at the expense of citizens at large. Even in fulfilling its apparently virtuous functions, government can be influenced by organized groups and state officials may receive bribes to act against the interests of the citizens at large. Government may lack sufficient incentives for officials (who are less than publicly spirited) to act in the public interest. These officials may choose to divert resources to their own ends or simply slack on the job.[2]

This book strives to understand a view of government and its potential that lies between these two extremes. Its intellectual origins lie in the so-called *Publius* view which is today often associated with the name of James Madison, one of the authors of the *Federalist Papers* (1788[1961]) and an architect of the US Constitution. This view recognizes the potential for government to act in the public interest but understands the tendency for things to go awry. Good government is in part associated with designing an institutional framework which affects the incentives of those who make policy decisions. But good government is not entirely about incentives: it also requires good leaders—persons of character and wisdom. These twin elements of incentives and selection in politics are central themes throughout.

Making progress on these questions requires models of how government allocates resources. At the heart of effective government lies the solution to a principal–agent problem between citizens and government. This approach is a focal point for this book. However, it is located more broadly in the modern political economy literature which develops theoretical and empirical tools for understanding public resource allocation.

The book shares with the Publius view the notion that there are institutional preconditions to effective government. But finding them requires an understanding of incentives and the process by which the political class is selected. It is broadly optimistic—good government *is* possible, but only when the conditions are right.

1.2 This book

This book comprises four relatively self-contained essays. This first essay (Chapter 1) provides an introduction to the issues studied here

---

[2] This view has been at the core of the Public Choice. In the context of public finance, see Buchanan (1967).

and discussions of government from a political economy perspective. We will place this in its historical context and the traditional public economics approach to the role of government. We will also discuss some of the empirical evidence on differences in the quality of government across countries that motivates these ideas. This essay also discusses the themes of incentives and selection in politics in general terms.

Chapter 2 is an essay on government failure. Most economists now agree that the idea of government failure needs to be placed alongside the idea of market failure in our discussions of government intervention. However, unlike market failure, there is no agreed upon definition of government failure. The economics literature is also obscure on which aspects of government failure are intrinsic to the fact that government has a monopoly of coercive power and which aspects are a consequence of democratic political competition. Chapter 2 provides an overview of these ideas and develops some simple economic examples to illustrate the main ideas.

In Chapter 3 we turn to political agency models. These explore the consequences of limited information in politics. The chapter develops a canonical model which is then used to discuss an array of issues that arise in such models. As well as providing an introduction to the literature, the chapter also throws up a variety of issues that have not been fully understood to date and merit further work. The chapter also emphasizes the empirical potential of these models in explaining real world policy choices. At the heart of the models is the notion of *political accountability*—a frequently used concept that often lacks precise usage. The political agency model is an ideal vehicle for thinking about this idea and exploring how accountability works in practice.

Chapter 4 applies the political agency model to public finance issues reporting on joint work with Michael Smart. The chapter develops a simple and tractable model which can be applied to thinking about the determination of taxes, debt, and public spending in an agency framework. The model is used to think about the merits of restraining government in an agency model. It also discusses how agency models can provide insights into the choice between non-governmental organizations (NGOs) and government in delivering public services.

Chapter 5 offers a few concluding comments and observations. One of its main themes is the need to devote more attention to issues of selection in political economy models and it introduces some of the main ideas that are relevant to this.

1.3 Background

The discussions in this book center around policy making in representative democracies. This achieves special poignancy in view of the fact that there is now an unparalleled consensus about the centrality of the market economy and some form of liberal democracy in allocating public and private resources. Indeed, much of the world is now committed to a broadly capitalist model of production regulated and augmented by a popularly elected government. It was not always thus. From 1945 to around 1990, the world was divided into two broad economic systems. On one side were the planned economies based on total subordination of the economy to the state via economic planning. On the other side were the mixed economy with private goods production dominated by the market and public goods production in government. This economic cleavage was largely paralleled by a political cleavage—planned economies being mainly autocratic with most mixed economies committed to some form of liberal democracy. The swing towards democracy in recent years is illustrated in Figure 1.1 which uses the Polity IV data set. There is a downward trend from the 1950s through to the mid-1970s with a real 'take-off' around 1990. The latter is due in part, but not exclusively, to the fall of the Berlin Wall.

While democratic values have triumphed in recent years, there is still a huge amount of discussion about the impact of different institutional choices.[3] Moreover, there are many debates about the consequences of democratic policy making in economics. The dominant early traditions in political economy emanating from Virginia and Chicago offered competing analyses of how democracy generates policies and whether there are endemic forms of 'democratic failures' that need to be avoided. The key challenge remains understanding how government resource allocation works and uncovering the institutional preconditions to effective democratic governance.

1.3.1 *The size of government*

The remarkable growth in government that occurred in the twentieth century brings the two competing perspectives on government

---

[3] See Acemoglu and Robinson (2005) for some important insights about the differences between democratic and non-democratic government.

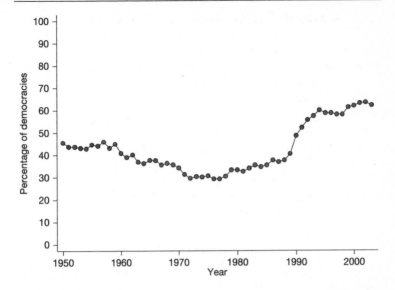

Source: Polity IV (version 2003)

Notes: A country in a given year is classified as a democracy if the variable Polity2 in the Polity IV data set is greater than zero. The percentage of democracies is calculated as the ratio of the number of democracies to the number of all countries in the Polity IV data set for each year. Note that the Polity IV data set only includes countries with a population of more than 500,000 in 2003. Also note that the number of all countries in the data set changes over time due to the independence of colonies, the break-up of a country, and the integration of countries.

Figure 1.1   Democracies in the world, 1950–2003

that we began with into sharp relief. Government growth could be seen as confirmation that government is 'out of control' with insufficient safeguards in place to restrain its power to tax. However, it could equally be viewed as confirmation of the effectiveness of government in acting in the common interest.

Table 1.1 reproduced from Maddison (2001) illustrates this. Whereas government in Western Europe in the early part of the century consumed only around 10 percent of GDP, it consumed more than 40 percent by the end of the century. The trend holds also in Japan and the United States, even though the latter has not adopted the full-scale 'welfare state'.

Figures 1.2 and 1.3 look at these patterns from 1960 onwards.[4] They graph the size of government as measured by the percentage

---

[4] Data from the World Development Indicators is only available from 1960 onwards.

Table 1.1 Total government expenditure as percent of GDP at current prices: Western Europe, the United States, and Japan, 1913–99

	1913	1938	1950	1973	1999
France	8.9	23.2	27.6	38.8	52.4
Germany	17.7	42.4	30.4	42.0	47.6
Netherlands	8.2	21.7	26.8	45.5	43.8
United Kingdom	13.3	28.8	34.2	41.5	39.7
Arithmetic average	12.0	29.0	29.8	42.0	45.9
United States	8.0	19.8	21.4	31.1	30.1
Japan	14.2	30.3	19.8	22.9	38.1

Source: Maddison (2001).

Notes: The data for the Netherlands is for 1910 rather than 1913

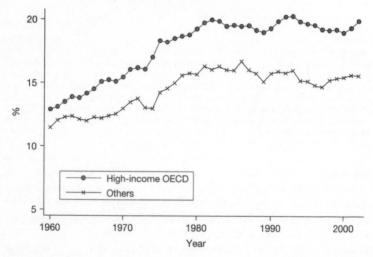

Source: World Development Indicators 2005
Notes: Size of government (in nominal terms) is measured as the percentage of general government final consumption expenditure in current local currency units over GDP in current local currency units. The simple average for each group of countries is calculated. High-income OECD countries are Australia, Austria, Belgium, Canada, Denmark, Finland, France, Germany (the unified Germany before 1990), Greece, Iceland, Ireland, Italy, Japan, Luxembourg, The Netherlands, New Zealand, Norway, Portugal, Spain, Sweden, Switzerland, the United Kingdom, and the United States. The data for year 2003 are excluded as eight out of the 23 high-income OECD countries are missing. For the sake of comparability to Figure 1.3, country-years for which the data on the size of government in real terms is unavailable are dropped.

Figure 1.2 Size of government (in nominal terms) in high-income OECD countries and the others

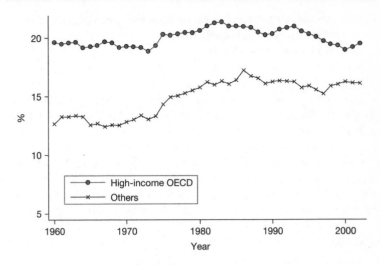

Source: World Development Indicators 2005

Notes: Size of government (in real terms) is measured as the percentage of general government final consumption expenditure in constant local currency unit over GDP in constant local currency unit. The simple average for each group of countries is calculated. High-income OECD countries are Australia, Austria, Belgium, Canada, Denmark, Finland, France, Germany (the unified Germany before 1990), Greece, Iceland, Ireland, Italy, Japan, Luxembourg, The Netherlands, New Zealand, Norway, Portugal, Spain, Sweden, Switzerland, the United Kingdom, and the United States. The data for year 2003 are excluded as eight out of the 23 high-income OECD countries are missing. For the sake of comparability to Figure 1.2, country-years for which the data on the size of government in nominal terms is unavailable are dropped.

Figure 1.3 Size of government (in real terms) in high-income OECD countries and the others

of government consumption in GDP in both real and nominal terms, separating out the experience of the (rich) OECD countries and the rest. These figures show that government is larger in rich than in poor countries. The size of government in nominal terms has, however, grown as a share of national income in both countries, although with signs of a leveling off towards the end of the period. The graph in real terms shows that the trend is largely flat in rich countries while the drift upwards is still seen in the non-OECD sample. This suggests that the increase in the size of government in nominal terms is largely due to an increase in the cost of providing a given bundle of services along the lines of the unbalanced growth story suggested by Baumol (1967). He argued that government growth in rich countries is significantly affected by the fact that it provides labor intensive services which have not benefitted from labor saving technological change. Borcherding

estimates that around 31 percent of the rise in the size of
government can be explained this way.

how democratization has affected the growth of government is
moot. From a theoretical point of view, democracies should put more
weight on popular opinion. Acemoglu and Robinson (2005) model
democracy as a system of government in which the poor have greater
influence which leads to greater redistribution. Mulligan et al. (2004)
argue that the data give little support to the proposition that democracies have substantially different economic and social policies from
non-democracies. However, their data end in 1990, before the important recent increase in the incidence of democracy. In addition, while
the Polity IV data they use may be useful for looking at broad trends,
they do a poor job in modeling policy incentives in the aggregate.

Figures 1.4 and 1.5 look at the size of government in democracies
and autocracies as measured in the Polity IV data. They show that

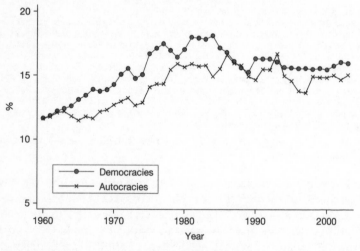

Sources: World Development Indicators 2005 and Polity IV
Notes: Size of government is measured as the percentage of general government final
consumption expenditure in current local currency units over GDP in current local
currency units. The simple average for each group of countries is calculated. A country
in a given year is classified as a democracy if variable Polity2 in the Polity IV data set is
greater than zero and as an autocracy if Polity2 is zero or negative. Note that a country
that is a democracy in some year can be an autocracy in another year. For the sake of
comparability to Figure 1.5, country-years for which the data on the size of government
in real terms is unavailable are dropped.

Figure 1.4 Size of government (in nominal terms) between democracies and
autocracies

there is little difference in terms of government size between democracies and autocracies. The difference in real terms prior to 1990 is largely an income effect—reflecting the larger difference in income levels between democracies and autocracies in this period.

Perhaps the most persuasive lesson from recent research is that democracy comes in many forms and looking for an effect of democracy per se is probably misguided. The important work of Persson and Tabellini (2003) shows that there are distinct patterns in terms of the form of government and policy outcomes. Most notably, there is a robust relationship between both parliamentary (rather than presidential) government and proportional representation (rather than majoritarianism) and the size of government.

The growth of government to its modern proportions may constitute a remarkable act of public trust. Government spends a significant fraction of national income and is expected to do so wisely. Such

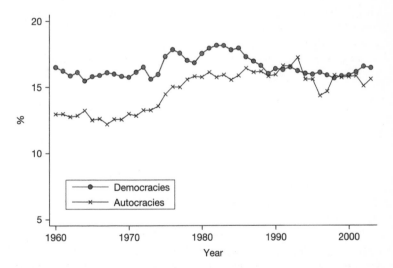

Sources: World Development Indicators 2005 and Polity IV

Notes: Size of government is measured as the percentage of general government final consumption expenditure in constant local currency units over GDP in constant local currency units. The simple average for each group of countries is calculated. A country in a given year is classified as a democracy if variable Polity2 in the Polity IV data set is greater than zero and as an autocracy if Polity2 is zero or negative. Note that a country that is a democracy in some year can be an autocracy in another year. For the sake of comparability to Figure 1.4, country-years for which the data on the size of government in nominal terms is unavailable are dropped.

Figure 1.5 Size of government (in real terms) between democracies and autocracies

trust can be supported in one of two ways—either we are confident that government is populated by publicly spirited officials or else there must be sufficient safeguards in place to curtail self-interested behavior. Either way, it does seem remarkable that this position has changed so markedly over 100 years. This faith in government to deliver benefits in return for taxes, which are remarkably high in any long-run perspective, is a core part of the institutional consensus that has emerged.

1.3.2 *Corruption*

While it is debatable whether the size of government tells us much about government quality, there is one aspect of government quality that has received a lot of empirical attention, namely corruption. While there is still debate about how far corruption is damaging to the economy as a whole, it is widely agreed to be an important symptom of low quality government. That said, corruption is often used *sui generis* to stand for a variety of distinct problems in state performance, many of which should require separate analyses. One important distinction is that between bureaucratic and political corruption.[5] The institutional structures that perpetuate these may be related, but can also be quite different. For example, the incentive mechanisms for the control of bureaucrats and politicians tend to be rather different.[6]

As we shall see in the next chapter, there are a number of ways to think about the costs of corruption from a normative point of view. Corruption could be viewed primarily as a distributional problem as those who receive illicit returns from the state are rarely socially deserving: it is pretty hard to think of a social welfare function that would value transfers between public officials and citizens that arise as the product of corruption.

Corruption also leads to resource misallocation. There are many different ways in which this can happen. For example, corruption could lead to misallocation of investment and public infrastructure away from their most productive use. It can also lead to misallocation of talent as self-interested individuals seek rewards in occupations where

[5] Hellman et al. (2000) distinguish 'state capture' (corruption to change the laws) from 'administrative corruption' (corruption to alter the implementation of laws), and empirically show that the type of firms engaging in state capture is different from that in administrative corruption.

[6] See Alesina and Tabellini (2004) for a recent analysis of this.

returns are inflated by corrupt activities.[7] Corrupt government may also lead to more self-interested individuals choosing to enter public life in order to capture rents.

While corruption is not easy to measure, there are a number of measures now available, the main ones being those from the International Country Risk Guide (ICRG) and Transparency International. A mini-industry has sprung up that correlates corruption with various historical and institutional factors.[8] Some useful empirical regularities have emerged.

Whether as cause or effect, corruption is associated with low income (see Mauro 1995). While it is extremely difficult to establishing the direction of causation here, it is clear that part of being a poor country is having a lower quality government. Moreover, this observation has affected debates about how to promote economic development. The World Bank and other organizations have pushed a 'governance agenda' which puts weight on combating corruption as a means of improving government performance throughout the developing world.

Figures 1.6 and 1.7 illustrate these two claims. Figure 1.6 graphs the ICRG corruption measures between the mid-1980s and late 1990s. Over the entire period rich countries had significantly lower corruption levels.[9] As illustrated in Figure 1.7, corruption is also lower in democracies compared to autocracies over the same period.

In support of this, there are a number of strong correlations between corruption and other measures of government performance. La Porta et al. (1999) investigated the empirical links between corruption and (i) ethnolinguistic fractionalization, (ii) religion, and (iii) legal origins. They find that less diverse societies are less corrupt, as are those with a larger fraction of Protestants. Common law legal origin is also correlated with lower corruption. Even setting aside the question of causation, the policy consequences of these correlations are far from clear. However, they motivate the need to treat quality of government as endogenous and to explore how structural factors affect government performance through their impact on incentives and selection. Some of our findings in Chapter 3 which look at determinants of government performance in an agency model are helpful in thinking this through from a theoretical point of view.

[7] See, for example, Murphy et al. (1991).
[8] The empirical literature is surveyed in Treisman (2000).
[9] A high score on this index denotes low corruption.

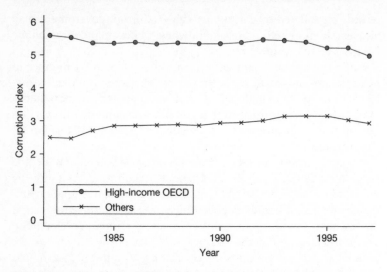

Source: International Country Risk Guide (http://www.countrydata.com/datasets/)
Notes: Corruption index (variable 'corruption in government' in the dataset) ranges in values 0–6 with higher values indicating *less* corruption. The simple average for each group of countries is calculated. High-income OECD countries are Australia, Austria, Belgium, Canada, Denmark, Finland, France, Germany (West Germany before 1990), Greece, Iceland, Ireland, Italy, Japan, Luxembourg, Netherlands, New Zealand, Norway, Portugal, Spain, Sweden, Switzerland, the United Kingdom, and the United States.

Figure 1.6   Corruption in high-income OECD countries and others

The link between openness and corruption has also generated interest. For example, Ades and Di Tella (1999) argue that countries whose economies are more open to trade are less corrupt. This type of analysis is expanded and developed in Bonaglia et al. (2001). The main theoretical argument that these studies make is that openness acts as a constraint on the behavior of politicians. In Chapter 4, we locate such arguments in broader terms, using the political agency model to investigate the quality of government when there is tax competition between nations.

Corruption has also been related to freedom of the media by Ahrend (2000) and Brunetti and Weder (2003) who relate press freedom and corruption in cross-country data. Both of these papers find that press freedom is associated with lower levels of corruption. Djankov et al. (2003b) focus more directly on the effect of media ownership patterns on a variety of outcomes. They develop a remarkable data set on media ownership patterns in 98 countries to do so. They find that corruption

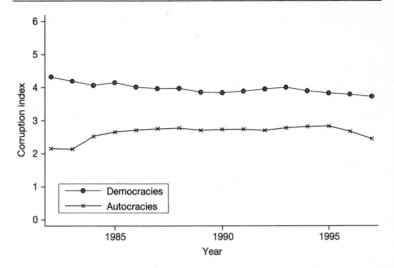

Sources: International Country Risk Guide (http://www.countrydata.com/datasets/) and Polity IV

Notes: Corruption index (variable 'corruption in government' in the data set) ranges in values 0–6 with higher values indicating *less* corruption. The simple average for each group of countries is calculated. A country in a given year is classified as a democracy if Polity2 the variable is greater than zero, and as an autocracy if Polity2 analogously variable is zero or negative. Note that a country that is a democracy in some year can be an autocracy in another year. The International Country Risk Guide data set covers years 1982–97.

Figure 1.7   Corruption in democracies and autocracies

is related to state ownership of newspapers. We show in Chapter 3 that such findings can be understood in a political agency framework where press freedom affects the extent of information available to voters.[10]

Corruption has also been related to political institutions and political outcomes. For example, Persson et al. (2003) consider the link between corruption and political/constitutional variables. They test the idea that majoritarian systems and larger voting districts are less prone to corruption, finding strong evidence in favor of this. Treisman (2000) and Persson et al. (2003) document the fact that corruption is negatively correlated with political turnover. In Chapter 3, we will return to the links between political turnover and corruption that

---

[10] This is based on Besley and Prat (2006).

are suggested by the political agency framework which treats *both* turnover and corruption as endogenous.

Empirical studies of corruption provide one of the most thoroughly researched areas of government quality. That said, the links to theory tend to be quite limited. This shows up the choice of what is treated as endogenous or exogenous. For example, the rate of turnover among politicians is often treated as an exogenous variable whereas many theoretical approaches would determine this endogenously. There are also great difficulties in establishing the direction of causation in cross-country data. Nonetheless, it brings into sharp relief the proposition that, even measured in this crude way, there are significant differences between government quality across the world that cry out for explanation.

1.3.3 *Property rights*

Enforcement of property rights has been studied extensively. To motivate this, observe that at the heart of the Weberian view of the state is the notion that the state has a monopoly on the legitimate use of coercion. This coercive power can be used in a benign way to raise taxes to finance public goods and regulate externalities. However, that same power can be used to expropriate wealth. A key aspect of government quality concerns the extent to which this is done. Without suitable restraints on the power of government it is harder to foster a climate for private investment incentives.

This problem of expropriation arises when government is too strong and overbearing. Alongside government expropriation of wealth is private expropriation in situations in which the government is too weak. In such cases, private contracts may not be enforced which will also have a deterrent effect on trade and investment, leading to lower income per capita. Here the problem is one of private rather than public predation. The role of government is to support market arrangements between private actors and to uphold contracts.

In light of these observations, Djankov et al. (2003a) see the role of effective government as steering a path between the two evils of authoritarianism and disorder. Effective institutional solutions are those that create the right balance between them. It is clear that political incentives shaped by political institutions provide only a partial picture in understanding these issues. Another key issue is whether

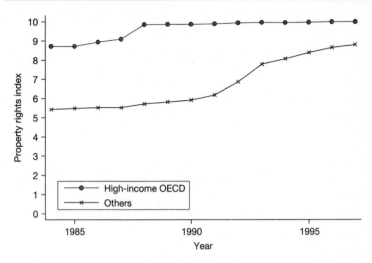

Sources: International Country Risk Guide (http://www.countrydata.com/datasets/)
Notes: Property rights index (variable 'risk of expropriation' in the data set) ranges in values 0–10 with higher values indicating *more* secure property rights. The simple average for each group of countries is calculated. High-income OECD countries are Australia, Austria, Belgium, Canada, Denmark, Finland, France, Germany (West Germany before 1990), Greece, Iceland, Ireland, Italy, Japan, Luxembourg, The Netherlands, New Zealand, Norway, Portugal, Spain, Sweden, Switzerland, the United Kingdom, and the United States. Although the data set covers years 1982–97, years 1982 and 1983 are excluded because 21 of the 23 high-income OECD countries are missing in the data set for these years.

Figure 1.8 Property rights for high-income OECD countries and others

there is an effective legal system with sufficient judicial independence to curtail predation by government and uphold private contracts. Djankov et al. (2003a) review the extensive empirical evidence relating market performance to the operation of legal systems.

As in the case of corruption, there is a strong correlation between income per capita and enforcement of property rights. This is illustrated in Figure 1.8 using the ICRG measure of 'risk of expropriation' by government. The difficult issue is again to establish the direction of causation. In a recent paper, Acemoglu et al. (2001) suggest the use of settler mortality in colonial times as an instrument for property rights enforcement, arguing that this has lead to institutional legacies. They argue on the basis of this that causation runs from poor property rights to low income. Moreover, the quality of government, in so far as it contributes to property rights enforcement, has long-lived historical roots.

Competing views of government

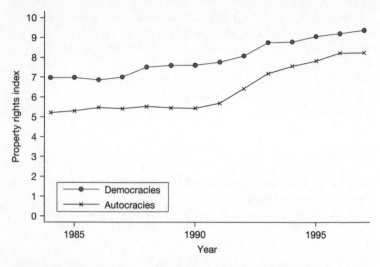

Sources: International Country Risk Guide (http://www.countrydata.com/datasets/) and Polity IV

Notes: Property rights index (variable 'risk of expropriation' in the data set) ranges in values 0-10 with higher values indicating *more* secure property rights. The simple average for each group of countries is calculated. A country in a given year is classified as a democracy if Polity2 the variable is greater than zero, and as an autocracy if Polity2 analogously variable is zero or negative. Note that a country that is a democracy in some year can be an autocracy in another year. The International Country Risk Guide data set covers years 1982–97 though figures for years 1982 and 1983 are dropped because about half of democracies are missing for these two years.

Figure 1.9   Property rights for democracies and autocracies

The work, however, says little directly about the exact theoretical route by which this effect is mediated. While Figure 1.9 shows that there is a predictable link between protection of property rights and democracy, it is unclear whether it is causal. In an effort to get at this, Persson (2004) relates settler mortality to modern day political institutions using Acemoglu et al.'s (2001) variable as an instrument for the *form* of democracy. He finds that parliamentary (as opposed to presidential) democracies[11] and proportional representation (as opposed to majoritarian) systems are growth promoting. In tune with the Acemoglu et al. (2001) results, these government types also tend to have better protection of property rights.

[11] Parliamentary systems are defined as those that have a vote of confidence procedure for the executive.

Even though political institutions are only part of the story, the structure of government incentives and the quality of the political class are an important input into aims to improve the functioning of a market economy, especially in the creation of secure property rights. The models and analysis in Chapters 3 and 4 which study principal—agent problems are therefore a useful input into this aspect of government quality.

1.3.4 *Trust and turnout*

The pattern of democratization illustrated in Figure 1.1 suggests that liberal democracy has been riding high as an institution since around 1990. However, there is an underlying concern about the declining health of the more established democracies.[12] One major symptom of this is the observed decline in voter turnout.[13] This is illustrated for OECD countries in Figure 1.10 which documents this trend by plotting turnout over time for OECD countries. This fell from an average of 84 percent in 1946–50 to 74 percent in 1996–2000, the most dramatic decline being in the latter part of the period. This OECD experience is mainly driven by the older democracies. The new democracies of Central and Eastern Europe which have enjoyed very high participation rates would not show this pattern.

In general, there is a difficulty in assessing the welfare consequences of declining turnout in the absence of any agreed upon theory of voting. The low likelihood that any voter will be decisive in mass elections makes models based on the probability of being pivotal, a questionable basis for the theory of voting. As discussed by Aldrich (1997), political scientists tend to work in frameworks where some extra component of utility (such as social duty) is invoked to explain why people vote in such large numbers. In this case, election turnout could be a barometer for how such feelings of duty extend in the population. To the extent that these are correlated with perceived satisfaction with government, this could create a link between turnout and the quality of government, but the link is tenuous at best. If social duty is the main basis of deciding to vote, then declining turnout could also be linked to a general decline in 'social capital', i.e. a willingness by citizens to privately provide public goods.

---

[12] See, for example, Pharr et al. (2000).
[13] See Levi and Stoker (2000) for a wide-ranging discussion of these issues.

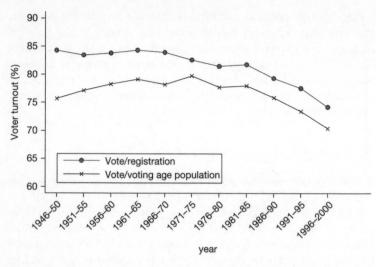

Sources: International Institute for Democracy and Electoral Assistance (IDEA) (www.idea.int/vt)
Notes: 'Vote/registration' is the ratio of the total number of votes cast to the number of registered voters. 'Vote/voting age population' is the ratio of the total number of votes cast to the population over the age of 18. The five-year period is chosen so that each country, except for Greece, Portugal, and Spain during their dictatorial rules (see below), held at least one election in each period, which avoids the composition bias. The five-year average turnout for high-income OECD countries is calculated as follows. For each country and each five-year period, the turnout (variables Vote/registration or Vote/voting age population in the IDEA data set) for legislative elections is averaged. For countries whose form of government is presidential (e.g. the United States), the average turnout for presidential elections is calculated separately, and averaged with the legislative counterpart, in order to ensure that the same weight is given for each type of election. The simple average over countries is then calculated for each five-year period. This makes sure that those countries that held more elections within each period than others are not over-represented. High-income OECD countries are Australia, Austria, Belgium, Canada, Denmark, Finland, France, Germany (West Germany before 1990), Greece, Iceland, Ireland, Italy, Japan, Luxembourg, The Netherlands, New Zealand, Norway, Portugal, Spain, Sweden, Switzerland, the United Kingdom, and the United States. There were no national elections in Spain for 1946–76, Greece for 1965–73, and Portugal for 1946–74. The data on the number of registered voters (hence Vote/Registration) is not available for Greece in 1946–50 and the United States in 1946–63.

Figure 1.10 National election turnout in high-income OECD countries, 1946–2000

Other theories of voting put weight on the role of being informed in affecting the decision to turnout—see Feddersen and Pesendorfer (1996). If elections were purely a common values problem, then nobody would mind if only one voter showed up and caste their vote decisively provided that individual was informed.

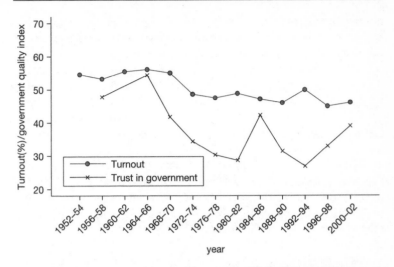

Sources: Trust in government is taken from National Election Surveys (NES); Turnout obtained from Michael McDonald for 1952–98 and his website (elections.gmu.edu) for 2000–2.

Notes: Turnout is the ratio of the total vote cast for the highest office to the voting age population. Shown in the Figure is the simple average over each presidential year and its following mid-term election year with the same weight on each state. Trust in government (variable CF0656 in the NES data set) is the aggregate index of survey responses to the following four questions: 'How much of the time do you think you can trust the government in Washington to do what is right?', 'Would you say the government is pretty much run by a few big interests looking out for themselves or that it is run for the benefit of all the people?', 'Do you think that people in the government waste a lot of money we pay in taxes, waste some of it, or don't waste very much of it?', and 'Do you think that quite a few of the people running the government are crooked, not very many are, or do you think hardly any of them are crooked?' The survey was conducted each other year when national elections were held. The simple average across US states shown in the Figure is calculated as follows: the simple average is taken across respondents in each state; then the simple average across the states is calculated for each survey year; finally, each presidential election year figure is averaged with the figure for the following mid-term election year (except for 1958 where the survey in 1956 did not take place). For both turnout and trust in government, the states of Alaska and Hawaii and the District of Columbia are not included.

Figure 1.11 Trust in government and turnout (simple average across US states)

This argument has less force when there are important ideological divergences between groups of voters. This is a particular issue if the informed voters are mainly from one particular ideological grouping.

To get a feel for whether turnout and declining voter satisfaction with politics and politicians are linked requires more than evidence on turnout alone. The National Election Surveys (NES) from the United States provide an interesting perspective. They ask a variety of interesting questions about attitudes to government which can be correlated with the indicators of what governments do and the pattern of turnout. Of particular interest is the composite variable which gauges trust in government over the period 1958–2002. It is, however, important to bear in mind that these are subjective assessments and there is always the possibility that they are a poor reflection of actual government performance. Figure 1.11 shows a declining trust in government. This Figure also looks at turnout and shows that these two are broadly moving in the same direction—both trust and turnout having decline over the period. Trust showed some evidence of recovery towards the end of the period. While only suggestive, this illustrates why declining trust is often linked to declining turnout in many discussions.

1.4 Economic policy making

The two views of government discussed above have their parallels in approaches to the study of economic policy. The benevolent government view which focuses on the good that government can do has important figures such as Arthur Pigou, James Meade, and James Mirrlees in its ranks. The more cautious view is associated with equally distinguished figures such as James Buchanan, George Stigler, and Anne Krueger. The latter place political economy issues at the heart of their approach.

Among the latter group it is Buchanan who has developed at length the importance of using constitutional rules to improve the workings of democratic institutions.[14]. As we noted above, this is the spirit of the approach used by the Founding Fathers of the United States as expressed in *The Federalist Papers* (Madison 1961). This approach argues that there is a need for both a *procedural* constitution—rules that define the workings of democratic institutions, and a *fiscal* constitution—rules that define constraints on policy making.[15]

The main purpose of this section is to survey in brief the main elements of the normative approach to policy making. This is important

[14] This is particularly true in his joint work with Geoffrey Brennan: Brennan and Buchanan (1980, 1985)

[15] These themes are taken up in Chapter 4.

for the discussion in Chapter 2 which rigorously tries to understand the idea of government failure. It is also important as a backdrop to the discussion of political economy issues in policy making.

1.4.1 *Foundations*

Making sense of good government requires a performance metric. The standard economic notion is *social welfare*. This is usually invoked in a context where the 'inputs' into social welfare are individual utility levels. (The idea that social welfare is solely a function of such data is known as *welfarism*.) The task is then to provide a means of aggregating these utility levels to form a societal measure of well-being. Once a criterion for social welfare is established, then policies and other social states can be evaluated and ranked. From this, the notion of good government can be defined.

This approach can be applied to policies, political processes, and institutions. It provides an intellectual underpinning for ideas of government operating for the common good or in the public interest. Its historical antecedents include classical utilitarianism as well as Rawls's theory of justice. But some have taken issue with the coherence of the notion of the common good and hence its usefulness for thinking about good government.

There are two levels of attack. The first questions the very idea of the common good. This would include concerns following the discovery of Arrow's impossibility theorem. Arrow (1951) examined the possibility of *deriving* social welfare from individual preferences in the absence of interpersonal comparisons of utility. By producing his impossibility theorem, his work appeared to be a significant set-back in the quest for giving a scientific foundation for social welfare and hence for notions of common good. However, as Sen (1977) has emphasized, one key issue concerns the assumptions made about interpersonal comparisons. If interpersonal comparisons are allowed, social welfare functions can be derived which satisfy Arrow's axioms. These include utilitarianism and Rawlsianism.

The second attack on the notion of common good views notions of social welfare, even if logically coherent, as inherently contested. The choice of a social welfare function will hinge to a significant degree on value judgements—for example, notions of inequality aversion—on which no consensus prevails. The problem is then that there are too many competing notions of the good for an idea of *common* good to make sense. While the social choice literature has produced elegant axiomatizations of certain kinds of social welfare functions, they are not a particularly helpful way of resolving this issue on a practical level. It is clear that the practical question is whether there are *procedures* that are regarded as reasonable ways of making collective choices, especially when it allocates coercive power to particular individuals. The remarkable thing about representative democracy is how readily it has been accepted as a legitimate way for this to be done.

The fact that there is no readily agreed upon social welfare function for making social decisions is important for the issue of defining good government. Such concerns are echoed in Schumpeter (1943) who rejected classical notions of democracy that saw the aim of democratic institutions as trying to find ways of pursuing the common good. He recast the problem of democracy in terms of the positive problem of understanding how candidates competed to secure votes, eschewing normative comparisons entirely.

One option is to work without any distributional judgements—focusing exclusively on the implications of Pareto efficiency. As we shall discuss further below, the standard economic model puts weight on Pareto efficiency as a criterion for good policy. The use of Pareto efficiency is broadly uncontroversial in standard economic models. However, it can conflict with other principles that many have invoked as constraints on policies. Respect for individual liberty is one important example. As argued persuasively in Sen (1970), a policy can be Pareto efficient and yet violate the most minimal notions of individual liberty. In fact any side constraint on welfare is likely to have the property of picking Pareto inferior policies (see Kaplow and Shavell 2001).

Even if this concern about Pareto efficiency as a normative criterion is set aside, there is still the problem that it provides a very weak and ambiguous idea of the common good. There are typically many different Pareto efficient policies with varying degrees of inequality associated with them. It may be an achievement of sorts that policies or institutions guarantee Pareto efficiency, but many policy outcomes become non-comparable on these terms. Having a criterion which allows distributional comparisons would certainly provide a richer theory of good government. But that would require invoking some kind of social welfare function.

Even though it is hard not to have some sympathy with these difficulties, a wholly nihilistic take on normative metrics that invoke some distributional criteria for good government is probably too strong. First, some aspects of distribution, such as helping the poor or particular disadvantaged groups, are frequently viewed as broadly desirable. Second, narrowly targeted policies, those that lead to the enrichment of small elite groups, are frequently frowned upon and the language of common good can be powerful in getting them thrown out. Indeed, more generally, the calculus of gainers and losers in the policy process often reveals whether there is broad support in societies for particular policies with specified distributional ends.

As we shall see in Chapter 2, there is an important tradition in political economy, which has not had much sway in mainstream economics, of appraising the case for good government attaching weight to what would happen in the absence of government intervention. This is central to the normative framework put forward by James Buchanan which we discuss further below and which has its historical roots in Wicksell (1896). They advocate a criterion for good government which emphasizes the principle of *unanimity rule* relative to what would happen in the absence of government. This approach has a libertarian flavor since the government cannot do anything that reduces an individual below his/her status quo (no government) utility. Thus, each individual is given an effective veto over some aspects of government intervention. Below, we will return to a discussion of its implications.

1.4.2 *Good policies*

In the traditional welfare economic model which has dominated modern public economics, good government is largely identified with good *policy*. The latter is typically defined with reference to both efficiency and distribution. Hence, it sets aside worries about the coherence of ideas like social welfare.

Consider a community of individuals (citizens) who have to make a policy choice. There is a set of feasible policies from among which they must choose. Feasibility requires taking into account both technological feasibility and budget balance, and so on, as well as information constraints on what government knows about its citizens.[16]

---

[16] The seminal contributions on incentive compatability in normative public economics are Mirrlees (1971) and Hammond (1979).

In the first instance, the appropriate benchmark for good policy is second best Pareto efficiency, in other words, taking into account appropriate restrictions on policy instruments. A whole tradition of policy analysis in this vein has been developed (see, for example, Atkinson and Stiglitz 1980). The modern theory of planning has also taken such incentive constraints seriously and sees the difficulties in getting citizens to reveal private information as at the heart of designing good policy. The individuals in that community have heterogeneous policy preferences. The aim is to pick a policy from the feasible set.

The study of *efficient* policies is incredibly powerful. There are many examples of well-known policy rules in economics that are derived from considerations of Pareto efficiency. For example, the Lindahl–Samuelson rule for the efficient provision of a public good says that the sum of marginal rates of substitution should be set equal to the marginal rate of transformation. However, this does not define a unique policy—it is consistent with many different levels of the public good being provided, depending on the distribution of resources in society. The Ramsey tax rule is also an example of a second-best Pareto efficient policy. A further important class of second-best policy rules are variants on marginal cost pricing. In all cases, the Pareto efficient policy levels vary according to the distributional criterion being used, the information available to policy makers, and the form of the budget requirement for the industry in question.

Invoking a specific social welfare function permits the study of *optimal* policy. The exact policy depends on the form of social welfare function that is selected and, to the extent that social welfare is egalitarian. Second-best policy models can formalize the idea of an equity efficiency trade off. Society may be willing to have a lower level of total income or average utility in exchange for policies that promote the well-being of socially favored groups.

The welfare economic model is often referred to as the 'Pigouvian' model of government, an important antecedent being Pigou (1920) who was the first to systematize the idea that intervention in the economy is guided by a benevolent government pursuing social objectives. Pigou also played an important role in recognizing market failure as a motivation for designing 'corrective' policies—taxation to reduce pollution levels being an important example.

The welfare economic model can be thought of as generating 'rules for good government' using a systematic model of the economy and what drives human well—being. The model constitutes one of the crowning achievements of twentieth century economics. The welfare economic approach displaced the rather ad hoc policy reasoning displayed in classical economics.

For example, when Adam Smith discussed the role of government in *The Wealth of Nation* ([1776] 1976), he did so by cataloguing what government should do rather than putting forward a framework. The following passage from the wealth of nations is quite typical:

According to the system of natural liberty, the sovereign has only three duties to attend to...first, the duty of protecting the society from the violence and invasion of other independent societies; secondly, the duty of protecting, so far as possible, every member of the society from the injustice or oppression of every other member of it, or the duty of establishing an exact administration of justice, and thirdly, the duty of erecting and maintaining certain public works and certain public institutions, which it can never be for the interest of any individual, or small number of individuals, to erect and maintain

(Smith [1776] 1976: IV, chap. IX)

Even in Book V of *The Wealth of Nations* where Smith develops various principles of good policy, he does not develop an overarching set of principles, but a catalogue of functions.

The great attraction of the welfare economic model is precisely that it does give a unified way of thinking and a set of powerful lessons. Arguably it is this that elevated the position of economists over other branches of the social sciences in the policy sphere. That said, it has tended to say little about the process of policy choice and implementation. To that extent, it gives a highly technocratic perspective.

1.4.3 *The public choice critique of welfare economics*

The welfare economic approach to policy has been criticized by those working in the public choice tradition, for failing to consider how actual policy choices are made and implemented. Even if we were to understand what optimal policies are, there need be no guarantee that the kinds of decision making institutions that we observe in reality will bring them about. The *public choice* critique of welfare economics says that, by failing to model government, it provides a misleading view of the appropriate role for government (see Buchanan (1972) for a forceful plea for a level playing field). The landmark contribution in this regard is Buchanan and Tullock (1962) which showed how choices in a democratic system need not conform to any kind of normative ideal.

The main point of the critique is to remind us that the welfare economic case for intervention offers no guarantee that actual governments making real decisions about policies will actually pick the optimal policies according to a welfare economic criterion. While Pigou (1920) is sometimes thought of as one of the main instigators of the welfare economic tradition, it is clear that he was well aware of this point when he argued that:

It is not sufficient to contrast the imperfect adjustments of unfettered enterprise with the best adjustment that economists in their studies can imagine. For we cannot expect that any State authority will attain, or will even wholeheartedly seek, that ideal. Such authorities are liable alike to ignorance, to sectional pressure and to personal corruption by private interest.

(Pigou 1920: 296)

While such concerns may sound rather abstract, they have force in real world contexts. A good example concerns designing interventions when corruption is a possibility. In addition to the standard economic benefits from intervention, it is necessary to weigh up the consequences for corruption.

To address these issues requires models of public resource allocation that enable us to understand when and if government will behave in accordance with a welfare economic model. This requires a significant increase in the competence of economists, requiring them to become experts not only in market resource allocation but also in the study of politics and bureaucracy. Moreover, unless economists engage in this analysis, there is a risk that they will become sidelined in many debates about economic policy. Although there is a long-standing interest in these issues, it is only in the past 15 years or so that mainstream economics has put incentives in government at the heart of the study of policy problems.

1.5 Political economy

The term 'political economy' has been used in many contexts to refer to different intellectual projects. Hence, it is useful to set the newer usage of this term in its wider historical context. The classical economists used the term political economy synonymously with economics. Sometime in the late nineteenth century, scholars of the economy came to use the term economics apart from political economy and, ultimately, use of the term political economy lapsed in mainstream economics.

Of particular note in this era is the work of John Maynard Keynes's father—John Neville Keynes—who published his *The Scope and Method of Political Economy* in 1891. On page 34, he identifies three branches of economics: positive science (what is), normative or regulative science (what ought to be), and the art of political economy—which he refers to as 'formulation of precepts'. As for John Stuart Mill, it is apparent that John Neville Keynes views the art of political economy as the branch of economics by which practical maxims are formulated. He remarks:

when we pass … to problems of taxation, or problems that concern the relations of the State with trade and industry, or to the general discussion of communistic and socialistic schemes—it is far from being the case that economic considerations hold the field exclusively. Account must be taken of the ethical, social, and political considerations, that lie outside the sphere of political economy regarded as a science.

(Keynes 1891: 55)

There is little evidence, however, that studying the art of political economy as described here was of great interest to mainstream economists in the first half of the twentieth century. Nonetheless, the modern political economy literature is re-engaging with the art of political economy as envisaged by the classical economists.

Throughout the twentieth century, the term 'political economy' remained in use in discussions of comparative economic systems—particularly in debates about the relative merits of socialism and capitalism. This brand of political economy was in part the preserve of Marxist thinkers. But it was also evident in Austrian thinkers such as Hayek and Schumpeter.

Political economy considerations surfaced particularly in the market socialism debates of the 1930s where once again they intersected with mainstream economics. Lange (1936, 1937) and Lerner (1944) had proposed a centralized system which could replicate the market system by using a social planner. Hayek's position turned on two key problems of planned systems: (i) that government is not omniscient and that the informational requirements assumed are too demanding (ii) that it hinged on a model of government that was too optimistic in assuming benevolence. Von Hayek ([1944] 1976) argued persuasively that recognizing the role of markets provided the answer to the first of these. The resolution of the second problem was less clear. Clearly some guarantees of liberty were necessary given the limitations on personal freedom under socialism. However, how democratic systems could be organized to improve the workings of the economy and government was left unclear. Resolving this issue would require a model of democracy which Hayek plainly did not have.[17]

With the fall of socialism, these debates make interesting history of economic thought but offer little of concrete relevance to contemporary economics and politics. But it is clear that modern political economy does have its roots in a prior set of debates in which political and economic issues were jointly influential.[18]

The immediate postwar period saw debates about what drives government quality being muted in mainstream economics. The move towards systemization and formalization of economics saw mainstream policy economics largely dominated by a technocratic mode descendant from Pigou's economics of welfare. By systematizing the notion of market failure, Pigou seemed to promise an economic theory of the mixed economy and the role of government. Much economic theory saw the problem of planning as purely technical.[19]

In continental Europe, the schism between economics and politics was less marked than in the English-speaking world. This was particularly clear in the field of public finance which remained imbued with law and political science throughout.[20] But it was not until the postwar period with the creation of the field of public choice that these ideas were systematized into a body of understanding and integrated with mainstream economics in the English speaking world. The key

[17] See Boettke (2003) and Boettke and Lopez (2002) for discussion.

[18] Referring back to the quote above from John Neville Keynes, it is clear that he saw debates about the merits of socialism as falling under the 'art of political economy'.

[19] See, for example, Heal (1973).

[20] The excellent collection edited by Musgrave and Peacock (1958) brought these contributions to the attention of the English-speaking world.

contributors in this enterprise were Buchanan and Tullock whose 1962 book *The Calculus of Consent* provides a landmark analysis of problems of log-rolling and implications of democratic governance for taxation and public expenditures.

In some circles the term 'public choice' is used to refer to *any* analysis that links economics and politics.[21] But here, I am using it more narrowly to represent the work beginning in the Virginia School in the 1950s. This has three distinctive features.

The first is the assumption of rational self-interest in the study of political interactions. Thus, Buchanan says, 'Individuals must be modeled as seeking to further their own narrow self-interest, narrowly defined, in terms of measured net wealth position, as predicted or expected' (Buchanan 1989a: 20).

To most economists, this may seem innocuous. After all, economic agents as rational egoists is a firmly established tradition in a market context. However, below we will argue that setting aside issues of selection in politics constitutes a blind-spot.

The second key idea in public choice analysis is the importance of constitutions as constraints on self-interest. Here, Buchanan says, 'To improve politics, it is necessary to improve or reform rules, the framework within which the game of politics is played. There is no suggestion that improvement lies in the selection of morally superior agents who will use their powers in some "public interest"' (Buchanan 1989b: 18). In this sense, he is firmly interested in the project of designing effective political institutions.

The third key aspect of public choice is its normative framework. Economists have tended to work with a particular (broadly utilitarian) framework in which good and bad outcomes are seen in terms of their impact on the individual's utilities taken as an indicator of well-being. Various proposals have been made for how to trade these off to get measures of 'social welfare', which allows the analyst to engage in policy debates about good and bad policies. But the public choice approach is rooted in a quite different normative tradition—one that goes back to classical eighteenth-century views of the state (particularly those of John Locke). The main idea is that the legitimate domain of the state is related to what freely contracting individuals would be willing to agree to, but only that.

21 For example, Mueller (2003).

While Buchanan has been a champion of these ideas, it was the Swedish economist, Knut Wicksell, who first applied these ideas in a concrete policy setting—the provision of public expenditures (see Wicksell 1896). He studied the problem of public provision via unanimity rule and observed that, with benefit taxation, the allocation would obey the contractarian ideal. This approach conflicts with a standard welfare economic framework which appeals to some other authority (the guardian of social preferences) as the arbiter of the justness of the allocation.

This intellectual framework gives rise to the public choice critique of welfare economics observing a conflict between its recommendations and the kind of idealized world that Buchanan and Wicksell envisaged. On the whole, the case for intervention is less permissive than the welfare economic view. Moreover, the framework of the analysis has a libertarian flavour.

As we will discuss in the next chapter, the public choice approach also offers a particular slant on the concept of *political failure*—the allocation of resources in a democratic process which does not meet Wicksell's test. Moreover, it was a key insight of Buchanan and Tullock (1962) that there is no guarantee that a system of representative government based on majority rule would be immune to such failures.

The public choice approach has been influential in thinking about many of the broad issues concerning the proper role of government. However, it is less associated with the creation of specific models for the study of politics.[22]

Chicago political economy views politics as a process of competition for support with policies tending towards those that maximize political support offered either through votes or direct monetary transfers. Its pioneers are Gary Becker, Sam Peltzman, and George Stigler.[23] These tend to downplay the significance of particular institutional differences in the policy process.[24] The Chicago approach tends to be associated with relatively reduced form models which does make the models fairly easy to use in complex policy environments. While

---

[22] The Leviathan model of Brennan and Buchanan (1980) is perhaps the main exception. This supposes that government picks taxes and public spending to maximize the size of government.

[23] See, for example, Becker (1983); Peltzman (1976); and Stigler (1971).

[24] Mulligan et al. (2004) even argue that a failure to find a significant difference in policies between democracies and non-democracies is consistent with the Chicago approach. This is because the latter puts so little weight on the importance of voting per se in determining policy outcomes.

policies can be distorted by political resource allocation, one of the main intellectual thrusts of the Chicago approach is a tendency for policies to be efficient. This comes from the observation that support maximizing politicians have a tendency to prefer efficient policies. As we shall see, this turns out to be important in thinking about different notions of government failure.

The most influential economic model for the study of political resource allocation is that due to Downs (1957). While Downs's book was filled with many important ideas, the main one that caught on among economists was a justification for the idea that politics would converge to the preferences of the median voter. Downs described politics in the language of competing firms called 'parties' where customers were voters. He observed that if parties cared only about winning, then they would have an incentive to converge to the centre. Similar ideas were also being developed in Black (1958) who recognized the importance of preference restrictions (*single-peakedness*) to this prediction.

While it came to dominate economists' approaches to political economy, there are deep-seated problems with the approach. First, the reason that parties pick the median outcome in simple models is that this outcome is a *Condorcet winner*: an outcome that beats all others in pairwise comparisons.[25] In the absence of a Condorcet winner, there can be *cycles*. This would happen if there are three alternatives (A,B,C) where A can beat B in a simple majority vote, B can beat C, and C can beat A. Such Condorcet cycles present an insurmountable problem for the Downsian approach since one party can always win an election by proposing something different from the other party whatever that party is proposing. This matters since in just about any interesting policy problem—particularly those with multiple policy dimensions—no Condorcet winner exists.[26]

Countless papers have been written elaborating this point and trying to propose ways around it.[27] But the bottom line is clear. There is relatively little to commend median voter predictions from a theoretical point of view, except in very special circumstances. Even so, the model has gained enormous influence among economists

---

[25] This term is named after the French aristocrat, the Marquis de Condorcet.

[26] This is closely linked to the fact that the idea of a median outcome does not make much sense for a multi-dimensional distribution.

[27] See Mueller (2003) for a discussion of many of these.

and is presented as a cornerstone of political economy analysis to generations of students.

There is another important theoretical problem with Downs's approach. The model assumes that citizens care about policies while politicians are infinitely pliable—adopting any position to get elected. But if politicians have even a little preference for policies then they will have an incentive to renege after the election. Thus, the model needs to build in reasons why the policy pledges of politicians are credible. One way to approach this is by supposing that politics is a repeated game in which individuals build reputations as in Alesina (1988). However, he shows that this will not typically result in complete convergence. Another is to see credibility as coming from picking candidates with appropriate policy preferences as in Osborne and Slivinksy (1996) and Besley and Coate (1997).

The Downsian approach held much more appeal for economists than political scientists. The latter had long been aware of the evidence from polling data suggesting systematic divergence between median preferences and policy outcomes on key dimensions.[28] The model could offer little insight into where convergence might happen and where it would be absent.

The final problem with an agenda building on the Downsian model is the fact that it is not particularly useful in looking at institutional differences. Indeed if politics is about seeking out median preferences among the electorate, there would be little scope for institutional structure in shaping preference aggregation. There is plenty of good evidence that structures matter in practice and hence that something is at work beyond voter preferences in determining policy outcomes.[29]

The more recent literature has not solved the problem of studying political competition in the absence of a Condorcet winner posed by the Downsian model. But it has made sure to keep this firmly in the background. There are some new modeling approaches, but the approach is not built around any kind of dominant political paradigm. A few key approaches are, however, gaining popularity.

Part of the difficulty in the Downsian paradigm is the fact that there is little institutional restriction on policy *proposals*. It is very difficult to get a stable point when any policy can be proposed by any political

---

[28] See, for example, Weissberg (1976).
[29] See, for example, Persson and Tabellini (2003).

actor at any time. By adding more institutional structure to a model, the degree of freedom open to political actors is diminished and it may be easier to understand policy formation. This idea was a key insight of Shepsle and Weingast (1981) who discuss how restrictions of the structure of proposal power within a legislature can be used to generate a stable point in a multidimensional policy space. Roemer (2001) restricts proposal power by modeling within-party conflict. Such restrictions improve the odds of developing a model that predicts an equilibrium outcome in a particular policy context, providing a basis for empirical analysis. Restricting proposal power is also at the heart of the 'agenda setter' model of Romer and Rosenthal (1978).

Another way to create the possibility of an equilibrium is to relax the requirement that the equilibrium be in pure strategies. A number of authors have investigated this (see, for example, Banks and Duggan (1999)).[30] Predicting the outcome now becomes an involved process and lacks the simplicity of the median voter outcome. Hence, the Downsian model loses many of its attractions after going down this route.

Probabilistic voting features in many recent contributions. This recognizes that there are random shocks to voter intentions which make the mapping from policy choices into political outcomes uncertain. This simple device is powerful in making concrete progress in studying political strategy.[31] The influential monograph by Persson and Tabellini (2000) makes extensive use of this device in exploring the policy implications of different models. This approach often assumes that there are some fixed and some pliable policy dimensions with competition taking place on the latter.[32]

Old style political economy paid little attention to the selection of politicians. For example, the Downsian model sees policies, not politicians, as the currency of political competition. But in a representative democracy, it is politicians who are elected and are charged with making policy. This idea has been formalized recently by Osborne and

[30] See also Myerson (1993).
[31] It also helps to overcome some of the technical difficulties associated with finding an equilibrium point in a Downsian model which has an inherent 'discontinuity' in the payoff function around the point at which a party switches from winning to losing or vice versa. A probabilistic voting model tends to make the probability of winning a smooth function of policy choices over some range.
[32] Lindbeck and Weibull (1987) is an important precursor. They assume that parties care solely about winning. Calvert (1985) and Wittman (1977) consider parties with policy preferences.

Slivinski (1996) and Besley and Coate (1997). These models suppose that citizens elect politicians who then implement their preferred policy outcomes. An implication of the candidate centred view of political competition discussed above is that the identity of candidates matter to policy outcomes.[33] Such models can work in complicated policy environments although equilibria may also be in mixed strategies.

Models of extra-electoral policy making are important as well in the political economy literature. Recent contributions have been heavily influenced by Grossman and Helpman (1994) who formulated the problem of lobbying using an approach in which policy favors are auctioned to the highest bidder. Policy outcomes then reflect the 'willingness to pay' of organized lobbies. This approach has provided a much more transparent way of thinking about lobbying compared to the previous generation of models which typically had a black box 'influence function'.[34]

The recent literature has a core concern with empirical testing of ideas. There is a wealth of data to be exploited as well as scope to generate new data sets. There are many studies that look at cross-country variation—exploiting the many differences in institutions that we see between national governments.[35] The great advantage of this is that the extent of institutional variation is vast creating many possibilities for comparisons of institutions. However, on the downside, such institutions tend to be relatively fixed over time and there are many sources of heterogeneity across countries which it is difficult to control for in a convincing manner. The difficulty then lies in discerning the difference between the effect of institutions on outcomes versus some other unmeasurable factor that is correlated with institutions. This can only be overcome with extreme ingenuity.

Another class of studies exploits variation within countries—where there are differences in politics across subjurisdictions.[36] This is not immune to the problems of unobserved heterogeneity discussed in relation to cross-country studies. The fact that many institutions remain fixed over time is also an issue. However, there are sometimes

---

[33] Lee et al. (2004) has looked at close elections (i.e. those determined by a few points) and argue that the data support the candidate centered view of politics for US elections.

[34] See, for example, Becker (1983).

[35] Persson and Tabellini (2003) is an excellent compendium of what can be achieved using such sources.

[36] See Besley and Case (2003) for a review of what has been achieved for cross-state variation in the US.

cases where a change in institutions or some suitable interaction with a time-varying factor can be exploited. More generally, subnational data probably suffer less than cross-country data in having highly heterogeneous cross-sectional units. But such studies typically have less variation in interesting outcomes and institutions to exploit.

Finally, there is scope for increasing collection of bespoke data sets to examine specific policy issues. Economists have long undertaken household survey work to investigate economic behavior. There is similarly a tradition of collecting data sets to examine political behavior: voting, activism, and so on. But only rarely have the two been put together to get a more complete picture. There is growing interest in doing so and in developing pictures of how policy choices evolve. Bespoke data sets can also be used to supplement standard data from official sources.

Public resource allocation has both short- and long-run effects on the economy. One distinctive feature of the recent political economy literature is the attention that it pays to the dynamics of politics and economics. A key aspect of democratic political life is that governments are typically short-lived while the consequences of many policies are not. Kydland and Prescott (1977) observed that even benevolent governments would have an incentive to make promises that were not credible—for example promise low taxes to encourage investment and subsequently renege on the promise. But the problem is much worse with short-lived government.

A variety of issues have been studied in models that emphasize this feature of political life. A key example is the incentive to incur public debt as a strategic measure to constrain future governments.[37] The political business cycle is another example. Accounts of government incentives to inflate the economy before an election have been around for a long while. But only fairly recently has it been understood how to think about this when voters are not being systematically fooled.[38]

It is also now clear that long-run patterns of development are tied up with the process of political development. Problems of state failure are endemic in low income countries and their study has been to central to appreciating the forces that shape economic development.[39]

---

[37] See the discussion and references in Persson and Tabellini (2000).

[38] Rogoff (1990) uses a dynamic model with imperfect information to develop a 'signalling theory' of equilibrium business cycles.

[39] See Acemoglu and Robinson (2003) for a recent insightful discussion of these issues.

It is clear from this brief overview, that there is already a lot of work on issues of incentives in politics—most of the approaches to political resource allocation discussed above are concerned with understanding how particular assumptions about the structure of political institutions and organization shape policy choice. For the most part, the conflict of interest being resolved in the models discussed here is that between different groups of citizens who have divergent policy interests—the classic spatial model of politics is the 'ideal type' of this kind. Politics is then predominantly about the problem of preference aggregation. In the next section, we look at models which focus more on the conflict of interest between citizens and government: political agency models.

1.6 Incentives and selection in politics

Most of the analysis of this book—especially that in Chapters 3 and 4—is focused on how elections can resolve the conflict of interest between citizens and government. When political authority is delegated to politicians, then they hold the public trust between elections. Constitutions offer only limited provisions for the control over politicians—punishing them only for the grossest of abuses. The main sanction for poor performance is electoral—those who perform badly will not be re-elected. Hence, politics is about achieving *accountability* of politicians to voters.

The importance of elections as an accountability mechanism has long been recognized. For example, Alexis de Toqueville viewed US presidential elections in this way when he noted that

The President is chosen for four years, and he may be re-elected, so that the chances of a future administration may inspire him with hopeful undertakings for the public good and give him the means to carry them into execution

(de Tocqueville [1835] 1994: 121)

In similar vein, Madison recognizes this in *The Federalist Papers* when he notes that:

the House of Representatives is so constituted as to support in the members an habitual recollection of their dependence on the people. Before the sentiments impressed on their minds by the mode of their elevation can be effaced by the exercise of power, they will be compelled to anticipate the moment when their power is to cease, when their exercise of it is to be reviewed, and when they must descend to the level from which they were raised; there forever to remain unless a fairful discharge of their trust shall have established their title to the renewal of it.

(Madison 1961: LVII)

Information is important in thinking about electoral accountability. Voters who hold politicians to account are likely to do so more effectively when they can observe what they are doing. This brings to the fore the role of information providers such as the media and civil society (think-tanks and policy analysts) in increasing accountability.

As we shall see in Chapter 3, it is useful to think about the distinction between formal and real accountability. A politician is formally accountable if there is some institutional structure that allows the possibility of some action to be taken against him/her (such as being voted out of office) in the event that he/she does a poor job. But there is no guarantee that such accountability mechanisms are used effectively. *Real* accountability requires that those who hold politicians to account have sufficient information (for example about the politician's action) to make the system work.

This approach to studying political life was pioneered by Barro (1973) and Ferejohn (1986). They showed how the threat of not being re-elected could curtail rent extraction by politicians. The focus, therefore, is on elections as an incentive mechanism. The problem of opportunism is then essentially like a problem of moral hazard in the contracting literature.

The second generation models—such as Rogoff (1990) and Coate and Morris (1995)—have looked at the implications of agents who differ in their type, thus adding concerns of adverse selection. Elections then serve two key roles: creating incentives and selecting the best candidate.

The idea that there are some individuals who are better suited to public life than others is an interesting one. The great American political scientist V.O. Key certainly regarded political selection to be an important issue when he remarked,

The nature of the workings of government depends ultimately on the men who run it. The men we elect to office and the circumstances we create that affect their work determine the nature of popular government. Let there be emphasis on those we elect to office.

(Key 1956: 10)

Selection could matter for two main reasons: differences in competence between individuals and differences in motivation. With motivation comes concerns about integrity, honesty, altruism, and policy interests. The quote from Madison at the beginning of this chapter suggests that he had both in mind. Having 'wisdom' is akin to competence and 'virtue' is akin to motivation.

The idea that individuals differ in terms of their competence as politicians is similar to the idea that individuals have match-specific skills in models of the labor market. Whether this is innate or acquired is far from clear. It is also unclear whether previous career experience is a reliable guide to whether an individual has greater competence. Madison's reference to wisdom suggested that he had in mind the need to have politicians with generally high levels of human capital and innate ability.

Dealing with differences in motivation provides more of a departure from standard economics. We are used to assuming, for most aspects of market behavior, that individuals are self-interested. Whether this should be extended to their behavior in public life is debatable. As we noted above, Buchanan puts weight on the idea that ruthless self-interest is the correct assumption to make. The idea of modeling political choices from the premise that actors are self-interested is also characteristic of the Chicago approach to political economy. Thus, Peltzman (1980) assumes that 'political preferences are motivated purely by self-interest' (page 16). The self-interest model is also thought to underpin the growth of government that we observed above. For example, Holsey and Borcherding (1997) comment that the 'political paradigm... views public services as selfishly redistributive [i.e. transfers of purely private goods to politically favored groups], hence government expenditures are determined by the most influential agents' (pp 565–6).[40]

The idea that self-interest assumption should be applied to the conduct of public life is far from new. The philosopher and economist David Hume, a contemporary of Adam Smith, argues eloquently in favor of this when he says:

In contriving any system of government and fixing several checks and controls of the constitution, every man ought to be supposed a knave and to have no other end, in all his actions, than private interest. By this

---

[40] Although explaing the *growth* of government requires that the self-interest of politicians has increased over time due, say, to a decline in civic virtue.

interest, we must government him, and by means of it, notwithstanding his insatiable avarice and ambition, cooperate to the public good

(Hume 1742)

Smith himself had a somewhat schizophrenic view. He viewed markets as the perfect outlet for self-interest channeled in the common good. But his theory of moral sentiments attached great weight to altruism in non-market contexts. Hayek proposed the following extension:

Smith's chief concern was not so much with what man might occasionally achieve when he was at his best but that he should have as little opportunity as possible to do harm when he was at his worst. It would scarcely be too much to claim that the main merit of the individualism which he and his contemporaries advocated is that it is a system under which bad men can do least harm. It is a social system which does not depend for its functioning on our finding good men for running it, or on all men becoming better than they are now, but which makes good use of men in all their given variety and complexity, sometimes good and sometimes bad.

(von Hayek 1948: 11–12)

This has echoes of Madison: the key question is how institutions shape actions and how they can, if at all, promote selection of those most suited to public office.

Of course, accepting that individuals are broadly self-interested is consistent with a wide variety of utility functions for politicians. For example, liking policies that help the poor can be regarded as a form of self-interest in so far as politicians gain satisfaction from doing this. Hence the real issue is how narrowly this assumption is interpreted. It is clear that very often self-interest is defined in terms of something like consumption of private goods.

Applied to politics, it is this kind of narrow self-interest motive which underpins accounts of political corruption. It is this notion of self-interest which underpins the agency models of Barro (1973) and Ferejohn (1986). There is little doubt that this kind of self-interested behavior is important in practice and its importance has been recognized increasingly in recent discussions of the role of the state. The most egregious examples—the overwhelming kleptocracies of the world—have been in non-democratic systems where electoral sanctions are limited or non-existent.

There are three other models of motivation in politics: ego-rent, policy preference, and fiduciary duty. We discuss each in turn.

Political economy models often assume that politicians seek solely to win office. Perhaps the best-known political model founded on this is Downs (1957) which assumed that parties do whatever it takes to win office. The desire to win could be interpreted as another manifestation of self-interest. However, conceptually, the desire to hold office could be distinct from narrow self-interest. Moreover, the psychology literature attaches weight to the way in which winning an election can bolster self-esteem which would create a reward to holding office which was neither dependent on policy nor on extracting private goods. This model has been invoked by Rogoff (1990) and Maskin and Tirole (2004) among others to describe the preferences of politicians who are otherwise benevolent. This is often referred to as an 'ego rent' derived as a non-pecuniary benefit from being in office. Pure ego rents are distinct from a monetary rent since reducing the possibility of malfeasance while in office does not diminish the re-election incentives of agents who earn them.

As we mentioned above, the motive to enter for office could be to influence policy.[41] As citizens, politicians are affected by policies and hence have self-interested reasons to be policy motivated. This view encompasses at one extreme a very narrow view in which individuals care about specific issues such as the environment or tax policy. However, policy preference can also be mediated through vaguer ideas like ideologies—world views that shape a broader set of policy predilections.

One important model of motivation in politics that has received less attention in modelling the behavior of politicians, but which, in line with the models developed in the chapters below, is the *fiduciary* model. The term fiduciary comes from the Latin verb *fidere*: to trust. It is most often applied in describing the duties of trustees and directors of company boards.[42]

Fiduciarity has two main aspects—a duty of care and a duty of loyalty. The idea of political office as trusteeship runs through Madison's

---

[41] See especially Calvert (1985) and Wittman (1977). Persson and Tabellini (2000) reviews the literature.

[42] This trustee view of political representation is most closely associated with Edmund Burke who put it forward in a speech to the electors of Bristol in 1774. It also found favor in the writings of J.S. Mill.

essays in *The Federalist Papers* who refers to leaders as upholding public trust. In modern parlance, the duty of care could be interpreted as refraining from moral hazard. The duty of loyalty is less clear in some models, but broadly refers to the duty of politicians to act in the interest of citizens at large, eschewing narrow self-interest. The models that we develop in Chapters 3 and 4 have politicians who if elected would fulfill their fiduciary duty on behalf of voters. These are contrasted with narrowly self-interested politicians.

Just why some individuals take their fiduciary duties seriously while others do not is not clear. Performing a fiduciary duty could be thought of as a form of *intrinsic motivation*. This idea, which originated among psychologists, has only recently been brought into economic thinking.[43] It refers to a case where actions are driven by internal factors and are pursued 'for their own sake' rather than because of some well defined external reward. Thus, a politician who upholds his duty of loyalty may be willing to do so even though he is forgoing an increase in his utility by doing so. On this view, being a trustworthy politician is a type rather than a consequence of incentives. The role of elections is to find ways of sorting in such politicians rather than incentivizing them.

To assume that politicians who take their fiduciary duties seriously are completely immune to influence by incentives is perhaps too strong. The extent of incentives may depend on whether they agree wholly with the ends that they are pursuing. Besley and Ghatak (2005) develop a model of agent motivation in which the extent to which agents take care depends on the extent to which they agree with the *mission* being pursued by an organization. Thus, a politician could be much more motivated when he/she agrees with the cause. This naturally creates some ambiguity in the exercise of the duty of loyalty in such cases. Those voters whose mission preferences are most closely aligned with politicians will tend to receive more attention from incumbents. This suggests that citizens may care about which sort of fiduciary politician they select.

Invoking broader notions of motivation is consistent with wide-ranging evidence on behavior in public and private life—especially that emerging from laboratory experiments. It has long been known that narrow assumptions about human motivation have not fared well in explaining individuals' contributions to public goods when

---

[43] See, for example, Frey (1997); Murdock (2002); and Bénabou and Tirole (2003).

these are studied in the laboratory. The evidence from experimental work reviewed by Ledyard (1995) catalogs many important anomalies to narrow self-interest models. Even in the context of market interactions, Fehr and Falk (2002) document how concerns about fairness in resource allocation are needed to explain behavior.[44]

Once it is recognized that politicians are heterogeneous in important ways, it is necessary to develop models that explain who will be selected. Let us suppose that there are some individuals who will make better politicians and that all citizens would prefer a better politician in office—politician quality is a valence issue. Then, we can study the process by which political selection takes place and understand why some low quality politicians can survive. The citizen—candidate approach of Osborne and Slivinsky (1996) and Besley and Coate (1997) provides a useful framework for thinking about this. They model the entry, voting and policy making stages when citizens can choose to become candidates for political office.

This approach suggests three main reasons why some low quality politicians get into office. First, there is the possibility of restrictions on entry and voting. If the cost of political campaigns differs across candidates of different quality, then either poor or high quality candidates may be deterred. Political elites may also prefer corruptible candidates in order to preserve their rents. If they control entry (through party systems) then high quality candidates may also be deterred. This mechanism can also work by controlling the voting process to prevent high quality candidates from being elected, even if they stand.[45]

The second reason for low quality candidates is informational. Bad politicians may enter since there is some chance that the voters will not be able to identify them during election campaigns. This has been studied by Caselli and Morelli (2004). This results in bad candidates

[44] Moving beyond narrow self-interest is necessary to create a satisfactory theory of voting. The possibility that individuals vote on the basis of narrow self-interest runs foul of the fact that the probability of being decisive is so low in mass elections. This has led to a wide variety of alternatives being proposed which are based on some kind of broader motivation such as duty (see Aldrich 1997 for a review). This notion of duty fits very well with the fiduciary model that we are suggesting.

[45] Poutvarra and Takalo (2003) develop a model in which the value of holding office impinges on candidate quality via its effect on election campaigns. Gehlbach and Sonin (2004) apply a citizen candidate framework to ask when economic elites (such as businessmen) will choose to run for political office. Running for office is in this world an alternative to lobbying for influence. They argue that business candidates lead to greater misuse of public office.

entering as rent seekers if there are significant private benefits from running for office.

The third reason for existence of low quality politicians is developed in Besley and Coate (1997) which considers the implications of coordination problems among voters. Suppose that there are two low quality candidates running for office who are polarized in the policy space. Then entry by high quality candidates can be deterred if these candidates fear that voters would be unable to coordinate on the high quality candidates. Otherwise, the result would be for entry by high quality candidates to increase the probability that a candidate with the opposite policy preference will win.

If the process of entry, campaigning and voting cannot weed out low quality politicians, then observing their performance while in office will play a role. But the initial situation is one of uncertainty about the type of the incumbent (adverse selection). Hence, combining this model with one where incentives matter requires taking the twin informational problems of moral hazard and adverse selection in politics seriously.

To summarize, while it is clear that incentive issues are important in understanding conflicts of interest between government and citizens, there are good reasons to think that selection is important too. This could be selection of more competent politicians or those who will take their fiduciary duty seriously. Much of this book is devoted to understanding how politics and public resource allocation works when both incentives and selection are taken seriously.

1.7 Concluding comments

If government is to work well, then problems of incentives and selection must be dealt with. In situations where either good politicians are selected and/or incentive problems are dealt with, we have a world approximating the standard normative model of government. At the other extreme, there is a preponderance of self-interested politicians who use public office to further their personal ends. To the extent that the incentive mechanisms available are weak, this will result in low quality government. In this sense, understanding the political economy of public resource allocation in settings where selection is an issue is a useful step along the way to understanding the possibility of benevolent government.

Following in the footsteps of the pioneers whose work we refer to above, there is now a considerable body of knowledge to draw upon. The remaining chapters of this book are largely synthetic. They develop frameworks which are useful to explaining the main ideas. However, by developing their own frameworks there is some hope of bringing unity to the area. But this is a preliminary report on work in progress.

The modern political economy literature is having some success in extending the competence of economists in the direction of understanding policy processes as well as policy outcomes. The project coheres well with Madison's vision in *The Federalist Papers*. This is not a project about restraining government, but of understanding the institutional preconditions for government to work. With this in mind, we turn to the project at hand.

2

The anatomy of government failure

[E]fficient government... is a standard by which performance can be measured, similar to corresponding standards by
which performance of households and firms in the private
sector are assessed. Actual performance will differ among
governments and periods of time, but efficient conduct and
constructive leadership are not beyond reach.

(Musgrave 1999: 34)

2.1 Introduction

Government failure is a term that is often used, but rarely defined.
The basic and highly intuitive idea is that there are systematic reasons
why government fails to deliver the kind of service to its citizens that
would be ideal. It is invoked, in particular, as a reason to be doubtful
about the usefulness of the standard welfare economic recommendations for government intervention. An analyst will frequently say
that government failures need to be weighed against market failures
in making the case for government intervention according to welfare
economic prescriptions.

However, unlike its sister notion of market failure, no systematic
account can be found of this idea in the political economy literature.
This chapter tries to remedy this by discussing alternative notions of
government failure. It will do so through some general discussion as
well as developing a simple example to illustrate the main ideas.

It is important to distinguish *government* failure from a narrower
concept of *political* failure. Government failure refers to problems

that arise when one actor in the economy (the state) monopolizes the legitimate use of force. Political failure refers to the narrower idea of problems that arise when power to control this monopoly is allocated in *democratic* political systems. Political failures as described here are therefore a subset of government failures.

Two examples will help to make this distinction clear. The first example is the problem of imperfect information and the provision of public goods. It is well known since the seminal work of Clarke (1971) and Groves (1973) that the inability of governments to measure accurately the valuations that individuals place on public goods may lead to a suboptimal level of government provision. This implies that the Lindahl–Samuelson rule for public goods provision cannot be achieved. The problem is generic to the operation of government and is likely to arise (to some degree) under *any* system of government. Hence, imperfect information of this form may constitute a government failure. But it has nothing to do with politics.

For the second example, consider the problem of finding rules for the operation of a legislature charged with making decisions about public resource allocation. Suppose that the legislature concentrates the power to set the policy agenda to a single individual, with the others able to vote on his/her proposals. Suppose that this agenda setter represents a particular district, but through self-interest, fails to internalize the impact that spending in his/her own district has on other districts. This will lead to a suboptimal pattern of resource allocation—it may be possible to construct a Pareto improvement in public resource allocation (assuming that suitable compensatory transfers can be made). Imperfections in the operation of legislative bodies can result in political failures.

It is often not important whether a particular problem in the functioning of government is a government failure or is specifically associated with democratic resource allocation. However, there are two reasons to be interested especially in political failure. First, studying political failure may give a sense of the potential drawbacks of democracy which as we argued in the last chapter is becoming a dominant institution. As with studies of markets which motivated ideas of market failure, it is useful to know how democracy really works. Second, studying political failures may give concrete insights into how democratic systems of government may be improved, in particular how changing the rules of the game can lead to improvements in resource allocation.

The standard way in which economists discuss market resource allocation provides a model for thinking about government failure. As we discussed in the previous chapter, the primary criteria of assessment are equity and efficiency. While the term *market failure* is typically reserved to describing situations where market resource allocation results in Pareto inefficiency, government failure, as we shall discuss below, has been used rather differently. In fact, there are three main notions that the literature has suggested. Only one of these corresponds straightforwardly to the standard definition of market failure.

As with market failure, it would be useful to understand just how prevalent the use of the term 'government failure' is. There are those, for example Wittman (1997), who have argued that democratic systems will tend to produce efficient results. However, the Public Choice tradition as typified by Buchanan and Tullock (1962) sees the world quite differently. In part, these conflicting views stem from using the term government failure rather differently. Either way, with such conflicting claims, it is necessary to look closely at these issues.[1]

The title of this chapter borrows unashamedly from Bator (1958) which pulled together various ideas of market failure for the first time. He defines his quest as 'an attempt ... to explore ... those phenomena which cause even errorless profit- and preference-maximizing calculation ... to fail to sustain Pareto-efficient allocation' (p. 352). He argues that non-appropriability, non-convexity, and public goods are the main sources of market failure. In principle, we would like to catalog government failures in terms of similarly simple categories.

The procedure we will adopt is similar. We will assume that actors in government and political processes maximize their payoffs under appropriate constraints. We will then explore when this leads to policy outcomes and patterns of private influence activity that are Pareto inefficient. The overall aim is to identify the basis of inefficiencies. We will also broaden the set of possible normative criteria to include cases where political resource allocation is inegalitarian. Finally, we will consider the implications of certain non-consequentialist criteria.

---

[1] Acemoglu (2003) in many ways shares the ambition of this chapter. He frames the issue as understanding why the Coase theorem fails in a political arena. Much of the discussion of government failure here—especially the examples of Pareto inefficiencies—could be framed in this way. Acemoglu (2005) pursues the more ambitious task of looking at institutions in a policy setting in order to understand institutional failure (in the language of this chapter).

As we discuss in greater detail below, ideas about government failure are central to understanding constitution design. However, it also plays a central role in thinking about economic policy reform and reasons why apparently beneficial reforms are not undertaken.[2] By appreciating the specific form that a government failure may take, it may be possible to understand when reforms are likely to work in the way that their architects intend.

2.2 Three notions of government failure

In this section, we discuss three ways of defining policy outcomes as government failures. The first parallels the classic definition of market failure—Pareto inefficiency. The second allows the possibility that the political process produces an 'undesirable' distributional outcome. The third is due to Wicksell and has been developed in the writings of James Buchanan. It is based on whether a particular intervention Pareto dominates what would happen in the absence of government.

As we shall see in the example studied in the next section, these notions of government failure can be applied to the policy *outcome* and to the policy *process*, in other words, to any resources used up in the decision making process. The latter refer, in particular, to standard 'rent-seeking' inefficiencies. Thus, we need to study the set of policy outcomes and a set of private and public actions that are made to achieve this outcome. A government failure might then arise either because the policies selected are poor or because the means of picking (even good) policies is very costly. A system of government free from government failure will pick good policies and policy processes. It will also encourage efficient private actions to affect policy outcomes.

2.2.1 *Pareto inefficiency*

The most obvious definition of government failure to an economist is based on *Pareto efficiency*. This most clearly parallels the textbook case of market failure. This is motivated by a long tradition in public economics which has studied (in particular) Pareto efficient taxation

---

[2] See Rodrik (1996) for an excellent discussion of such issues in general.

and public spending.[3] For example, the Ramsey tax rule and Lindahl–Samuelson rule for provision of public goods are policy rules that follow from the characterization of Pareto efficient policies.

The output of such an exercise is society's *utility possibility frontier*. This characterizes the set of government policies and private resource allocation decisions where an individual cannot be made better off without another being made worse off. Being Pareto inefficient means operating inside this frontier. Pareto inefficiency is the economists' free lunch—it should be possible to pick a different set of policies and/or private decisions so as to make *every* citizen better off.

Market failure is defined as a situation where markets fail to achieve an allocation on the Pareto frontier. Applied to government failure, this approach says that government fails when *policies* result in a society being inside its Pareto frontier. Given the obvious extension of market failure analysis in this way, it is somewhat surprising that this notion of government failure has received so little attention in the literature. It was suggested as the appropriate benchmark for government in Besley and Coate (1997) and developed further in Besley and Coate (1998).

Government failure as Pareto inefficiency is in many ways a weak criterion. As observed in Besley and Coate (1997), any situation where some citizen is given the right to pick policy from the feasible set will be trivially Pareto efficient in a static setting since it is certainly not possible to make the policy maker better off. However, we will see that there are some interesting non-trivial examples of government failure defined this way in dynamic models.

2.2.2 Distributional failures

As we discussed in the previous chapter, Pareto efficiency is frequently deemed too weak a criterion for normative analysis. After all, a political equilibrium in which a dictator transfers the whole of society's resources to himself/herself and a few of his/her cronies can be efficient. Yet few would regard it as a satisfactory state of affairs and many think that this could constitute a government failure. The only way to tackle such concerns is to bring in distributional concerns and to judge the policy outcome and process accordingly.

---

[3] See, for example, Atkinson and Stiglitz (1980).

Some authors, for example Mueller (1996), seem to regard transfers to farmers in rich countries, heavily subsidized public projects (such as the development of Concorde), or geographical targeting of public goods to particular regions as prima facie evidence of government failure.[4] If such transfers are made inefficiently, then this collapses back to the first definition of government failure. However, assuming that this is not a source of Pareto inefficiency, it is clear that there is an implicit appeal to particular social welfare function against which the policy produced by government is being judged. These examples therefore lie in the realm of distributional failures.

Thus, to make this operational requires some kind of distributional metric: a social welfare function. However, unless there is a fair degree of consensus on social preferences, the conclusions from such an analysis will probably be controversial. Since there is little reason to suppose that any kind of political process will maximize a well-defined social welfare function, then the danger is that any policy picked in a democracy will result in a government failure according to this definition.[5] Hence, this notion of government failure risks having no bite at all.

However, this is probably too pessimistic. There might, for example, be rather broad agreement that any decent government should limit the extent to which the government officials use the state for the purposes of self-enrichment, however efficiently they choose to do it. The experience of kleptocratic dictators such as Mobutu in Zaire or Marcos in the Philippines underline the generalized outrage that is felt when government is used as a vehicle for self-enrichment.

Another approach to thinking about government failure which invokes an element of distribution is *social surplus*. The notion of social surplus only makes sense as an efficiency criterion in the case of 'transferable utility': utility that is linear in money. It can then be motivated in terms of a compensation test—of the Hicks-Kaldor variety—where the gainers can compensate the losers. Thence if a policy choice maximizes social surplus there is no direction of policy change in which the gainers can compensate the losers. Conversely, moving towards a

---

[4] See, for example, Mueller (1996: 23).

[5] Proponents of probabilistic voting models have sometimes suggested that particular social welfare functions are maximized in political equilibrium. (See Coughlin (1992) for a discussion.) However, they rest on strong assumptions and it appears unlikely that technological assumptions are at the heart of the distributional conflict implicit in political competition.

surplus maximizing policy will guarantee that gainers from the change can compensate losers.

As is well understood, this logic only seems compelling when compensations are actually paid in which case it corresponds to a Pareto improvement. Moreover, payment of compensation can happen only with a very rich set of policy levers, including lump-sum taxes and transfers. If compensations are not actually paid, then the appeal of surplus maximization is less obvious. It is then best thought of as a distributional rather than an efficiency criterion. Indeed when preferences are linear in money, the social surplus optimum and the utilitarian social welfare optimum frequently coincide.

While surplus maximization often has appeal given the notion of 'making the cake as big as possible', it is better to think of it as a kind of social welfare maximization exercise with a particular social welfare function. In the sequel we will use it this way. In fact, we will use it as our main example for the investigation of distributional failures. This is because we make no pretence that compensations needed to generate a Pareto improvement are being paid.

In more pragmatic terms, there is a sense in which it serves as a powerful force for criticism in the context of government failures. If policies are captured by political elites or special interests and result in lower social surplus, then there will typically be more sympathy in reducing the political advantages of these groups to benefit the broader group of citizens. When employed in this context, the social surplus criterion can indeed be powerful since it can demonstrate that a small group is profiting at the expense of a much wider group. Thus weighing up the consumer surplus losses from tariff protection against the benefits generated for stakeholders within an industry can have influence on policy debates about protectionism.

As we have already mentioned, distributional considerations are also important in thinking through the implications of politicians earning rents from holding office. There are models that put this at centre stage—including the agency models that we discuss in Chapter 3. Another example is the Leviathan model of Brennan and Buchanan (1980) where politicians are assumed to maximize the tax revenue that they can extract from citizens while diverting some tax revenues to private use.

Just how to build a constraint that specifies a government failure in this context is moot even though to many the prima facie case is clear. However, it is worth bearing in mind that the decision to enter politics is likely to be a function of the rewards on offer to politicians and may affect the competence of those who choose to stand for office (with more competent politicians having a higher opportunity cost). Hence, specifying that there should be no reward to holding political office is probably too strong.

One criterion for government failure would investigate whether it is feasible to obtain the same policy outcome with fewer rents. A government failure would then constitute an outcome with 'excessive' rents relative to this benchmark. The surplus maximization criterion could also be useful here in demonstrating that enriching the politician is imposing a significant cost on the voters. Many would not find the case for compensating the politician for his/her loss of rents compelling and hence one of the objections to surplus maximization falls away.

2.2.3 *Wicksellian failures*

Our third notion of government failure is drawn from the writings of Wicksell (1896). He uses a criterion somewhat outside the standard welfare economic model and is best thought of as a rights based approach which is derived from classical liberalism. At the heart of this is the notion that policy outcomes and political decisions should lead to an outcome that Pareto dominates what would be achieved without government. The idea behind this idea is seen clearly in the following passage:

If any public expenditure is to be approved, whether it be a newly proposed or an already existing one, it must generally be assumed that this expenditure as such . . . is intended for an activity useful to the whole of society and so recognized by all classes without exception. If this were not so . . . then I, for one, fail to see how the latter can be considered as satisfying a collective need in the proper sense of the word . . . . It would seem blatant injustice if someone should be forced to contribute toward the costs of some activity which does not further his interests or may even be diametrically opposed to them

(Wicksell 1896: 89)

The main motivation for this idea is to think of government (like the market) as a process of exchange which results in Pareto improvements over some status quo point. Alternatively, it could be approached from a contractual point of view, thinking of citizens as signing up to a grand contract that defines what government will do, with every citizen having veto power over the contract.

This notion limits the extent to which the policy process can lead to redistribution of resources between its citizens. For example, it rules out pure redistribution except in so far as the losers feel altruistic towards the beneficiaries and hence benefit as altruistic donors from redistribution to others. For this reason, the approach is often thought of as providing a conservative way of judging the legitimacy of government intervention. This leads to a marked contrast with the main stream welfare economic tradition. One concern with the approach is the fact that an initially unjust allocation of resources would be perpetuated through history and could not legitimately be changed by government.[6]

2.2.4 *Comparisons*

We will now look at how these ideas of government failure relate to each other in an abstract sense. The example that we develop below will give this more precise content. Here we develop a graphical representation.

As we noted above, the first two criteria of government failure are based on a standard welfare economic approach. They are likely to be nested in the following sense—pretty much any reasonable social welfare function will also regard a Pareto inefficient policy choice as a failure too. Hence, government failures based on Pareto inefficiency tend to be a strict subset of those based on a broader social welfare criterion.

This is illustrated in Figure 2.1 which illustrates a social welfare function defined on the utilities of two citizens, 1 and 2. Point A is the full optimum according to these social preferences. If point B were attained through choice of government policy then this would be deemed a government failure using these social preferences. However, it is not Pareto inefficient. This makes it clear just how widespread

[6] This was clearly recognized by Wicksell (1896) who notes that 'It is clear that justice in taxation tacitly pre-supposes justice in the existing distribution of property and income' (page 108). He goes on, 'if there are within the existing property and income structure ... priveleges ... in open contradiction with modern concepts of law and equity, then society has both the right and duty to revise the existing property structure' (p. 109). Just how this is done is left to something of a fudge and he entertains some kind of qualified majority rule without specifiying the exact procedure or rule.

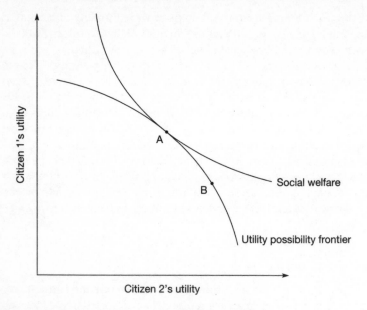

Figure 2.1 Pareto inefficiency and distributional failures

government failures based on distributional preferences are likely to be. Any point away from A is a government failure.

The Wicksellian criterion provides quite a different slant on government failures. Figure 2.2 illustrates the difference between this criterion and that based on Pareto inefficiency. Suppose that at the status quo (no government), the economy would operate at a point like A. This is inside the Pareto frontier representing the possibility that, say, by fixing market failures, the government can make everyone better off. Suppose that point B is the outcome after government intervention. Point B is now on the Pareto frontier and hence is (second best) efficient. However, it does not constitute a Pareto improvement over point A. Hence, if chosen by government, it would constitute a Wicksellian government failure. However, it would not be a government failure according to the Pareto efficiency definition as there is no scope for improving government efficiency. Now consider point C. According to the Wicksellian definition, it is not a government failure as it is a Pareto improvement relative to A. However, the definition based on second best Pareto efficiency would regard it

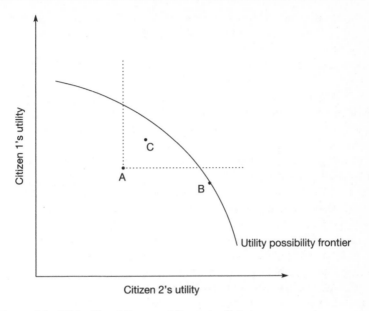

Figure 2.2 Wicksellian failures and Pareto inefficiency

as a government failure. It is possible to make all citizens better off beginning from this point.

Using Wicksell's definition, a government can intervene efficiently in the welfare economic sense and yet still create a government failure. Indeed, a Wicksellian government failure is possible even if the outcome generated in political equilibrium is social welfare maximizing according to an agreed social welfare function.

2.3 An example: financing a public project

As we have shown, these three notions of government failure are distinct. But whether this matters can only be assessed by thinking about concrete policy problems. This is at its starkest in thinking about policies aimed at redistributing income. Suppose that the government does this in the most efficient way. In the case of full information, this would be using lump-sum taxes while otherwise, it would use an optimal income tax or any other appropriate optimal tax system. This is normally studied with reference to a specific social welfare function and any government that did not use this social welfare function would be deemed to have failed on the basis of distributional failure while the Pareto efficiency criterion for government failure would deem *any* tax system which is optimal for some set of welfare weights to be free of government failure. The Wicksellian definition would reject any form of redistribution—so if the economy were Pareto efficient without government intervention, this would mean that there is no legitimate government intervention of this form.

Such abstract discussions of the logic of government failure suggest that pure redistribution is not going to be a case where ideas of government failure have much bite unless there are some predefined notions of acceptable income redistribution. Hence, we will focus for the remainder of the discussion on cases where government can intervene when there is some form of inefficiency—specifically private 'under-provision' of a public good. This canonical example will allow us to have a richer discussion which does not run into the dead end that we have found for pure redistribution. The competing notions of government failure can then have real bite.

Suppose that a community of N individuals has to make a single social decision: whether to build a public project. We denote the decision to build the project by $e \in \{0, 1\}$ where $e = 1$ denotes the case in which the project is constructed. If the project is built, the community must decide how to finance it. Here, we will assume that if the government funds the project then it uses a head tax (equal per capita financing) if the project goes ahead.[7]

There are two groups of citizens: those who value the project and receive utility b from it and those who do not value the project, receiving a utility of zero. The citizens who value the project comprise a fraction γ of the population. All citizens have an income of y and the project costs c to implement. Assume that $y > \frac{c}{N}$, each citizen has an endowment sufficient to pay their per capita cost.

2.3.1 *Private provision*

Before proceeding to public provision, observe that we can motivate public provision of the project as fixing a classic market failure.

---

[7] This is a simplification as such tax systems are not seen in practice. However, the main points that are illustrated using the example do not hinge on this. It is key that there is no optimal lump sum taxation (see below for more on this).

Suppose that the project is to be funded through private subscriptions where each citizen contributes $s_i (i = 1, \ldots, N)$ to its cost. If $\sum_{i=1}^{N} s_i \geq c$, then the project goes ahead and each citizen has any surplus returned to them on an equal sharing basis, in other words, they get $\frac{1}{N} \left(\sum_{i=1}^{N} s_i - c \right)$. If $\sum_{i=1}^{N} s_i < c$, then the project does not go through.

Suppose that we look for a Nash equilibrium in contribution levels. Then, our first observation is that there is no equilibrium in which any citizen who does not like the project makes a positive contribution. However, there are a variety of Nash equilibria where those who value it make a contribution. In each of these, all of the contributors must be pivotal so that the value of the contributions just adds up to c.

As long as $b < c$ then there is always a Nash equilibrium where $s_i = 0$ for all citizens. There may also exist a Nash equilibrium where $s_i = \frac{c}{N\gamma}$ if $N\gamma b > c$. This Pareto dominates the zero provision equilibrium in this instance and hence failure to achieve it leads to a classic 'market' failure.

To motivate government intervention, therefore, we will focus on the case where there is zero private provision. This discrete case is arguably artificial in the sense that an efficient equilibrium exists. It rests here on a coordination failure due to the free-rider problem rather than the free-rider problem per se. However, inefficiency in private provision of public goods is generic. Hence, it is reasonable to overlook this issue here and the gain from the simplicity of the example more than outweighs this (slightly) artificial feature.

2.3.2 Government provision

Suppose now that government finances the project and uses a head tax. To create a social welfare calculus, we adopt a utilitarian perspective which is identical to the social surplus criterion in this context. In this case, the Samuelson rule applies to optimal public provision.

Figure 2.3 gives the payoffs to all of the parties in this instance.

Observe that $e = 0$ and $e = 1$ are both Pareto efficient policy choices in this setting. This is because we have supposed that the government has to tax *all* citizens. Thus those who do not value the project are worse off under government provision. This implies that a system of political resource allocation that costlessly decides whether to have the project go ahead or not cannot constitute a government failure using the Pareto criterion.

	Citizens who value the project	Citizens who do not value the project	Social welfare
$e = 0$	0	0	0
$e = 1$	$b - \frac{c}{N}$	$-\frac{c}{N}$	$\gamma Nb - c$

Figure 2.3 Citizens' payoffs and social welfare under government provision

Using our posited social welfare criterion, the project is worthwhile if the sum of benefits to all citizens exceeds the resource cost which boils down to:

$$N\gamma b \geq c.$$

If this condition holds, then *any* political mechanism in which the project fails to go ahead constitutes a government failure. (The converse would be true if we assumed that $N\gamma b < c$.)

Turning now to Wicksell's unanimity test, observe that this always fails if $e = 1$. This is because the group who does not favor the project have a payoff of $-c/N$ as they do not value the project. Hence any model of political resource allocation in which the project goes ahead would generate a government failure. However, if the government could levy a benefit tax in the amount $c/N\gamma$ on all those who value the project, then going ahead with the project would indeed generate a realized Pareto improvement if $N\gamma b > c$. In fact this achieves the same payoff as with the 'good' Nash equilibrium in this case. Except for where we make specific mention, we assume that $N\gamma b > c$ for the remainder of this.

The simple example makes clear why the Wicksellian model is likely to lead to the most conservative criterion for government intervention when the benefits of public intervention are unevenly distributed among the citizens. Unless benefit taxation can be used to fund public projects, then the case for government intervention will be extremely limited. In contrast, Pareto efficiency does not have any bite in this situation whereas social surplus allows trade-offs between the payoffs of gainers and losers.

The example also illustrates why the set of instruments available to government matters for a government failure. If we had assumed that lump-sum taxation were feasible for government, then the Wicksellian criterion and social surplus could always be fulfilled together in this model by suitable use of such transfers. Moreover, there would be a unique Pareto optimal policy which coincided with the surplus maximizing outcome. Thus, interesting conflicts between competing notions of government failure require us to work with a world where there are restrictions on policy instruments.[8]

This example provides a useful building block that we will now use to study public resource allocation and the reasons for government failure. While simple and stylized, it does embody many of the ideas that make the study of government intervention in political economy settings interesting. In particular, there are gainers and losers from government intervention with limited policy instruments for compensating losers.

2.4 Sources of government failure

This section discusses three aspects of government failure using the example above to illustrate their implications. We begin by discussing government failures that arise whether or not a democratic political process is used to make policy decisions. These problems are due to ignorance, the use of private influence and the quality of leadership.

In each case, we begin by supposing that there is a leader in office who is charged with deciding whether or not to set $e = 1$. He/she is assumed to have their own preference over the project outcome. We do not model the process of leadership selection. We then study how this policy authority will be exercised and its welfare consequences.

2.4.1 *Ignorance*

Governments who intervene in the economy typically lack the kind of omniscience that simplistic models of the policy process invoke. This was the basis of Hayek's critique of state planning that we discussed in Section 5 of Chapter 1. However, it runs through the modern welfare economic literature based on mechanism design. At some level, it is hardly deep or surprising that some forms of ignorance can lead to policy mistakes being made, at least when compared to the omniscient

---

[8] The uniqueness of the Pareto optimal outcome with lump-sum transfers is also an artifact of the assumption of transferable utility.

outcome. In our example, a government that was ignorant of b or c would be unlikely to make the correct decision all of the time over whether to go ahead with the project. This would be true regardless of the criterion being used to evaluate the quality of public decision making. However, it is equally unclear, a priori, whether ignorance leads to a systematic bias in policy decisions towards too much or too little government intervention.

Ignorance can clearly lead to a Pareto inefficient policy, at least when compared to the case of full information. It can also lead to social decisions that fail specific welfare criteria and to situations where policies are implemented that do not Pareto dominate the status quo.

While ignorance is undoubtedly a pervasive feature of the policy landscape, the most interesting issues concern situations where the quantity of information is endogenous and when different individuals are differentially informed about policy. In these cases, the question is whether particular decision making processes are better at eliciting and managing information. In general the quality of policy outcomes will fall short of what happens with perfect knowledge—the issue is whether all information is incorporated into making social decisions. However, the relevant criterion is now *second best*, in other words, information constrained efficiency about policy.

One key difference between democratic and non-democratic systems of government lies in the way in which information is collected and disseminated in the policy process.[9] This could mean democratic systems of government less prone to government failure if it leads to policies that are more reflective of common underlying information about policy needs. Suppose, for example, that the government is uncertain about the fraction of individuals in the population who value the project (the parameter γ in our example). Then, direct voting over policy may be a good way of revealing common values when citizens are differentially informed about policy.

To look at these issues in more detail would require us to develop a specific model of information aggregation in the political process. This raises interesting and important issues. We will not, however, be addressing them to any extent in this book. However, clearly the form in which social decisions are made has a bearing on the way in which information can be incorporated in the policy process. Laffont

---

[9] These issues are explored in Feddersen and Pesendorfer (1997).

(2000) provides many insights into political processes viewed from this perspective.[10]

The agency models discussed in Chapters 3 and 4 take informational issues seriously. However, they focus on situations where the government retains an informational advantage about policy. In the current setting this might be because b or c is known to the government and not to the citizens. This does not, however, create a problem unless the policy maker also faces a conflict of interest—has an incentive to pick a policy outcome that does not suit voters. Hence, to make the model interesting, we will also need to assume that politicians are not always benevolent. One way of doing this is to suppose that they face external influence in choosing policy. It is to the issue of influence that we now turn.

2.4.2 *Influence*

Whether democratic or not, governments are subjective to influence from powerful organized groups. This will lead, in general, to policy benefits being skewed towards such groups. In this section, I discuss how this can be brought into the example above and discuss the implications for identifying government failures. I consider two models. The first is 'pure' corruption whereby influence is purely redistributive. The second is costly 'rent-seeking' where resources are used up in the policy process.

CORRUPTION

We define pure corruption as a situation where a monetary payment—a bribe—is paid to the policy maker to influence the policy outcome. It is not particularly surprising that, in such circumstances, corruption can change the alignment of citizen and leader preferences. Whether this is for good or ill depends on the notion of government failure under scrutiny.

To be specific, suppose that the policy maker can earn a private monetary rent of $r > 0$ for setting $e = 1$ regardless of whether the project is a good idea. We suppose that this payment r is a transfer made by a subset of 'organized' citizens. We will not model the transfer

---

[10] It is difficult to say a priori how problems of ignorance by government bear on government failures from either a distributional or Wicksellian point of view. This would depend heavily on the specifics of the situation.

process explicitly. However, the general considerations of this section could be approached using the menu auction model due to Bernheim and Whinston (1986) which was first applied to political influence by Grossman and Helpman (1994). The basic idea in that approach is that government auctions off a policy to the highest bidder(s). Each of the bidders offers a menu which specifies a payment in exchange for a policy outcome. Here, for simplicity, we fix the size of the transfer made and the identity of those who make it.

Suppose that:

$$r > c/N.$$

In this case, the policy maker will implement the project regardless of his personal preference for or against it since the transfer he receives exceeds any share of the taxes that he will have to pay. The policy outcome is, therefore, always $e = 1$.

The utility of the citizens depends on whether they finance the transfer. Suppose that a fraction of $\beta < \gamma$ of citizens who favor the project collectively finance this transfer on an equal per capita basis. Those who favor the project and share the cost of the transfer, therefore, get utility of:

$$b - c/N - r/N\beta$$

while those in favor who do not pay receive:

$$b - c/N.$$

Citizens who do not favor the transfer receive a payoff of $-c/N$.

Assuming that $b - c/N - r/N\beta > 0$, corruption of the form modeled here cannot generate a Pareto inefficient policy outcome in this setting. The transfers made are individually rational so that both the organized citizens and the policy maker are better off than they would be in the absence of corruption. The effect is purely a movement around the Pareto frontier. In general, we should expect this for pure bribery—those who pay and receive the bribe ought to be better off and hence it is unlikely that this can be Pareto inferior.[11]

---

[11] This does depend, however, on the kinds of instruments that are available to compensate gainers and losers. Besley and Coate (2001) develop a model in which there are coordination failures between lobbyists that can result in a Pareto dominated policy outcome.

Since we have assumed that $\gamma Nb > c$, corruption here actually increases social surplus relative to any policy which generates $e = 0$. Of course, things could go the other way. Had we assumed that $\gamma Nb < c$, the opposite would have been true. The point is that there is no presumption that bribery raises or lowers social welfare in the abstract. However, in general corruption will reduce welfare when the benchmark is one where the government is purely benevolent. Thus, if our policy maker had done the right thing in social welfare terms to begin with, then clearly bribery could only make things worse. On the other hand, in any model where there is already some potential imperfection in the resource allocation process to begin with, there is no a priori prediction about this. This 'second best' theme is echoed in the analysis in Chapter 4.

In terms of the Wicksellian definition, corruption only strengthens the tendency towards government failure by making it more likely that the project goes ahead. However, there is no need for things to go in this direction in general if we allowed for bribery to be among the group who wants smaller government. There may, however, be a tendency towards those who favor specific projects being more organized. Nonetheless, if the government were inclined towards implementing the project and the transfers were from those citizens who are against it, then this could reduce the chances that the project goes ahead. However, those who are bribing to prevent the project from going ahead would be worse off than if the government were constitutionally prevented from implementing the project, while the policy makers would be better off. Hence, the *possibility* of government intervention can generate a set of transfers that constitutes a government failure! This is true even if no intervention takes place. This further motivates the public choice preoccupation with constitutional constraints—this being the only way to prevent this from happening.

Corruption here is only a label. Influence activities could equally well lead governments to do 'good' as well as bad things. In cases where there are two sides to an issue there will always be a group who feels that the policy process is stacked against them and will voice their concern about the way in which political influence is used.

Of course, there are good reasons to frown on corruption for other reasons than those emphasized here. First, we may not like per se the distributional effect of making transfers to politicians. It could also distort the allocation of talent if individuals enter public life to capture private benefits. Third, corruption could also induce a deadweight loss of its own if it is directed through inefficient means in order to keep it secret. Thus we could introduce a transactions cost on bribery whereby the citizens lose τr to deliver r to the policy maker where $\tau > 1$.

All of this notwithstanding, this analysis paints a somewhat more benign view of corruption than does a lot of other literature. That is not to say that the general opprobrium that greets corruption is not correct. First when the policy maker is elected in a legitimate democratic process, then we might expect bribery to undermine the democratic process. Moreover, one suspects that many of the policy favors granted through the process of corruption have no distributional merit according to any reasonable social welfare function. There are also hard to model systemic costs whereby corruption undermines norms of good behavior and the legitimacy of the state.[12]

COSTLY RENT-SEEKING

In our model of bribery, no resources were expended in influencing politicians' decisions. In this section, we allow policy makers to be subject to costly influence activities—which can be thought of as rent-seeking or lobbying. In reality individuals expend resources in order to secure political favors. To the extent that such activities involve hiring labor, people are drawn out of productive occupations.

The extensive literature on rent-seeking originating with Tullock (1967) and Krueger (1973) has studied how private actions influence policy. Following Tullock (1980), formal analysis has focused mostly on modelling competition among individuals or groups to obtain an indivisible policy favor, the aim being to characterize the aggregate expenditure on rent-seeking activities (see, for example, Baye et al. (1994) and the references therein). This fits very well the structure of the example that we are studying. It is frequently asserted that rent-seeking is a cause of government failure and hence it is important to see how it fits into our framework.

Suppose that citizen i can pay r_i to influence the policy maker either to go ahead with or desist from the project. We assume that r_i is a real resource cost, such as labor time, which cannot be appropriated by the policy maker. In fact, we assume that the policy maker gets no payoff from the influence (positive or negative). Suppose that each citizen commits resources $r_{ia} (\geq 0)$ in favor of the project and $r_{if} (\geq 0)$ against.

---

[12] See Tirole (1996) for a model of collective reputations with mutliple equilibria which he applies to the amount of corruption.

Let total resources committed in favor of the project be $R_f \left(\sum_{i=1}^{N} r_{if} \right)$ and the total against be $R_a \left(\sum_{i=1}^{N} r_{ia} \right)$. Then assume that the probability that the project goes ahead is captured by the following simple function:

$$\frac{R_f}{R_f + R_a}$$

This kind of 'contest' function is popular in the rent-seeking literature and will serve to make the main points of interest. We look for a Nash equilibrium in influence levels where all citizens have access to the influence technology and there is symmetric behavior within the two groups of citizens. It is easy to see that citizens who favor the project will not commit any resources lobbying against it and that the converse is true for those who oppose the project.

Consider the decision of citizen i who favors the project. His payoff if he contributes r_{if} is:

$$\frac{\left(\sum_{k=1}^{N} r_{kf} \right)}{\left(\sum_{k=1}^{N} r_{kf} \right) + R_a} \left(b - \frac{c}{N} \right) - r_{if}.$$

Citizen j who opposes the project has a payoff of:

$$-\frac{R_f}{R_f + \left(\sum_{k=1}^{N} r_{ka} \right)} \frac{c}{N} - r_{ja}.$$

We now solve for a Nash equilibrium where each citizen in favor and each against puts in the same effort level. Solving for the Nash equilibrium in the usual way, it is straightforward to see that the equilibrium probability that the project goes ahead is:

$$\left(1 - \frac{c}{Nb} \right).$$

The key magnitude here is c/bN: the ratio of the cost of construction per capita to the benefit to having the project for those who favor it. As the cost per capita becomes small (high N or low c), then the probability that the project is constructed goes to one. This is because only those who gain a benefit engage in influence activity—the cost of the project to those who are against is negligible.[13]

---

[13] This is a feature of the project being a pure public good so that the cost of the project does not increase with the population size.

The total expenditure on 'rent-seeking' at a Nash equilibrium is:

$$\frac{c}{N}\left(1 - \frac{c}{Nb}\right).$$

Using this, it is now straightforward to consider the welfare consequences of costly rent-seeking.

Evaluating the welfare consequences of costly rent-seeking requires considering two complications. First, the outcome needs to be evaluated both in terms of the policy that is chosen and the resources spent on influencing the decision which impose a social cost. The second issue is whether ex ante or ex post evaluation of the outcome is appropriate. For example, if the ex post policy outcome is $e = 0$ then everyone who committed positive resources to influence is worse off than they would have been without the possibility of political influence. But from an ex ante point of view, engaging in influence activities is still individually rational. The ex ante view point therefore makes more sense.

The outcome with influence is ex post Pareto efficient. However, it can be Pareto dominated from an ex ante point of view by fixing the probability that the project is implemented at $q = \left(1 - \frac{c}{bN}\right)$. If citizens knew that this was fixed, they would not expend any resources on rent-seeking and would have the same probability distribution over the project outcome as in the Nash equilibrium with influence activities described above. In this sense, costly rent-seeking is always a source of government failure in the Pareto sense. However, to bring about the Pareto improvement would require having a policy technology in which the policy-maker could commit to a (possibly random) policy allocation up front. Only by committing to this ex ante would influence activity be closed down.

Closing down costly rent-seeking without using the same probability distribution over policy achieved in the Nash equilibrium of the influence game does not necessarily create a Pareto improvement. For example, an ex ante commitment of $e = 0$ is not Pareto superior to the Nash equilibrium with influence activity as the citizens in favor of the project going ahead are made worse off.

Turning now to ex ante total surplus (i.e. before the rent-seeking activity has been undertaken), we need to take into account the resources spent on influence. Aggregate (ex ante) surplus at the Nash equilibrium in influence is given by:

$$\left(1 - \frac{c}{bN}\right)\left(N\gamma b - c\frac{(N+1)}{N}\right). \tag{2.1}$$

The first term is the equilibrium probability that the project goes ahead and the second is the surplus that it generates. Whether the latter is positive or negative depends on comparing the total benefit $(N\gamma b)$ with the total project cost c and the per capita project cost c/N. Where c/N is small, it is clear that whether total surplus is positive or negative is not really affected by influence. However, the welfare economic calculus which compares $N\gamma b$ with c clearly neglects the costs of rent-seeking activity and requires a stronger criterion for the project to go ahead.

From a surplus maximization point of view, the outcome with costly influence activities could be better or worse than what would happen without rent-seeking. If the outcome would be $e = 1$ with probability one without influence, then influence makes things worse—recall that we have assumed that $\gamma Nb > c$. But if it were $e = 0$, the effect on social surplus is ambiguous.

All the same, (2.1) gives us a sense of how to compare market failure and government failure in the decision to go ahead with a public project from a surplus maximization perspective. Our 'market failure' arose because we assumed that coordination failure lead to suboptimal private provision of the public project. The additional influence costs now need to be weighed alongside the traditional welfare economic costs and benefits.[14]

From a Wicksellian point of view, there is also an ambiguity as to whether a government failure has occurred. This depends on what the policy outcome would have been without the influence activity. If this were $e = 0$, then allowing influence makes things worse in a Wicksellian sense as there is now a positive probability that the project goes ahead. However, if $e = 1$ were to be the outcome in the absence of influence, then permitting influence could improve the situation from a Wicksellian point of view by empowering those who disapprove of the project.

We used a special and highly stylized model of how influence works. An important area of recent concern is influence activity in the form of campaign finance. Recent literature (see, for example, Grossman and

---

[14] See Acemoglu and Verdier (2000) for a related analysis.

Helpman (1996)) has studied how influence in the form of campaign contributions can distort policy in a model of electoral competition.[15]

Coate (2004a,b) develops a model where the process of political influence through campaign contributions is modeled explicitly. This boils down to something whose reduced form looks rather similar to rent-seeking models. He shows that, in some cases, the probability distribution over policy is not affected at all by campaign finance and hence that banning campaign finance will result in a Pareto improvement. This provides an excellent illustration of the general principle that we have discussed and one that may have practical relevance.

However, as we have emphasized, dismissing of all influence activities as government failures is not very convincing. It depends on assuming that there is up front commitment to the ex post policy outcome. This does not seem the kind of scenario that most crude analyses have in mind. Without this, there are distributional effects as well as losses in resources that need to be weighed up in any careful welfare analysis.

There may of course be intrinsic concerns about the exercise of non-democratic influence. However, with any approach that emphasizes outcomes rather than processes, the trade-offs revealed here seem likely to prevail. As we observe in the case of bribery, once it is recognized that the policy mechanism that will prevail in the absence of influence is also flawed in some way or another, there is really no reason to believe that the exercise of political influence is damaging in a wholesale way from a welfare economic point of view. That does not mean that empirically many cases of influence are indeed not damaging. Whether influence activities are socially costly has to be assessed on a case by case basis and by bringing empirical evidence to bear. Sweeping claims are far from self-evident.

2.4.3 *The quality of leadership*

The models that we studied above attach no weight at all to the quality of the leaders that hold policy authority.[16]We now consider the possibility that the policy maker has an effect on policy. There are broadly two reasons why the type of the policy maker can matter. First, the quality of the policy could be embodied in policy makers.

---

[15] See also Persson and Tabellini (2000) and Besley and Coate (2001).
[16] This theme is discussed in Besley (2005).

For example, some individuals can implement policies more cheaply or may even have more insight into what works. In this case, the only way to improve politics is to change the individuals who make policy. Second, some policy makers may be better at carrying out the citizens' wishes. Whether this actually happens depends on the kinds of incentives that can be offered to policy makers for good behavior—good incentives might yield good policy regardless of the policy maker's type. These issues will be discussed in greater detail in the models of Chapters 3 and 4. Here, we discuss—in a very simple way—how this can be a source of government failure.

Suppose that the policy maker in office is drawn from a pool of potential policy makers that are differentiated according to the cost of implementing the public project. Thus, we think of the task of policy formation depending on the human capital of the policy maker. Specifically, let $c_i \in \{c_L, c_H\}$ for i in the set of potential policy makers. Thus c_i is a measure of policy maker competence with cost type c_L being a competent policy maker. Suppose initially that:

$$b > \frac{c_H}{N} > \frac{c_L}{N}.$$

This implies that any policy maker who in office will desire to implement the project as long as he/she values it personally. Moreover all citizens who value the project also prefer that the project be implemented.[17]

To think about government failure issues the outcome has to include both a policy outcome (here whether e is zero or one) and a policy maker (type c_i) who implements that outcome. This generalized approach to think about policy making was suggested in Besley and Coate (1997) which used the citizen–candidate model of political competition to generate a policy outcome as well as a policy maker's identity.

With any type of citizen in office, the outcome where $e = 1$ is itself Pareto efficient. However, if a type H citizen is in power, then all citizens (including the policy maker!) is worse off than if a type L were choosing policy. Even those who don't like having the project go forward would prefer that it was implemented by a citizen with cost type c_L.

---

[17] By focusing on competence as a 'common value', policy makers do not get any benefit from their own incompetence. This differentiates competence and rent-seeking models of low quality leaders. In the latter, low quality leaders earn a rent from being in office. This makes it more difficult to create a Pareto improvement.

Thus, having a type H citizen in office constitutes a government failure since a Pareto improvement can be generated by replacing that citizen with a type L. Thus, defining the outcome in terms of who is picked for office in addition to the policy outcome adds a further dimension to the set of possible government failures. This justifies a focus on issues on political selection in political economy models, in other words, worrying about who is selected to office. Clearly it would be in the interest of societies to generate systems of leadership selection that are sensitive to finding competent policy makers.

Turning to our other definitions of government failure, it is evident that having a type H policy maker in office may interfere with attaining a surplus maximizing policy outcome. Moreover, if:

$$\frac{c_H}{N} > \gamma b > \frac{c_L}{N}.$$

a type H policy maker might implement the project even though it reduces social surplus.

Allowing for heterogeneous policy makers can work for or against the creation of Wicksellian government failures. To see this, consider what happens if:

$$\frac{c_H}{N} > b > \frac{c_L}{N}.$$

In this case, having a type H policy maker in office leads to the project (which was a government failure anyway) not being implemented. Type L policy makers in this world will tend to implement government projects which are harmful to citizens who have to pay for them without deriving any benefit. Thus, it is better to have incompetent policy makers who then decide that it is simply too costly to go ahead with them. This is a rather perverse logic—once government fails it may be better to have more distortions. Again, it has to do with the nature of second best reasoning in these kinds of settings—the political system is already distorted, so adding a further distortion is not always welfare decreasing.

2.5 Sources of political failure

The issues that we discussed in the last section do not hinge on whether or not the government is democratic. In this section, we analyze two classic problems that arise in government in democratic settings. The first looks explicitly at the issue of when voting over policies and/or policy makers will result in a government failure. The second looks at decision making in legislatures and the problems of distributive politics. These are both areas where there has been extensive discussion of political failure. Thus a closer look at the basis of this merits some attention.

2.5.1 Voting

Voting is at the heart of democratic decision making and is the basis of political resource allocation in many instances. One important issue concerns whether voting is endemically linked to any form of political failure.

To explore this, suppose that the individual who has to make social decisions in this setting is chosen in an election and that there is a choice between two types of citizens—those in favor and those against the project.[18] In this case, voting is purely a method for aggregating competing views about policy. The conflict of interest is purely between the citizens who are for and against the project. It is reasonable to suppose that the outcome will be to pick a citizen to choose policy whose policy preference coincides with majority opinion—the median voter outcome in this context.

Formally, this yields the following policy decision rule:

$$e = 1 \text{ if } \gamma \geq 1/2 \text{ and } e = 0 \text{ otherwise.}$$

The outcome depends on which is the numerically largest group.

It is immediate from this that the *median voter outcome is always Pareto efficient*. However, there is some confusion about this point in some of the existing literature on political failure. For example, Bergstrom (1979) uses the Downsian model to analyze whether political competition will produce an efficient level of public goods. He shows that strong restrictions are needed for the median voter's desired level of a public good to satisfy the Lindahl–Samuelson condition for the provision of a public good. The latter requires that the good be provided if and only $\gamma Nb > c$. Thus, the outcome with voting seems to coincide with the Lindahl–Samuelson rule when $\gamma \geq 1/2$

---

[18] This could be modeled by means of a simple citizen–candidate game along the lines laid out in Besley and Coate (1997). In this simple setting, this will yield the same outcome as allowing direct voting over the policy outcome.

implies $N\gamma b \geq c$ which clearly does not hold in general. Indeed if:

$$\frac{b}{2} < \frac{c}{N}$$

then there is always a value of $\gamma \in (\frac{1}{2}, 1]$ which results in the project going ahead when the Lindahl–Samuelson rule rejects it.

But this disjunction between the Samuelson rule and the voting outcome is far from surprising. For the purposes of the voting analysis, we have fixed the tax system to be a uniform head tax. By contrast, the Lindahl–Samuelson rule *as an efficiency criterion* assumes that there are lump sum taxes and transfers, at least if the losers are to be compensated by the gainers. As we have seen from our example, holding the method of financing fixed, the majority voting outcome is trivially efficient.[19] These issues are bound to arise in models which work with restrictions on the policy space. But it is important to consider the welfare comparison holding the policy instruments fixed.

This discussion makes plain why the outcome achieved under majority voting and based on social surplus maximization will almost certainly diverge in general. Voting cannot be used to register preference intensity. However, it is essential to most distribution criteria that the intensity of preferences for and against—as well as the numerical strength of these groups—count.

The outcome achieved under voting is a Wicksellian political failure if $\gamma \geq 1/2$ since the group that is against the project going ahead would be better off in the no-government status quo. This observation that Wicksellian justice is inconsistent with majority rule is a core observation in Buchanan and Tullock's (1962) critique of democratic policy making.

The example makes clear that there can be no general presumption of efficiency or inefficiency from the median voter outcome (except in the Paretian sense). In fact the result on Pareto efficiency holds true whenever the political equilibrium picks a Condorcet winner. When it comes to distributional criteria and the Wicksellian ideal, then it is a fair to say that there is a good reason to think that voting will lead to political failure.

We now consider a different argument due to Fernandez and Rodrik (1991). They apply the argument to economic reforms in general. However, our public project could easily be thought of as a program

---

[19] This point was noted in an important article by Wittman (1989).

of economic reform as building a single public project. Suppose that $\gamma < 1/2$, in other words, a minority of the population would gain b for sure from the project. However, unlike the baseline model, we suppose that the remaining $(1 - \gamma)$ of the population do not know whether they will receive b from the project. Specifically we suppose that, with probability π, they receive b if the project goes ahead and with probability $(1 - \pi)$ they receive nothing. Suppose also that:

$$\pi b < \frac{c}{N}$$

so from an ex ante point of view, those who are uncertain about whether they will gain are opposed to the project, and so, would vote against it. Thus, with majority rule, $e = 0$ will be the policy outcome. We know, however, that if $(\gamma + (1-\gamma)\pi)b > c/N$, then this is a political failure in terms of ex ante social surplus. That said, this insight is not substantively different from the basic case without uncertainty.

More interesting is the observation by Fernandez and Rodrik (1991) that if:

$$\gamma + (1 - \gamma)\pi > \frac{1}{2}$$

a majority would vote for the reform *ex post*, i.e. if the identity of the gainers and losers were already known. Thus individual specific uncertainty is responsible for the fact that $e = 0$.[20]

Whether this kind of individual specific uncertainty is good or bad from a welfare point of view is unclear. It has no bearing on whether policy choices are Pareto efficient. It will, however, tend to reduce the probability of a Wicksellian political failure and hence could be viewed as welfare enhancing in models that value greater inertia in the policy process.[21] In terms of social surplus, things could go either way. For example, if:

$$(\gamma + (1 - \gamma)\pi)b < c/N,$$

[20] Fernandez and Rodrik (1991) draw the conclusion that this will lead to status quo bias in reform. This point turns out not to be robust in their framework—see Ciccone (2004).

[21] Observe that if $\pi b > c/N$ and $(\gamma + (1 - \gamma)\pi) < 1/2$, then a project that would be rejected under majority with certainty would be implemented were there was uncertainty about who gains and who loses. Thus, uncertainty need not be a device to minimize Wicksellian political failures. Note also that ex post a vote to abandon the project would be successful in this case. I am grateful to Sanjay Jain for discussion on this point.

then individual specific uncertainty can prevent projects that fail the surplus maximizing criterion being implemented even though they would be implemented under certainty.

Thus, while introducing uncertainty does yield some interesting insights, it does not give a new source of political failure in public decision making.

2.5.2 Log-rolling and legislative behavior

So far, we have discussed highly simplistic models of the policy process. However, in practice policy processes work with interactions among a group of politicians collectively charged with making policy decisions. One important example of this is policy making in legislatures. The question is how agreements are structured according to the rules of the legislature and how this affects policy outcomes.

The seminal work of Tullock (1959) and Buchanan and Tullock (1962) emphasized how log-rolling in legislatures could lead to policy distortions. Tullock (1959) contrasts two systems of social decision making—straight majority decision making (what he calls a referendum) and some kind of bargaining between subgroups of voters which he calls log-rolling. He gives the following insightful account of the main ideas:

A township inhabited by one hundred farmers who have more or less similar farms is cut by a number of main roads maintained by the state. However, these roads are limited access roads, and the farmers are permitted to enter the primary network only at points where local roads intersect it. The local roads are built and maintained by the township. Maintenance is simple. Any farmer who wishes to have a specific road repaired puts up the issue to vote. If the repairing is approved, the cost is assessed to the farmers as part of the real property tax. The principal use of the local roads by the farmers is to get to and from the major state roads. Since these major roads cut through the district, generally there are only four or five farmers dependent on any particular bit of local road to reach the major road.

Under these circumstances, the referendum system would result in no local roads being repaired as an overwhelming majority would vote against repairing any given road. The logrolling system, however, permits the roads to be kept in repair through bargains among voters.

(Tullock 1959: 573)

An instructive benchmark for legislative policy making is a Coasian view that supposes that a group of individuals will reach joint agreements which internalize any externalities between them due to differences in policy preferences. This kind of Coasian bargain will result in policies that are efficient for the legislatures and hence are Pareto efficient from the point of view of the economy as a whole.[22] Hence, the presumption will be that policies will be efficient. Even in this case, there is no reason to think that legislatures will satisfy Wicksell's concerns—there is plenty of scope for legislatures to pick policy outcomes which do not Pareto dominate the no-government status quo.

Whether efficient bargains can be generated in legislatures given the kinds of rules that obtain for reaching agreements is moot. Clearly it requires investigation by developing models of bargaining in legislatures and there are many important contributions that look at this. Here is not the place to discuss these models in general. However, it is useful to observe that these models can sometimes create sources of political failure in the sense of Pareto (in)efficiency.

One classic example of this is the well-known model due to Weingast et al. (1981). They consider a legislature which allocates a number of public projects to various districts. They suppose that each project benefits one district only. Each district is represented in a legislature by one elected representative. The notion they analyze is that the legislature operates according to a 'norm of universalism' in which each district gets a project provided that all the others do. But each district in deciding how far to fund a project will realize that it bears only a fraction of the cost—the remainder being born by residents of the other districts. The result is an inefficiently large number of projects being financed. The outcome can sometimes be Pareto dominated from the point of view of the members of the legislature—everyone could be made better off with a collective reduction in the levels of the public goods being funded. Thus, the outcome does constitute a political failure in the Paretian sense. However, this happens because the model simply excludes the possibility of Coasian bargains among the legislators without stating the reason. To tackle the problem of inefficiency would require developing some other rule of operation that can internalize policy externalities.

---

[22] Since legislators are citizens, they will pick some kind of agreement that is at least as good as any other for the group of legislators.

The anatomy of government failure

To explore this issue, we extend the model above in a very simple way. Suppose now that policy decisions are made in a legislature comprising representatives selected from geographic regions. The n districts that they represent are labeled $j = 1, \ldots, n$. Each district is of equal size containing m citizens so $m \times n = N$. A project can be undertaken in each district and is enjoyed solely by the residents of that district, i.e. there are no spillovers across districts. Thus the legislature can authorize the building of up to n projects (one for each district).

Let $e_j \in \{0, 1\}$ denote whether a project goes ahead in district j. We assume that there is common pool financing—the taxation levied on each citizen across the districts is equal to the total cost of projects that are financed divided equally by all citizens in the polity (regardless of residence). We also suppose (following Weingast et al. (1981)) that project allocation is governed by a rule in which the representative in each district can unilaterally decide whether to implement a project in its district as long as all other legislators enjoy that privilege.

For simplicity, we suppose that each representative maximizes the average utility of a district resident which is:

$$e_j \gamma b - \frac{\sum_{k=1}^{n} e_k c}{N}.$$

Note that this assumes that each district comprises an equal fraction (γ) of citizens who are in favor of the project.

It is apparent that the representative in any district will wish to have a project located in his district provided that:

$$N \gamma b > c.$$

In effect, he/she compares the benefits as if they accrued to the whole population with the cost—this is because the cost is shared with other districts. But, from a social surplus point of view, a project is desirable only if the surplus that it generates in the district that it is located in is positive, i.e., if $m \gamma b > c$.

Thus the legislative process that we have posited along with common pool financing will yield excessive publicly financed spending (according to the social surplus criterion) if:

$$N \gamma b > c > m \gamma b.$$

The policy outcome is Pareto inefficient if:

$$\frac{c}{\gamma N} < b < \frac{c}{m}.$$

Then even the citizens in favor of the project would prefer not to have it. Hence, it corresponds to a political failure. The outcome can be Pareto dominated by a cooperative solution in the legislature, i.e. one where all projects are simultaneously agreed upon rather than delegating that decision to the representative within a district. This raises the issue of why the norm of universalism would ever be seen in the first place. An efficient solution could also be found by using a tax system which tried to share the costs of project financing so that each district paid more taxes if it had a project located within it, moving away from common pool finance.

The outcome under the norm of universalism is a political failure according to the Wicksellian criterion of $N\gamma b > c$. Again the tendency for political resource allocation is to authorize too many projects. Thus, the posited rules of legislative decision making lead to an outcome which can fail according to all three definitions of political failure.

Since legislatures that are asked to allocate resources across space are a central feature of democratic policy making, it is clear that political failures generated this way merit close attention. However, it is also apparent that the policy outcome depends on the details of legislative processes, a key issue being why Coasian bargains among legislators cannot be struck. While the above kind of analysis has been influential among economists, the fact that the norm of universalism is maintained is puzzling and it is important to give persuasive microfoundations before using it. That said, those who have looked at legislative decision making in more detail confirm that this can be an important source of political failure.[23]

2.6 Dynamics

We now explore government failure in models where policy making takes place in more than one time period. This is important since it

[23] See Battaglini and Coate (2005) for an overview and development of a dynamic model of legislative bargaining applied to an economic policy model.

highlights the role of commitment issues and re-election concerns in shaping policy. We will develop an example with two time periods. The main issues arise because there are linkages between decisions made in period one and period two. We identify three sources of linkages that are potentially important.

1. **Investment linkages:** This refers to cases where private investment decisions are affected by future economic policies. The classic time consistency problem in government policy first identified by Kydland and Prescott (1977) falls into this category.
2. **Political linkages:** If policy choices in period one affect the type of policy maker who is in office in period two, then Period 1 policies are tied to those that are undertaken in Period 2.
3. **Policy linkages:** Policies that are undertaken in Period 1 affect the policy choices that incumbents make in Period 2.

With either political or policy linkages, period one policy choices acquire a *strategic* element if policy makers are forward looking.

2.6.1 *Investment linkages*

Suppose now that there are two time periods labeled $t \in \{1, 2\}$. A project can be implemented in each period and the policy decision in period t is denoted by $e_t \in \{0, 1\}$. As above, the cost of the project is c in each period and is financed equally by all N citizens. Citizen i receives a period one payoff from the project denoted by $b_i(e_1)$. But we allow citizens to make private investment decisions denoted by $x_i \in \{0, 1\}$ for citizen i which costs κx_i. The payoff to citizen i from the Period 2 project is denoted by $B_i(x_i, e_1, e_2)$, in other words, it depends on their investment decision in Period 1 and the actions of government in both time periods.

We consider two cases:

1. Commitment: The government chooses (e_1, e_2) and then citizens choose whether or not to invest.
2. No commitment: The government first chooses e_1, then citizens invest. The government then chooses e_2.

We study each in turn.

COMMITMENT

In this case, we will use * to denote the decisions made by government and citizens. Let $\{e_1, e_2\}$ be a fixed pair of government policies. Then the optimal investment decisions by the citizens are described by:

$$x_i^*(e_1, e_2) = \arg \max_{x_i \in \{0,1\}} \{B_i(x_i, e_1, e_2) - \kappa x_i\}. \qquad (2.2)$$

Suppose that the government is benevolent, caring about social surplus. Then:

$$\{e_1^*, e_2^*\} = \arg \max_{e_t \in \{0,1\}} \left\{ \sum_i (b_i(e_1) + B_i(x_i^*(e_1, e_2), e_1, e_2) - \kappa x_i^*(e_1, e_2)) \right.$$
$$\left. - c(e_1 + e_2) \right\}.$$

We make two assumptions:

Assumption 1

$$(B_i(1, e_1, 1) - B_i(0, e_1, 0) - \kappa) - \frac{c}{N} > 0$$

for all i and for all $e_1 \in \{0, 1\}$.

This says that any situation in which government chooses $e_2 = 1$ and citizen i chooses $x_i = 1$ for all i, Pareto dominates an outcome where $e_2 = 0$ and $x_i = 0$ for all i.

Assumption 2

$$B_i(1, e_1, 1) - B_i(0, e_1, 1) > \kappa > B_i(1, e_1, 0) - B_i(0, e_1, 0)$$

for all i and for all $e_1 \in \{0, 1\}$.

This says that only if citizens predict that the government will choose $e_2 = 1$, then it is optimal for them to invest in period one, i.e. set $x_i = 1$. In other words, the marginal return to private investment is increased by the Period 2 investment project. Together Assumptions 1 and 2 imply that it is surplus maximizing (and hence Pareto efficient) to have $e_2^* = 1$.

Assuming that the Period 2 policy is optimal, then the socially optimal Period 1 policy will be $e_1^* = 1$ if and only if:

$$\sum_i (b_i(1) + B_i(1, 1, 1)) - c > \sum_i (b_i(0) + B_i(1, 0, 1))$$

which simply compares the cost of the project with the benefit.

This provides a benchmark for studying the case where the government cannot commit up front.

NO COMMITMENT

Ever since the classic analysis of Kydland and Prescott (1977), it has been known that government's inability to commit to a policy ahead of time can reduce welfare. We now study this in our framework. We will use a 'hat' (^) above a variable to denote the equilibrium outcome in this case.

We work backwards beginning with the government's second period decision. The government will take $(x_1, \ldots, x_N, e_1)$ as given. Its optimal time consistent policy will satisfy:

$$\hat{e}_2(x_1, \ldots, x_N, e_1) = \arg \max_{e_2 \in \{0,1\}} \left\{ \sum_i B_i(x_i, e_1, e_2) - ce_2 \right\}.$$

We next consider the investment decision by the citizens. They take the Period 1 policy choice and form (rational) expectations about government policy in Period 2. Thus:

$$\hat{x}_i(e_1) = \arg \max_{x \in \{0,1\}} \{ B^i(x, e_1, \hat{e}_2(x_1, \ldots, x, \ldots, x_N, e_1)) - \kappa x$$

$$- \hat{e}_2(x_1, \ldots, x, \ldots, x_N, e_1) \frac{c}{N} \}.$$

The fact that the Period 2 policy outcome depends on the full vector of Period 1 investment decisions implies that private investment decisions are now interdependent. We thus look for a Nash equilibrium in private investment decisions.

Assumption 3

$$\sum_i [B_i(1, e_1, 1) - B_i(1, e_1, 0)] - c < 0$$

for all $e_1 \in \{0, 1\}$.

Then, if every citizen invests in Period 1, the government chooses $\hat{e}_2(1,\ldots,1,e_1) = 0$, i.e. not to implement the project in Period 2.

This implies that the time consistent policy without commitment has $x_i = 0$ for all $i \in \{1,\ldots,N\}$ and $\hat{e}_2 = 0$. The Period 1 policy will be $\hat{e}_1 = 1$ if and only if:

$$\sum_i (b_i(1) + B_i(0,1,0)) - c > \sum_i (b_i(0) + B_i(0,0,0)).$$

Assumption 1 implies that the policy achieved by a benevolent government is Pareto dominated. Thus, the failure to commit to $e_2 = 1$ constitutes a government failure in the Pareto sense.

This policy cum investment outcome will also constitute a failure according to any kind of social welfare function that respects the Pareto criterion, including surplus maximization. Hence, it is also a distributional failure.

It is less clear whether there is a government failure in Wicksell's sense. If:

$$b_i(1) + B_i(0,1,0) - c/N < b_i(0) + B_i(0,0,0)$$

for some i there will be a Wicksellian government failure if $\hat{e}_1 = 1$ since some citizens are made worse off by implementing the project. The fact that $\hat{e}_2 = 0$ means that a Wicksellian failure may be avoided in Period 2 compared to the full commitment outcome as long as some citizens prefer the Period 2 project not to be implemented.

This simple example illustrates the classic time consistency problem as it afflicts a benevolent government. It arises here because the government's policy preference changes once the private investment decisions have been made. However, this example of government failure has nothing to do with politics. There are no elections in the story—a benevolent dictator without commitment power would generate this kind of problem. However, the time consistency problem is due to an intertemporal linkage created from the fact that there is a durable private decision by the citizens—in this case the private investment decision—that affects government policy incentives. We now show how intertemporal political and policy linkages can induce government failures. Note also that the time consistency problem as generated here is not due to inefficiencies in Period 1 policy making. This will contrast with those that we demonstrate in the next section.

2.6.2 *Political and policy linkages*

As we have seen, commitment problems arise even when the identity of the (benevolent) policy maker remains fixed over time. But the essence of political economy models is the selection and turnover of policy makers through a political process. In this section, we explore the consequences of this for policy choice. To focus on the issue of political and policy linkages, we will now abstract from private investment decisions and hence suppress x_i from the analysis.

A key additional consideration in this section is to describe the process of survival and turnover which determines the probability that the policy maker remains in office as a function of his/her Period 1 policy choice. Here, we will develop a 'black box' approach to the process of turnover among policy makers. However, it could be given a micro-foundation. For example, Besley and Coate (1998) develop an analysis of turnover based on a citizen–candidate model of politics. The political agency models that we study in Chapters 3 and 4 can also provide a foundation for this. In these models, as we shall see, the key idea is that turnover reflects *political accountability*. They make sense of this using a model of imperfect information where either the policy outcome or the politician's type is uncertain ex ante. Considerations of political turnover could equally well be studied in a model of non-democratic politics as in Acemoglu and Robinson (2003).

We now suppose that there are two groups of citizens in the population—those who have a high level of demand for government projects and those who have a low demand. We use $\tau \in \{L, H\}$ to denote the type of each citizen. Let $\gamma_t (\in [0, 1])$ be the proportion of citizens who are of type H in period t. We allow for the possibility of turnover in the electorate which leads γ to change over time. There could also be some uncertainty about the future proportions of citizens of each type.

Let $b_\tau(0) = 0$ and:

$$b_\tau(1) = \begin{cases} \bar{b} & \text{if } \tau = H \\ \underline{b} & \text{if } \tau = L. \end{cases}$$

be the Period 1 payoff from implementing the Period 1 government project with $\bar{b} > \underline{b}$.[24] The Period 2 project payoff depends on whether

---

[24] We have not imposed the assumption that $\underline{b} = 0$ since we want it to be possible for *every* citizen to favor implementing the project in Period 1.

the project was undertaken in Period 1. Let $B_\tau(e_1, e_2)$ be the Period 2 valuation of a type τ. We assume that $B_i(e_1, 0) = 0$ and:

$$B_\tau(e_1, 1) = \begin{cases} \bar{B}(e_1) & \text{if } \tau = H \\ \underline{B}(e_1) & \text{if } \tau = L. \end{cases}$$

where $\bar{B}(e_1) > \underline{B}(e_1)$.

It is evident from this that we have a *policy linkage* between the two time periods since the demand for the Period 2 project could be affected by whether it is implemented in Period 1. As above, the cost of the project is c in each period and is divided equally across all N citizens.

We suppose that a citizen holds office in each period. This means that he/she must either be of type L or type H. Hence we consider only policy choices that are optimal for some kind of citizen as a policy maker. In addition to policy concerns, a policy maker may also care about the rent from holding office which we denote by $E \geq 0$. We suppose that a policy maker of a particular exogenously given type is in office in Period 1.

There are two aspects of political turnover to consider. First, there are concerns that the policy maker has about his/her own survival in office. This is particularly important in the presence of rents. Second, there is the issue of what type of policy maker will be in office in future. So a policy maker could lose office, but be guaranteed that he/she would be succeeded by someone with the same policy preferences. Hence, only the personal rent to holding office is lost.

Let $\sigma_t \in \{L, H\}$ denote the type of the policy maker in office in period t. We capture these two aspects of turnover as follows. Let $\pi(\sigma_1, e_1) \in [0, 1]$ denote the probability that an incumbent of type σ_1 is re-elected as policy maker for Period 2 as a function of the Period 1 project that he/she implements. There are three possibilities. The project is *politically neutral* if $\pi(\sigma_1, 1) = \pi(\sigma_1, 0)$, *politically advantageous* if $\pi(\sigma_1, 1) > \pi(\sigma_1, 0)$, or *politically damaging* if $\pi(\sigma_1, 1) < \pi(\sigma_1, 0)$. Let $q \in [0, 1]$ be the probability that the second period incumbent is of type L. There are a number of ways to motivate $q \neq 1$. For example, we could suppose that γ is a random variable due to changes in the electorate or turnout so the median type could be of type H or L. We let $\hat{e}_t$ denote the equilibrium project choice in each period.

The timing of the model is as follows. In Period 1 there is an (exogenously given) incumbent policy maker of type σ_1 in office who chooses e_1. Nature then determines whether the incumbent is replaced according to $\pi(\sigma_1, e_1)$. The latter could represent either the outcome of an election or a power struggle in an autocratic system. If the incumbent is replaced then nature determines the type of the new incumbent. The Period 2 incumbent then chooses e_2. We study the outcome working backwards beginning with the Period 2 policy choice.

It is straightforward to see that the Period 2 policy choice depends solely on the type of the Period 2 policy maker, so:

$$\hat{e}_2(\sigma_2, e_1) = \begin{cases} 1 & \text{if } B_{\sigma_2}(e_1, 1) \geq c/N \\ 0 & \text{otherwise.} \end{cases}$$

Now let

$$W^\tau(e_1, \sigma_2) = \left\{ \hat{e}_2(\sigma_2, e_1) \left[B_\tau(e_1, \hat{e}_2(\sigma_2, e_1)) - \frac{c}{N} \right] \right\}, \tau \in \{L, H\}$$

be the Period 2 utility of citizen of type τ as a function of the Period 1 policy choice and type of the Period 2 policy maker.

Now consider the Period 1 policy maker's choice. This has a forward looking element. The policy maker's preference is:

$$e_1 \left(b_{\sigma_1}(e_1) - \frac{c}{N} \right) + \pi(\sigma_1, e_1)(E + W^{\sigma_1}(e_1, \sigma_1)) + (1 - \pi(\sigma_1, e_1))\bar{W}^{\sigma_1}(e_1)$$

$$(2.3)$$

where:

$$\bar{W}^\tau(e_1, q) = qW^\tau(e_1, L) + (1 - q)W^\tau(e_1, H)$$

is his/her expected period two payoff if he/she is not re-elected. This reflects the uncertainty about the period policy maker's type.

The optimal Period 1 policy for an incumbent of type σ_1 is therefore:

$$\hat{e}_1(\sigma_1) = \arg\max_{e_1 \in \{0,1\}} \{e_1 \left(b_{\sigma_1}(e_1) - \frac{c}{N} \right)$$

$$+ \pi(\sigma_1, e_1)(E + W^{\sigma_1}(e_1, \sigma_1)) + (1 - \pi(\sigma_1, e_1))\bar{W}^{\sigma_1}(e_1, q)\}$$

This illustrates the strategic aspects of policy making that arise in a dynamic political economy setting. This equation embodies the three main considerations that shape policy making in dynamic political settings:

- **Short term policy considerations:** These are represented by $\left(b_{\sigma_1}(e_1) - \frac{c}{N}\right)$. This depends on whether the policy could be worthwhile or otherwise in terms of its current costs and benefits.

- **Long-term policy considerations:** These are reflected in the dependence of $W^{\sigma_1}(e_1, \sigma_1)$ and $\bar{W}^{\sigma_1}(e_1)$ on e_1. This term arises since the Period 1 policy may affect payoffs from *future* policies. This is the source of policy linkages.

- **Survival considerations:** This is represented by the way in which $\pi(\sigma_1, e_1)$ depends on e_1 and affects the probability that the incumbent will survive as a function of his/her Period 1 policy choice.[25] This is the source of political linkages.

We now study the implications of policy choices that maximize (2.3). We will illustrate both policy and political linkages. Before doing that, however, we develop a benchmark result based on Besley and Coate (1998). Suppose that

(1) The policy is politically neutral, therefore $\pi(\sigma_1, 0) = \pi(\sigma_1, 1)$ for $\sigma_1 \in \{L, H\}$
(2) The payoff from the Period 2 project choice is unaffected by the Period 1 project choice, so $B_\tau(0, e_2) = B_\tau(1, e_2)$ for $\tau \in \{L, H\}$.

Then the policy choices (e_1, e_2) will be Pareto efficient.

To see why this is true, observe that if conditions (1) and (2) hold then the expected Period 2 payoff of the current policy maker (and the citizens in the polity) do not depend on e_1 at all. Thus, the Period 1 policy choice is determined solely by whether $b_{\sigma_1}(1)$ is bigger or smaller than c/N. But then the model effectively reduces to a one period model with all intertemporal links having been severed.

Even though the outcome in this case is guaranteed to be Pareto efficient there is no reason to expect it to maximize social surplus or to avoid government failures of a Wicksellian variety. The reasoning here follows exactly that in the static model developed above.

We now consider what happens when either conditions (1) or (2) above fail. The first is the case of a political linkage and the second that of a policy linkage. We now show that in each case, we can construct an example where the policy choice is Pareto inefficient and hence a government failure in this sense.

---

[25] In principle we could also make q depend on e_1.

POLITICAL LINKAGES

Our first example illustrates a case where the desire of an incumbent to survive in office leads to a Pareto inefficient policy choice. Suppose that all citizens wish to implement the first period project, in other words, $\underline{b} > c/N$. The citizens disagree, however, about Period 2 policy. Specifically, we assume that

$$\underline{B}(0) > \frac{c}{N} > \underline{B}(1)$$

and

$$\bar{B}(1) \geq \bar{B}(0) > \frac{c}{N}.$$

The first of these says that the low types want the project in Period 2 only if it was *not* implemented in Period 1. The second says that the high valuation types want the project to be implemented regardless of whether the first period project is implemented.

Given these assumptions on preferences, any situation where the first period project is not implemented constitutes a government failure in the Pareto sense—all citizens are better off for *any* fixed policy decision in Period 2. We are interested, therefore, in studying cases where this does not happen. The starkest case of this is where it is politically costly to set $e_1 = 1$. Suppose that:

$$\pi(\sigma_1, 1) = 0 < \pi(\sigma_1, 0) = 1.$$

This says that the Period 1 incumbent will survive in office only if he/she fails to implement the Period 1 project.[26]

It is clear that for large enough E, the Period 1 project will not be implemented, so $\hat{e}_1(\sigma_1) = 0$ for $\sigma_1 \in \{L, H\}$. This makes sense. The incumbent has the desire to hold on to office since the rents are large, but he/she will lose office if he/she chooses to implement it. However, a government failure can also occur if $E = 0$. To see this, let $\underline{b} - c/N$ become small so that the direct benefits of the project are small to a type L. Then if $\sigma_1 = L$ and $e_1 = 1$, the incumbent will suffer a utility loss of $\underline{B}(1) - c/N$ if a type H policy maker holds office in Period 2 as the latter will set $e_2 = 1$. Thus as long as q (the probability of a

---

[26] A micro-foundation for this could be generated in an agency model of the type studied in the next chapter. This approach was used in the key contribution of Coate and Morris (1995). Besley and Coate (1998) also develops a model which is consistent with this kind of outcome using a citizen–candidate approach.

type L policy maker) is closer enough to zero, it will be optimal for a type L policy maker to set $e_1 = 0$. In this case, it is the decision rent from controlling the policy process rather than the direct rent from holding office which induces a government failure.

This example illustrates how the desire to survive in office affects the efficiency of policy choice and leads to a Pareto inefficient outcome. This arguments extends easily and unsurprisingly to other social objectives such as surplus maximization. It is more subtle in Wicksellian terms. From a Wicksellian point of view, the right outcome is $e_1 = 1$ and $e_2 = 0$. By failing to implement the project in Period 1, the type L incumbent prevents a Period 2 government failure.

Even though the welfare consideration is not always transparent, the idea that political survival can play an important role in affecting economic policy choice has been widely studied.[27] For example, Aghion and Bolton (1990) and Milesi-Ferretti and Spolaore (1994) develop models in which strategic policy choice can also lead to changes in who is elected. An incumbent may realize that if he/she runs a deficit then this can make election of the challenger less attractive. These ideas are applied to privatization policy in Biais and Perrotti (2002). Many governments have encouraged privatizations because they create a class of shareholders who then show favors towards right wing governments. This will encourage governments to underprice privatizations to create a class of stakeholders. Besley and Coate (1998) pull these ideas together and show that these strategic effects can be sources of real inefficiencies.

A variety of papers look at how political incentives for re-election shape the kind of public projects that are chosen. Glazer (1989) discusses how this can lead to projects which have long-run effects being preferred to those that pay off only in the short-run since these have effects on political equilibria. Coate and Morris (1995) use an agency model of the kind discussed in Chapters 3 and 4. They show how the fact that policy choice affects re-election chances leads to inefficient policies being chosen. This is driven by the desire of politicians to capture rents by being re-elected. Robinson and Torvik (2005) discuss how public project choices can provide a commitment device since only certain kinds of politicians will continue with these projects in future. Jain and Mukand (2003) extend the model of Fernandez

---

[27] Besley and Coate (1998) study the implications of political equilibrium in a dynamic model using the Pareto criterion.

and Rodrik (1991) to allow for an explicit dynamic political economy model where the government can compensate the losers in Period 2 for the consequences of a project choice in Period 1. They also find that whether the leader survives is important to understanding Period 1 policy choice.

These insights have also been useful in understanding how politics affects growth and development. There are now a number of models that develop this theme using the insight that government efforts to promote growth can have adverse political consequences for incumbents. For example, Acemoglu and Robinson (2003) build a theory of underdevelopment based on the possibility that governments are unwilling to invest in productive things because they affect the politician's tenure. In a similar vein, Krusell and Rios-Rull (1996) develop a model where politicians can affect the future political equilibrium via today's policy choices leading to stagnation.

POLICY LINKAGES

We turn now to policy linkages. To focus on these, suppose that the Period 1 policy is politically neutral, i.e., $\pi(\sigma_1, 1) = \pi(\sigma_1, 0) = 0$. This could describe a case where all politicians are term limited so that considerations of rents (E) cannot distort their policy choices. Hence, political rents play no role in this example.

We suppose that the type of policy maker who controls Period 2 policy is uncertain with an equal chance of any kind of Period 2 policy maker $(q = \frac{1}{2})$.[28] As above, we assume that there is universal demand for the Period 1 project, i.e. $b > c/N$. However, we now suppose that type H citizen demands the project in Period 2 only if the Period 1 project was implemented, i.e.

$$\bar{B}(1) > \frac{c}{N} > \bar{B}(0).$$

However, type L citizens never desire the project in Period 2:

$$\frac{c}{N} > \underline{B}(0) = \underline{B}(1).$$

As above, this implies that any situation in which the Period 1 project is not implemented is Pareto inferior.

[28] This could easily be underpinned by a political model where the two groups are of similar size and the policy maker is elected from a contest between one representative from each group.

Now consider what happens if the first period policy maker is of type L. He/she will be replaced by a type H with probability $\frac{1}{2}$. The latter will implement the project only if $e_1 = 1$. Thus if:

$$\underline{b} - \frac{c}{N} + \frac{1}{2}\left[\underline{B}(1) - \frac{c}{N}\right] < 0$$

then a type L incumbent will set $e_1 = 0$.

The logic here differs from the case of political linkages—the Period 1 project choice has no effect on whether the incumbent survives. The effect is driven from the fact that:

$$1 = \hat{e}_2(H, 1) > \hat{e}_2(H, 0) = 0.$$

Again, it is clear that this kind of logic can underpin government failures using a wide set of welfare functions. The Wicksellian implications are similar to the example with political linkages. The Period 1 policy maker of type L prevents a Period 2 government failure by setting $e_1 = 1$. Hence, this does not constitute a government failure in the Wicksellian sense.

A number of papers in the literature explore policy linkages and their implications. For example, Tabellini and Alesina (1990) and Persson and Svensson (1989) all explore why political equilibria can lead to excessive fiscal deficits if debt is used strategically to influence policy outcomes beyond a politician's current term. They show that a larger deficit prevents the future incumbent from spending on his/her own preferred policies. This is more likely to happen if there is greater ideological conflict between the incumbent and his/her potential challenger.

2.6.3 Investment and politics

To round off our discussions, we now consider the possibility that private investment decisions affect policy choices—an issue that we abstracted from in the last subsection. However, we study this using a somewhat different policy example than that which has run through the rest of this chapter—one where investments increase private productivity and government policy is in the form of tax and transfer policy.

Suppose that the citizens in a polity are divided into three groups. A fraction γ_H of high income citizens earn y_H, a fraction of γ_L low

The anatomy of government failure

income citizens earn income $y_L(< y_H)$ and a fraction γ_M of mobile citizens earn income y_L unless they make a private investment that costs κ in which case they earn y_H. We assume that $\kappa < (y_H - y_L)$ so that the investment is worthwhile. Let $x_i \in \{0, 1\}$ be the investment decision of the ith mobile citizen. We assume that the utility of each citizen depends solely on their consumption which equals their post-tax and transfer income.

The two period structure of the last subsection is maintained with these productivity enhancing investments being undertaken in Period 1 and realized in Period 2. As above, we suppose that a policy maker is a citizen and hence corresponds to one of the three types of citizen that we have described. As a policy maker, we assume that the government can set the rate of a tax on income that we denote by $t \in [0, \bar{t}]$ where $\bar{t} < 1$. The latter could be due to the ability of citizens to retreat into some kind of informal (non-taxable) activity. We assume that any tax proceeds are distributed back to the citizens in lump-sum fashion with the transfer being denoted by T. Let μ_s be the mean income in the society in period $s \in \{1, 2\}$. Then the government budget constraint is:

$$T_s = t_s \mu_s.$$

The timing is as follows. We begin with a Period 1 policy maker in place. In Period 1, the incumbent sets (t_1, T_1). Then the mobile citizens choose whether or not to invest. The type of the period two politician is then determined in a manner to be described below. This policy maker then sets (t_2, T_2).

We will consider an explicitly democratic political process where the type of policy maker is determined according to majority rule. We assume that:

$$\gamma_M + \min\{\gamma_L, \gamma_H\} > \frac{1}{2} > \max\{\gamma_H, \gamma_L\}.$$

This says that neither the high or low income citizens are a majority. However, each becomes a majority if they combine with the mobile citizens.

As a benchmark, suppose that there is no government so that $t_s = T_s = 0$ for $s \in \{1, 2\}$. In this case, all the mobile citizens find it optimal to invest.

We now study what happens with voting. As above let $\{\sigma_1, \sigma_2\}$ be the type of citizen in office in each period. First consider Period 2 policy making. It is easy to see that the optimal tax rate is:

$$t_2(\sigma_2, \mu_2) = \arg \max_{t \in [0,\bar{t}]} \{(1-t)y_{\sigma_2} + t\mu_2\}.$$

This implies that:

$$t_2(\sigma_2, \mu_2) = \begin{cases} \bar{t} & \text{if } y_{\sigma_2} < \mu_2 \\ 0 & \text{otherwise.} \end{cases}$$

A citizen with income y_H always prefers to set $t_2 = 0$ while a citizen of type y_L sets $t_2 = \bar{t}$.

It is now straightforward to see how policy in Period 2 depends on Period 1 investment decisions by mobile citizens. If all mobile citizens invest, then citizens with income of y_H are in the majority and hence $t_2 = 0$ while if all the mobile citizens choose not invest, then citizens with income level y_L are in a majority and the tax rate is $t_2 = \bar{t}$. This becomes interesting if:

$$(1 - \bar{t})(y_H - y_L) < \kappa,$$

since investment by mobile citizens then occurs only if these citizens anticipate that the other mobile citizens will also choose to invest. In other words the political system creates a strategic complementarity between the mobile citizens.

The political model now has multiple equilibria. In one equilibrium no mobile citizen invests so that the majority of citizens earn low income in Period 2 and $t_2 = \bar{t}$. In the other, all mobile citizens invest in Period 1 and there is no redistributive taxation in Period 2 since a majority of citizens have high incomes, i.e. $t_2 = 0$. National income is different in each case with the income level being higher when taxes are low.

To complete the model, we need only to determine the first period policy choice. However, this does not have any bearing on whether the mobile citizens choose to invest.[29] Hence:

$$t_1(\sigma_1, \mu_1) = \arg \max_{t \in [0,\bar{t}]} \{(1-t)y_{\sigma_1} + t\mu_1\}.$$

It is the fact that Period 1 policy does not affect private investment that differentiates this example from those above.

---

[29] This assumes that either κ is a purely non-financial (i.e. utility) cost or else that $\kappa < y_L$. Otherwise government redistributive policy could lead to an increase in investment.

We now consider whether this example constitutes a government failure and in what sense. Since government policy in this case is purely redistributive, any $t_s > 0$ constitutes a government failure in Wicksell's sense. This could be achieved either by passing a constitutional restriction that $t_s = 0$ or providing some form of guarantee that a high income citizen will always be in office. Social surplus will also be maximized in this example where redistributive taxation is zero in Period 2.

Turning now to Pareto efficiency. We will show that the outcome described may constitute a political failure. Consider the outcome where $t_2 = \bar{t}$ so that mobile citizens do not invest. Suppose that the tax rate is cut to:

$$\tilde{t} = \frac{(y_H - y_L) - \kappa}{(y_H - y_L)}.$$

This is the highest tax rate at which mobile citizens are willing to invest (they are indifferent between investing and not investing). We need to show that the low income citizens are better off at $\tilde{t}$ than at $\bar{t}$. This is true if:

$$\bar{t}\frac{y_H}{(1 - y_L)} < (y_H - y_L) - \kappa.$$

This requires that the gain from investing be large enough and that there be sufficiently many mobile citizens. This implies that transfers to the low income groups are small when the mobile do not invest and increase substantially when they do. This shows that the example that we are studying here is a political failure.

This example is an instance of a general phenomenon whereby private decision making affects policy outcomes. This general class of policy distortions includes the example studied by Coate and Morris (1999) who emphasize the fact that policies can persist due to individuals making private investment decisions to benefit from them. The endogeniety of groups affecting political support is also at the heart of the mechanism in Acemoglu and Robinson (2001) sustaining inefficient transfer policies.[30]

---

[30] Krusell and Rios-Rull (1996) is also related although in their model current policy (rather than just anticipated future policy) influences investment and hence future policy. Thus, it also has elements of the policy linkages studied in the previous section.

2.7 Implications

It seems harsh to call something a failure unless it can be shown that there is something better. The theory of market failure provides a framework for shaping the case for government to improve what the market can achieve. Indeed, many of the textbook functions of government—to provide public goods, regulate externalities and regulate monopolies—are rooted in the theory of market failure.

How to react to government failure is less clear cut. One widespread view is that identifying government failures should primarily provide a basis for constitution design. This view is often identified with the public choice approach, especially the work on Buchanan.[31] The idea is that the rules of the political game are codified ex ante, possibly behind a veil of ignorance, and that political resource allocation is shaped by these rules. The rules take on normative significance in responding to the kinds of difficulties that might arise in the operation of politics.

Buchanan (1967) divides constitutions into two parts. One of them is a set of rules laid down for the conduct of the policy process. He refers to this as a *procedural constitution*. This might include designation of specific policy authority, separation of powers, the electoral system and rules governing who may vote or hold political office. The other part of the constitution may refer to policies directly. Buchanan calls this a *fiscal constitution*. However, it is clear that the slightly broader term *policy constitution* might be more apt.

There are opportunities, particularly when new nations are founded, to specify the political architecture from the ground up. However, more commonly the focus is on more modest, piecemeal reforms. There are three main categories of democratic constitutional reform that are debated: democratic structure, government architecture and policy rules. We discuss the main elements of each in brief:

1. **Democratic structure:** There are many facets of a constitution which shape the conduct of democratic politics. These include
   (a) *Voting rules:* First, there are rules about who is eligible to vote and how they can register. The nineteenth and twentieth centuries saw a significant extension of the franchise, notably with women securing the right to vote. Second, there are the rules for

---

[31] See, for example, Frey (1983) and Mueller (1996) for development of these ideas.

aggregating votes and determining the spatial pattern of represesentation. There are countless alternatives which vary between a straight majoritarian system with single member districts through to list systems with proportional representation.

(b) *Electoral conduct:* Along with opening of the franchise came a decline in rules restricting who could hold public office. That said, most democratic systems still limit access to political office more than they limit the right to vote. Also important are rules about the conduct of campaigns which affect how elections are fought.

(c) *Legislative structure:* There are many aspects of rules within a legislature that can affect how politics is conducted post-election. This category also includes the possibility of directly elected authority as in the case of a president. Also important is the choice between uni-cameral and bi-cameral systems.

(d) *Direct democracy:* How and whether there should remain a direct voice for citizens remains open to debate. Some countries, notably Switzerland, allow a significant role for citizens' initiatives while most others rely very little on this.

2. **Government architecture:** This mainly includes the rules that determine who has policy authority and on what basis.

(a) *Independent agencies:* Even in democracies there are many agencies that have direct policy authority. These include independent central banks to determine monetary policy which operate alongside democratic legislatures. The role of the judiciary is also important in many polities. In common law countries, in particular, the judiciary plays a key role in shaping many policies through establishing precedent. The judiciary in the form of constitutional courts may also have the authority to limit the power of elected representatives.

(b) *Decentralization:* Most countries have multi-tiered governments and the degree of policy authority delegated below the central government level is an important policy parameter. This has been an extremely active policy area of late and includes some non-democratic polities such as China.[32]

(c) *Structure of the executive:* The way in which government agencies are structured within government and how this is accountable to legislative authorities varies greatly across democratic

[32] See, for example, Qian and Roland (1998).

systems. Parliamentary systems typically have ministers who are members of the legislature whereas some systems have appointed cabinet members.

3. **Policy rules:** There are also many legal rules that have a direct impact on policy outcomes. It is unclear, in some cases, how far these should be viewed as constitutional provisions or as merely policies that are subject to change. Nonetheless, they clearly have great practical force. They include:

   (a) *Fiscal deficit regulations:* Many countries use means to limit the ability of governments to run deficits. This is interesting in view of the large literature—which we referred to above—which looks at why deficit finance can be subject to political failure. We discuss this further in Chapter 4.

   (b) *Private property:* Many countries have evolved systems for the protection of property which place limits on the power of government to tax and regulate its citizens.

   (c) *Civil liberties:* Policy rules also have to function in the context of evolved rules for the protection of individual freedom. Policy choices that conflict with human rights provisions often require amendment to prevent inconsistencies between policies. Freedom of information provisions may also have a direct impact on the kinds of policies that can be implemented if their provisions are deemed to transcend those of particular policy provisions. These are areas where the role of courts is crucial.

This book will not be able to do justice to this rich array of constitutional issues. However, the welfare economic framework that we have developed here around the notion of government failure should be helpful for thinking about some of these issues. A general intellectual approach suggests itself:

- Step 1: Develop a theoretical and empirical model of the effect of a particular constitutional rule.[33]
- Step 2: Use Step 1 to identify who gains and who loses.
- Step 3: Use Step 2 to inform a process of discussion/aggregation to make a social decisions.

[33] See Besley and Case (2003) and Persson and Tabellini (2003) for progress in this area. Acemoglu (2005) discusses more broadly the idea of political equilibrium inducing preferences over institutions.

The ideas of government failure that we have discussed are implicit in the step from 2 to 3 where our different ideas of government failure correspond to ways of weighting gainers and losers.

This procedure is, of course, a highly idealized process and real debates about constitutional reform are messy and may appear to be influenced by idiosyncratic events rather than reasoned debate. Just as special interests may influence policy so they frequently try to influence constitutional reform and the idea of founding fathers reasoning behind a veil of ignorance is far fetched. But this makes the influence of social scientists even more crucial. It is imperative to have a space for structured and scientific reasoning, however slight that impact may sometimes appear to be.

But modesty too is needed. Economists have a comparative advantage in discussing many policies—especially those that involve the commitment of public resources. However, our competence in the field of human rights and calculating the value of freedom is more limited.[34] The Wicksellian approach that we discussed above is the only approach to government failure which gives a direct role for such concerns. But in discussing policies such as abortion rights, the decision to go to war or the incarceration of terror suspects, we should acknowledge that our welfare economic framework is limited. But that still leaves a vast domain in which the ideas discussed here are relevant and one that may be at the heart of many constitutional reform discussions.

The subsequent chapters will discuss some of the constitutional choice issues raised above. However, this will mainly be done through the lens of a specific approach to politics—political agency models. This is a class of dynamic models which take imperfect information issues in politics seriously. They also provide a vehicle for weighing the selection and incentives issues emphasized in the last chapter. We will use these models to explore issues concerning the quality of economic policy choices and politicians.

Reflecting on institution design in this way makes it clear that the reasoning of this chapter could also apply to institutions more broadly, in other words, to have a theory of institutional faliure. This project is anticipated in Buchanan (1967) when he says:

Theoretical welfare economics enables us to define the necessary marginal conditions that must be satisfied for an allocation of economic resources

---

[34] See Cooter (2000) for an attempt to tackle issues of rights in constitutional choices more directly.

to be efficient. Straightforward extension of this analysis to 'theoretical institutional economics' should enable us to define a similar set of conditions that would have to be met if an institutional arrangement or rule is to be classified as 'efficient.' It now seems quite possible that future developments will in fact allow for general statements of such conditions.

(http://www.econlib.org/library/Buchanan/buchCv4clg.html, 4.19.36)

Nearly 40 years on, the future developments that Buchanan refers to are not yet a reality. However, much progress is being made.[35]

2.8 Concluding comments

The main purpose of this chapter has been to identify sources of government failure. We have introduced three criteria by which such failures can be defined. We have also shown that they are distinct. Defining government failure in terms of Pareto efficiency—to parallel the classic definition of market failure—has little bite in static settings with unitary political actors. It can, however, be important when multiple actors are engaged in policy making. It is also non-trivial in dynamic models of government resource allocation.

Bator (1958) argued that non-appropriability, non-convexity, and public goods are the main sources of market failure defined as a Pareto efficiency. The parallel list suggested by the discussion here is non-Coasian legislative institutions, poor selection of policy makers, costly rent-seeking, and intertemporal investment, policy, and political linkages.

This discussion of government failure serves as a useful background to the specific discussion that follows, but also to more general debates about the achievement of government. In criticizing government intervention it pays to be specific about the sense in which government is failing and the remedy that is needed. To do this in a rich economic policy model is by no means straightforward. But the desiderata as laid out above are useful as an intellectual structure. Economists have benefited enormously from having a rigorous notion of market failure and there is every reason to think that putting government failure on a similarly firm intellectual footing should also pay off.

---

[35] See Acemoglu (2005) for further discussion.

3

Political agency and accountability

(I)n the large the electorate behaves about as rationally and responsibly as we should expect, given the clarity and the alternatives presented to it and the character of the information available to it.

(Key 1966: 7)

The problem is not how 180 million Aristotles can run a democracy, but how we can organize a political community of 180 million ordinary people so that it remains sensitive to their needs.

(Schattschneider 1960: 138)

3.1 Introduction

In the last chapter, we painted a broad picture of the issues at stake in thinking about whether government is likely to be run in the public interest. In this chapter, we explore a specific class of models which are ideally suited to pushing this debate forward: political agency models. Specifically, we look at the structure of political agency models with a focus on applications. We also lay out a canonical approach which should give the reader who is unfamiliar with the approach some idea of the model's potential. The simplicity of the model also provides a building block to look at many of the issues that have been studied in the literature.

At the heart of political agency models is the principal—agent relationship between citizens and government; the principals are the citizens/voters while the agents are the politicians/bureaucrats. This flips around the standard principal agent model that has been widely used in public economics and is at the core of the mechanism design problem.[1] In that approach, a welfare maximizing government tries to discern the privately observed characteristics of citizens which it will use to make good social decisions. For example, the standard optimal income tax problem assumes that each individual privately knows his/her own ability to earn. This implies that individualized redistributive lump-sum taxation may not be incentive compatible. Similarly, efficient provision of a public good requires that a government has sufficient information about the values that citizens attach to the good to discern the optimal level at which the good should be provided. The problem then lies in designing an optimal mechanism for public good provision.[2]

In the political agency approach, the incentive problem arises because the citizens have delegated authority to policy makers who enjoy an informational advantage. There are two main problems:

- Monitoring: The policy maker may act opportunistically. There is a need to establish whether this has happened and to reward/punish behavior accordingly in order to minimize opportunism.
- Selection: There is a need to select the most competent policy makers and/or those whose motivations are most likely to be in tune with the public interest.

As we discussed in Chapter 1, elections are the core mechanism for solving these problems. For the purposes of this book, this will simply be assumed. However, clearly this begs a host of important questions of constitution design. A full-blown attack on the issues would begin with the primitives of information constraints and limits on contracting and would seek to design the optimal set of constitutional rules.[3] It is less than clear whether the weight attached to the importance of elections in modern representative democracies would emerge from this approach. Moreover many of the assumptions of the political agency approach limit the incentive contracts that can be offered in apparently arbitrary ways. Clearly, in terms of theoretical purity, an approach rooted in mechanism design is on more solid ground. However, it is only as good as the available theoretical framework for capturing constraints on the set of mechanisms that are permissible. While this approach is strong when it comes to

---

[1] See Atkinson and Stiglitz (1980).   [2] See, for example, Laffont and Maskin (1980).
[3] See Laffont (2000) for an effort in this direction.

information constraints, it is hard to know how to capture other ideas like simplicity and fairness which may also be important in shaping institutional choices.[4]

Our main aim here is to analyze the properties of a stylized model of representative democracy with imperfect information. We are not asking whether it is the best possible institution. It could even be Pareto inefficient in some contexts. However, by studying a fairly simple model some insights might be gained about what goes into making democracy work and the kinds of piece-meal reforms that can make things work better.

The problem of monitoring (moral hazard) is at the heart of the classical statement of principal agent problems (see, for example, Holmstrom (1979)). In this problem, an agent is completing a task on behalf of a principal which yields a publicly observable payoff. The problem is that the action which generates the payoff cannot be observed by the principal. The principal's problem is then to design an incentive scheme for the agent which rewards him/her according to the payoff achieved. This model has been developed in a wide variety of ways to consider different problems.[5]

In the standard problem, agents are homogeneous. However, there are extensions to allow for unobserved types (in addition to unobserved actions) in particular applications (see, for example, Laffont and Tirole (1986)). This can mean offering the agent a menu of contracts which achieves self-selection. The literature on the dynamics of regulation has emphasized the importance of 'ratchet effects' in such settings in which information revealed by an agent is used in future periods, making information revelation harder to achieve in earlier periods.[6] Such models assume that firms differ in some core level of competence that is fixed over time. In a political agency setting with re-election incentives and unobserved types, such dynamic issues are central: incompetent incumbents may aim to disguise their type to get re-elected. In modeling political agency, issues beyond competency may be important. For example, the issue of selecting an agent with an appropriate motivation may be an issue.[7]

---

[4] This may explain why, even after two decades of research, the mechanism design approach has yet to give a persuasive account of the attractiveness of markets for allocating resources except in the most stylized of situations.

[5] See Prendergast (1999) for a survey.

[6] See, for example, Laffont and Tirole (1993) for discussion.

[7] See Besley and Ghatak (2005) for a model of bureaucracy along these lines.

In this chapter, we study a variety of agency models tailored to look at concrete issues. Each author in the literature has tended to take quite a specific approach depending on their ends. Even then, the development of political agency models owes much to the more general understanding of agency problems that has developed within economics over the past 30 years.

As we discussed above, achieving accountability is one of the key roles of elections. In the loosest sense, this means tying the performance of politicians to what they do while they are in office. It is important to distinguish in this regard between formal (de jure) and real (de facto) accountability.[8] It is in the nature of the institution of representative democracy that politicians are periodically subject to re-election. The formal rules, the term length and the rules governing electoral conduct, constitute the formal accountability rules. But they do not typically attempt to make any direct link between a politician's performance and his/her re-election chances. This depends on what happens in equilibrium, in other words, as a function of politicians' behavior and voters' strategies. The latter determines whether there is *real* accountability. In a poorly functioning democracy, politicians can perform acts which systematically displease voters without facing sanctions. This might be because voters are poorly informed or politicians intimidate voters.

The extent of real accountability might be thought of as a pretty good index of a well-functioning democratic system of government. It is through being accountable that politics is most likely to be *responsive* to voters' wishes. Responsiveness and accountability are frequently held up as self-evident values in political systems. However, there is no necessary link between accountability and the welfare of society. There is likely to be such a link when the issues at stake are mostly common values (valence issues in the language of political science), in other words, the electorate broadly agree on what should be done. As we discussed in Chapter 1, obvious examples include reducing corruption, improving public service efficiency, and collecting taxes at the lowest possible cost.

If there is a large measure of disagreement on the right policy, there is no obvious reason to believe that making sure that elections

---

[8] A useful definition of accountability in the political science literature can be found in Fearon (1999) who suggested that an agent A is accountable to principal B, if (i) there is an understanding that A is obliged to act in some way on behalf of B and (ii) B is empowered by some formal institution or perhaps informal rules to sanction or reward A for his/her activities or performance in this capacity.

outcomes are responsive to incumbent behavior increases any reasonable measure of social welfare. If the incumbent is accountable to the median voter then policies will be skewed towards these preferences even if (as argued in Section 2.5.1 of Chapter 2) these have no normative significance. To reflect this, we will work mainly here with models that assume that voters do have a common interest in achieving some outcome and discuss whether we would expect the political system to deliver it. We will return to this issue in our concluding remarks.

Our whole framework of analysis presupposes the existence of a legal system and a body of law governing the conduct of elections. For example, incumbents are supposed to leave office if they lose the election and to court voters fairly, i.e. avoiding bribery and intimidation. Similarly, there are legal limits on what politicians may do to serve their own interests and many politicians are threatened with legal sanction for using their offices corruptly.[9] Many of the failures of democratic systems are legal. For example, Robert Mugabe's unwillingness to leave his office in Zimbabwe makes real accountability impossible. We focus here on accountability within a well functioning legal system. However, it is clear that the extent to which the formal institutions are upheld might be an important difference in the way democracies function.

The remainder of the chapter is organized as follows. In the next section we discuss political agency models in general—the assumptions that go into them and general modeling issues. Section 3.3 puts forward a canonical agency model which serves to illustrate a number of the issues. Within that section (Section 3.3), we discuss a specific empirical application to data on US governors. This will offer an opportunity to get into some more general empirical concerns. Section 3.4 explores a number of extensions of the basic model. In Section 3.5, we discuss concrete policy driven applications from the literature. Section 3.6 concludes.

3.2 Elements of political agency models

Common to all of the agency models discussed here is the importance of re-election incentives in shaping the behavior of incumbent politicians. To model this requires a dynamic structure—the simplest

---

[9] Though in practice prosecutions for serving politicians are rare.

approach being a two-period setting. However, some contributions have looked at longer time horizons and we will do so in Sections 3.4.6 and 3.4.7.

The agency model can be thought of as a game in which the players are voters and politicians. At any point in time, one or more politicians have the power to make policy. If they are re-elected they retain this right. If they lose it then another politician replaces them. The politicians could, in principle, be drawn from the pool of voters. However, typically, this process of selection is not modeled. The simplest (and most popular setting) is one where voters are homogeneous while politicians differ in their type.

The key modeling issues are:

- The nature of the uncertainty.
- The motives for holding office.
- The nature of accountability.
- Retrospective voting.

We will look at each of these in turn.

3.2.1 *The nature of the uncertainty*

Models vary in what they specify as being unobservable to voters. At the core of many models are unobservable types of politicians. These could be their competence levels. For example some politicians may be skilled in choosing policies whereas others make poor choices. There could also be uncertainty about the motivations of politicians. Some may be honest while others are not. Some may have a strong sense of duty while others do not. Politicians may also vary in the utility they gain from being in office due to the thrill of being powerful or whether they like or dislike media attention.

One key issue is whether the politicians know their own types. In the case of competence, it seems less plausible to suppose that politicians know their own capacities completely and may be learning about this along with the voters. A model of uninformed politicians is more in tune with the celebrated Holmstrom (1999) 'career concerns' model in which individuals put in effort which reveals their type to the 'market'. Persson and Tabellini (2000) develop a political agency model along these lines, in which voters and politicians are symmetrically informed.

Voters may also be poorly informed about the best policy. There are good reasons to think that governments have access to a wide variety of policy advice which should enable them to make better policy decisions than voters left to their own devices. Indeed, the notion of asymmetric information is at the centre of the idea that voters are rationally ignorant as suggested in Downs (1957). In reality there are ways of informing voters about policy such as think-tanks, pressure groups, and the media.

A further source of uncertainty is over the exact policy implemented. An important example is the quality of policy choices which may be uncertain for a considerable time after a policy is chosen. A good example is the recent war with Iraq; it will take some time before the wisdom of the decision and the competence of its execution is known. In some cases, the welfare consequences of a policy may be uncertain for many years into the future, such as in the case of policies towards global warming.

In cases where politicians have a private interest in adopting some policy or other, voters may also find it hard to discern whether they have earned a rent from any particular policy. There is also a large literature which says that lack of transparency makes it difficult for voters to know exactly what is the true state of public finances. This may make it attractive for politicians to raise debt in order to postpone paying for certain policies in the short-run.

3.2.2 *The motives for holding office*

It seems to be accepted that a cast iron law of politics is that politicians like to be re-elected. However, the sources of re-election incentives differ between models. One possibility is simply to posit an 'ego rent' from holding office as in Rogoff (1990). This rent could be the intoxication effect from power or some sense of pride at having been approved in a ballot by one's fellow citizens.

Another source of benefits from holding onto office may come in the form of material gain. This could be because politics provides an opportunity to reward cronies or an opportunity for corruption. It could even be because politicians' wages and perks are attractive.

The desire for re-election may also stem from public goods concerns; this would be true, for example, if incumbents have strong policy preferences. We would expect these forces to be most important when there is a large degree of polarization in the political system.

In such cases, the incumbent will be keen not to have another policy maker take over. Related to this, Maskin and Tirole (2004) discuss the possibility of a 'legacy effect' associated with holding office whereby politicians care about the value created while they are in office.

In all three cases, incumbent politicians will desire re-election either instrumentally or for its own sake.

3.2.3 *The nature of accountability*

The agency model works best when applied to individual, directly elected representatives such as mayors, presidents, and governors. In this case, the incumbent is an individual who has certain responsibilities and spheres of discretion. The basis of accountability is then defined relative to these responsibilities.

In some contexts, this model has only limited applicability. For example, the individuals being held to account may be part of a collective such as legislature or a committee. In this case, there is the problem of untangling responsibilities for outcomes. In general, this may be expected to weaken the mapping from outcomes to re-election decisions on individuals.

In almost all democratic settings, parties play an important role in the workings of political competition. How they affect the process of political accountability is not altogether clear. Parties may have longer time horizons and may therefore make individuals who hold power take a longer view, leading to less opportunistic behavior by incumbents. Obviously the degree of attachment of the incumbents to parties and the kinds of sanctions that parties have are crucial here.

When thinking in terms of parties, it is less clear how to interpret the politicians' types. For example, it could reflect some underlying collective reputation or competence of the party members. Voters may then cast their votes based on party rather than individual characteristics. This view is intriguing. However, modeling it clearly requires some kind of model of the internal workings of the party.

3.2.4 *Retrospective voting*

A key idea in agency models is that voters hold incumbents to account for their actions while in office. This constitutes an optimistic view of the political process in which sufficient numbers of voters are informed about policy outcomes and use this information when deciding for whom they will vote. This is still an issue which is hotly debated by political scientists. But influential contributions by Key (1966) and Fiorina (1981) have significantly shifted the presumption towards the view that voters are rational and make their assessments based on the records of candidates while in office.

Fiorina (1981) identifies three distinct theories of retrospective voting: the first, which he identifies with Downs (1957), is that voters use retrospective information because such information is to hand and is cheaper than scrutinizing the records of candidates. The second, which he associates with Key (1966), is that voters are result oriented. Fiorina's own view attaches more weight to party identities in shaping retrospective voting decisions.

Both Fiorina (1981) and Key (1966) argue that there is evidence of retrospective voting in the context of US presidential elections. Their work has also been a key force behind accepting a model of political behavior based on standard postulates of rational choice applied to voters. That said, they did not have a framework of the kind that political agency models provide which permits an analysis of the *equilibrium* implications of retrospective voting. This requires some notion of why past records provide information about future performance. This is captured in the political agency model by assuming that voters are learning from past actions and use Bayes rule to update their beliefs. One key implication of this approach is that there really is no meaningful distinction between prospective and retrospective voting. It is precisely because there is information content in past actions about future behavior that retrospective voting is rational.

3.2.5 *Model types*

The models break down into three basic types. The first generation political agency models focused on hidden actions—specifically shirking by incumbents. Barro (1973) and Ferejohn (1986) both focused predominantly on moral hazard problems in government. In this framework, all politicians are alike in their desire to use political office as a means for pursuing their own agendas. The question is how well a re-election mechanism based on retrospective voting can discipline incumbents. The basic idea is that voters will choose a threshold that gives the politician an incentive for restraint. The latter always faces a choice between extracting maximal rents in the current period or showing restraint and continuing to enjoy rents in future. The main modeling assumptions concern the extent to which voters can observe the actions of incumbents and whether there is an unobservable state of nature. Since such models avoid different kinds of politicians, voters are always indifferent between re-electing the incumbent and the challenger.[10]

In a pure *adverse selection* model, the only issue is selecting the right kind of incumbent for the job. There is nothing that an incumbent can do to affect the electorate's opinion of them. The key question is how the observations that voters can make allow them to detect the type of the incumbent. This is the core model of Besley and Prat (2004). In reality, these models have fairly limited appeal as most politicians are likely to have some ability to disguise or reveal their type via their actions.

The most interesting and challenging types of models come from combining hidden action and different types in the same model. Among the earliest efforts in this direction are Banks and Sundaram (1993) and Austen-Smith and Banks (1989).[11] They assume that politicians differ in their competence and that the actions that they take are not observed by voters. Politicians that differ in their motivations are central to the analyses of Besley and Case (1995a); Coate and Morris (1995); Fearon (1999) and Rogoff (1990). One of the key issues that arises in these models is the use of policy choices as a signaling device as different types of politicians try to differentiate themselves from one another. Two types of distortions are possible. Good politicians may try to exaggerate their behavior in a way that cannot be mimicked by bad ones. Alternatively, bad politicians may try to pool with good ones to enhance their re-election chances. Such pooling behavior may or may not be optimal in political equilibrium.

Persson and Tabellini (2000) develop political agency models that are more in tune with the original career concerns model of Holmstrom (1999) in two senses. First, neither public servants nor the public know the competence level of their public servant. Second, the decisions made by incumbents are chosen prior to the election taking place. They take the form of an investment that will payoff after the election.[12] This differs from the main thrust of the literature

---

[10] This is quite a severe restriction. As we shall see below, even a little bit of heterogeneity can have a big effect on the predictions.

[11] See also Banks and Sundaram (1998).

[12] More precisely, the model in Section 4.5.1 (and Section 9.1) of Persson and Tabellini (2000) assumes that an incumbent chooses rents in Period 1 and consumes these whether or not he/she is re-elected.

which focuses on retrospective voting. Models based on the classic Holmstrom career concerns model are also developed by Ashworth (2005) and Ashworth and Bueno de Mesquita (2005a, b). This kind of approach also gets away from some of the signaling issues as the politicians do not know their own types. For some applications (for example where a type is some kind of competence issue) this may be natural. However, when preferences are part of the type, this is a less plausible assumption. Obviously, what is reasonable will depend largely on the application in question.

For the most part agency models work with situations where re-election incentives are a force for good either by improving selection of politicians or by creating greater discipline. Essentially, this works by giving incentives for politicians to build reputations.[13] However, there are circumstances in which such reputation building can be counter-productive. This happens when incumbents are deterred from doing the right thing because they know that voters will not reward them for doing so. In Section 3.4.3 we discuss a specific example of this.

3.3 The baseline model

This section develops a very simple approach to political agency problems.[14] It provides the simplest agency framework which puts adverse selection and moral hazard together. At the heart of the agency model is the notion that some politicians are more able/willing to give voters what they want. We begin by setting out a very simple model that looks at behavior of politicians in such a world. We then consider a variety of modeling choices and assumptions.

3.3.1 *The environment*

There are two time periods denoted by $t \in \{1, 2\}$. In each period, a politician is elected to make a single political decision, denoted by

---

[13] Political agency models have much in common with models where experts are hired to make decisions. They typically assume that payoffs cannot be made contingent on the agent's performance and hence being re-appointed is the main incentive—see, for example, Prendergast and Stole (1996) and Ottaviani and Sorensen (2001).

[14] The closest cousins to the model used here are Barganza (2000) and Smart and Sturm (2003).

$e_t \in \{0, 1\}$. The payoff to voters and politicians depends on a state of the world $s_t \in \{0, 1\}$ which is only observed by the incumbent. Each state occurs with equal probability. Voters receive a payoff Δ if $e_t = s_t$ and zero otherwise. Voters and politicians discount the future with common discount factor $\beta < 1$.

There are two types of politicians—congruent and dissonant—the type is denoted by $i \in \{c, d\}$. Let π be the probability that a randomly picked politician from the pool is congruent. All politicians (congruent or dissonant) get a payoff of E from holding office. This can be thought of as comprising any pure ego rents plus any wages from holding office. It could also depend on office perks such as pensions and free housing. We normalize the politician's outside option to zero.

Congruent politicians' payoffs are $E + \Delta$ in every period because they always choose $e_t = s_t$, i.e., they share voters' objectives exactly. Dissonant politicians get a private benefit (dissonance rent) of $r \in [0, R]$ from picking $e_t \neq s_t$, where r is drawn independently from a distribution whose cdf is $G(r)$. The mean of r is μ and we assume that $R > \beta(\mu + E)$.[15] Let the realized value of 'dissonance rents' in period t be denoted by r_t. The action of a politician at time t is denoted by $e_t(s, i)$ with $s \in \{0, 1\}$ and $i \in \{c, d\}$.

The interpretation of dissonance could be quite broad. It could include politicians whose competence is limited and who find it costly, therefore, to do what voters want. It could also capture the case of a politician who gives into a special interest group which wants the opposite of what voters want. It could also include a politician with a private agenda of his/her own (say an ideological disposition) which he/she wishes to pursue. In the case of a legislator, it could also capture the idea of delivering 'constituency service' to the voters. The exact interpretation is not important for most of the discussion.

Timing is as follows. Each period, nature determines the state of the world and the type of politician (if that politician is newly elected) neither of which is observable to the voter. Nature draws r_1 from the distribution $G(r)$. The incumbent politician then picks his/her preferred action. Voters observe their payoff and then decide whether or not to re-elect the incumbent or select a challenger at random from the pool of potential politicians. After the election, a dissonant politician receives a fresh draw from $G(r)$, denoted by r_2. The Period 2 action

---

[15] This assumption guarantees that dissonant politicians pick the wrong action from voters' point of view some of the time.

then follows after which Period 2 payoffs are realized. Thereafter the game ends.

3.3.2 *Equilibrium*

The equilibrium concept most commonly used in solving a model like this is perfect Bayesian equilibrium. This requires that in every period each type of politician behaves optimally given the re-election rule that the voters put in place. Voters use Bayes rule to update their beliefs.

It is very easy to work out the equilibrium behavior of politicians in this model. In Period 2, every kind of politician takes his/her short-term optimal action. Thus $e_2(s, c) = s_2$ and $e_2(s, d) = (1 - s_2)$. Anything of interest in political behavior must, therefore, happen in Period 1.

To explore this, it is useful to introduce two key notations. First, let λ be the probability that a dissonant politician does what voters want in Period 1. It is therefore an index of political discipline. Congruent politicians always do what voters want provided that they are re-elected for doing so.[16] If a dissonant politician does the right thing for voters with probability λ and voters use Bayes rule, their belief that the politician is congruent conditional on having received a payoff of Δ is:

$$\Pi = \frac{\pi}{\pi + (1 - \pi)\lambda} \geq \pi.$$

Thus good behavior always improves a politician's reputation (now measured by Π). This implies that there is always an equilibrium in which any politician who produces Δ for voters is re-elected, assuming voters are retrospective, in other words, use the incumbent's perform-ance during Period 1 as their basis for voting. A politician who fails to produce Δ for voters is not re-elected since such an agent is dissonant for sure and will yield voters a zero payoff in Period 2.

Based on this, it is straightforward to determine the optimal Period 1 action of dissonant politicians. By now the value of their dissonance rent r_1 has been revealed. This must be compared with the longer term benefits of doing what voters want and being re-elected which is $\beta(\mu + E)$. Thus, the probability that a dissonant politician takes the

---

[16] In Section 3.4.3, we explore a variant of the model in which this is not the case.

action that voters want is:

$$\lambda = G(\beta(\mu + E)).$$

Under our assumptions on the distribution of the dissonance rent, $\lambda \in (0, 1)$. Thus we have:[17]

Proposition 1: *Congruent politicians always set $e = s$. Dissonant politicians choose $e = (1 - s)$ in Period 2 and will choose $e = s$ in Period 1 if they earn sufficiently small rents from being dissonant. All politicians who choose $e = s$ in Period 1 are re-elected.*

Thus the model makes clear how elections can motivate politicians—the non-congruent politicians are now willing to mimic the congruent ones some of the time. Moreover, voters hold politicians to account for not delivering a return. At the same time, the re-election mechanism is imperfect. Some of the time dissonant politicians survive to the second period. This provides a starting point for thinking about how political accountability works.

3.3.3 Implications

We now consider some normative and positive implications of the models before proceeding to some discussion of empirical testing.

THE QUALITY OF GOVERNMENT

The model provides a useful way of thinking about determinants of the quality of government. In doing so we will abstract from the payoffs of politicians and measure quality of government in terms of whether voters get what they want.[18] To this end, we consider ex ante voter welfare in both time periods. In Period 1, it is:

$$V_1(\lambda) = [\pi + (1 - \pi)\lambda]\Delta \tag{3.1}$$

---

[17] If $(1 - \beta(1 - \pi))\Delta < \beta E$, there is also an equilibrium where all politicians pool on the action $e_1(s, i) = (1 - s_1)$ and voters believe that any politician who generates Δ is dissonant. However, this equilibrium is ruled out by applying Cho and Kreps' (1987) intuitive criterion. Hence, we focus on this equilibrium throughout.

[18] The time-honored tradition of ignoring the payoffs of politicians means that we cannot assess whether the outcome is efficient. For that we would have to consider whether a politician could be given a transfer by voters which makes everyone better off. But that, in turn, raises issues of whether we should consider different kinds of contracts for rewarding politicians. The tradition in political economy of ignoring the payoffs of politicians in the welfare calculus is strange and contrasts with analyses of efficiency in a market context which seem always to look at the payoffs of all market participants.

while in Period 2, it is:

$$V_2(\lambda) = \pi[1 + (1 - \pi)(1 - \lambda)]\Delta. \qquad (3.2)$$

It is clear that Period 1 welfare is increasing in λ (incumbent discipline) while Period 2 welfare is decreasing in λ. The latter is due to the fact that fewer dissonant incumbents are caught when there is more Period 1 discipline.

Discounted welfare, which is

$$W(\lambda) = V_1(\lambda) + \beta V_2(\lambda), \qquad (3.3)$$

is increasing in λ. This is because the loss in Period 2 welfare is of the order $\beta\pi(1-\pi)$ while the gain in Period 1 is of the order $(1-\pi)$. Voters gain from ill-discipline only when a dissonant politician is replaced by a congruent one in Period 2 whereas they gain from improved discipline whenever there is a dissonant politician in office in Period 1.

Voter welfare is also increasing in π—the quality of the pool of politicians. This is obvious as it increases voter payoffs in both periods and does not affect the quality of dissonant politicians' actions. This captures very simply the idea that a polity with more civic virtue (a higher quality political class) is better for the voters.

The model also predicts that voter welfare and political turnover are negatively related. To see this, observe that turnover is equal to $(1 - \pi)(1 - \lambda)$ which is decreasing in λ and π, while as we saw above, voter welfare is increasing in λ and π. This is due to the fact that a lack of political turnover is symptomatic of voter contentment—only politicians who do what voters want get re-elected. This is not always true as we shall see below.

THE INCUMBENCY ADVANTAGE

As discussed in Ashworth (2005), the agency model can be used to make sense of an incumbency advantage in politics. To see this simply, suppose that there is a random popularity shock δ to the incumbent which is uniformly distributed on the interval $\left[-\frac{1}{2\xi}, \frac{1}{2\xi}\right]$ and determines the election outcome along with the reputation of the incumbent.[19] Then, the probability that the incumbent is re-elected

---

[19] This is equivalent to the challenger and the incumbent experiencing a shock with the *difference* in the reputations ($\Pi - \pi$) being represented by δ.

is:

$$\min\left\{\frac{1}{2} + \xi\left[\frac{\pi(1-\pi)(1-\lambda)}{\pi + (1-\pi)\lambda}\right], 1\right\} > \frac{1}{2}.$$

This incumbency advantage is natural because of the asymmetry in opportunities between challengers and incumbents; the challenger has no way of signaling his/her congruence to the voters.

THE TERM LIMIT EFFECT

Political agency models predict that the behavior of politicians depends on how far their political careers extend into the future. This is the reason that, in this two period setting, voter welfare and politicians' behavior differ across the two time periods even though the policy environment is the same. Comparing politicians who can and cannot run for re-election, the model predicts a term limit effect—*politicians behave differently when they can and cannot run for re-election*. Specifically, discipline from a dissonant politician is λ in Period 1 and zero in Period 2. While this is quite stark in the current setting, the existence of a last period effect is quite general in agency models.

However, even though Period 2 dissonant politicians' behavior deteriorates, it is still a good idea to re-elect politicians on the basis of their first period behavior. Thus, expected performance among the pre-selected group of surviving Period 2 politicians is higher than a randomly selected politician.

This observation from agency models motivates empirical tests of last period effects in political life. For example, one strand of the political science literature focuses on data on representatives in the US Congress. It aims to test whether representatives who are not going to run behave differently from those who plan to. Lott and Bronars (1993) analyze congressional voting data from 1975—1990, and find no significant change in voting patterns in a representative's last term in office. However, it is far from clear that congressional representatives who announce they are stepping aside provide an adequate picture of the behavior of politicians who are bound by law not to run again for re-election. A provocative paper on potential end-games in the US Congress is provided by McArthur and Marks (1988), who observe congressional behavior in a lame duck session of Congress: in post-election sessions, members who have not been re-elected are at times called upon to vote on legislation before the swearing in of the new Congress. McArthur and Marks observe that lame duck representatives were significantly more likely in 1982 to vote against automobile domestic content legislation than were members who were returning.

The US House of Representatives does not (yet) have term limits. Hence, whether these kinds of studies can pick up exogenous variation in the time horizon of politicians is moot. In the next section, we look at the evidence from US governors. Here, the term limits imposed are genuine and there is the possibility of comparing the behavior of a given politician in their term-limited and non-term-limited period in office. While the model predicts that there is a selection bias into second terms, this provides a much more convincing basis for testing whether the time horizon matters.

EMPIRICAL EVIDENCE FROM US GOVERNORS

Models of political agency have had many applications. But one of the most compelling is to US governors. This is for two main reasons. First, US governors correspond fairly well to the standard agency model—a single agent being held accountable for their actions with well defined election dates and rules. Second, there is plenty of data available for US governors making this context a rich testing ground for the models. The contrast with US presidents who may also be important examples of political agents here is clear—there is roughly 50 times more data available at the Gubernatorial level. Our look at the data here is sketchy. However, it will still serve as a useful means of breathing life into the theoretical model.

On the downside, the case of governors is made less clear-cut since they must work together with state legislatures to determine policy outcomes. Hence, on some specific policy issues, they may have only limited input into the policy process. However, this is hard to know a priori. The institutional rules affecting the powers of governors also vary across states. For example, only a subset of governors have a line-item veto which allows them to strike out specific budgetary provisions. Governors also receive very different levels of remuneration and they may also face different degrees of media scrutiny. While in principle these many aspects of state-to-state heterogeneity could be brought into the empirical study, we will stick here to a straightforward empirical analysis. The role of this subsection is to illustrate the potential of the political agency framework as a way of explaining patterns in the data.

The period for our data is 1950–2000. We will study two things: (i) the determination of re-election chances of governors who are eligible to stand again, and (ii) the effect that not being able to stand (being term limited) has on policy choices. In the first case, we will look for evidence that governors are being held to account by voters for their actions while in office. In the second, we will look first at whether governors who are unable to run appear to behave differently from those who cannot.

Accountability

The idea that voters respond to changes in the economy is widely documented in a variety of empirical contexts—see, for example, Nannestad and Paldam (1994) for a review of the literature. For the US states this means linking voting outcomes to general indicators of state-level economic health. Chubb (1988) considers the determinants of state elections as a function of the performance of the state economy and other factors using data from 1940 to 1982. He finds very little evidence that changes in state income levels affect election outcomes. These results are consistent with the findings of Adams and Kenny (1986) and Peltzman (1987) who show that whether a government is re-elected is not correlated with economic growth in the state in question.[20]

We begin by looking at whether voters hold incumbents to account as follows. Let r_{gst} be an indicator variable that denotes whether the incumbent Governor g is re-elected in state s at time t. Suppose that this can be modeled as a linear probability model:

$$r_{gst} = \alpha_s + \beta_t + \rho x_{st} + \gamma z_{gt} + \theta \Delta_{st} + \varepsilon_{st}$$

where x_{st} is a vector of state level controls in part proxying for differences in the electorate, z_{gt} are personal characteristics of the governor, and Δ_{st} are policy (and other economic) changes during the term that the incumbent has been in office. The model also includes state fixed effects α_s and year effects β_t.

We will control for state population and the incumbent's lagged vote share in x_{st}. Our incumbent specific characteristics are age, years of education, experience in both political and non-political careers, and the proportion of that experience that has been in politics. For

---

[20] Lowry et al. (1998) find that state income growth relative to the national average affects the incumbent's vote share in Gubernatorial elections.

Table 3.1 Means of accountability variables

Variable	Mean	Standard deviation
Governor won election	0.57	0.50
Vote share (percent)	57.51	8.73
Two year growth rate of real taxes per capita (percent)	7.15	10.28
Two year growth rate of state income per capita (percent)	14.31	6.36
Two year growth rate of state spending per capita (percent)	6.77	9.56
Log of population	14.65	1.07
Governor's age (years)	52.06	7.95
Governor is lawyer	0.54	0.50
Years of work experience before governorship	28.61	9.58
Fraction of previous experience in politics	0.35	0.24
Governor's years of education	18.77	3.52

Sources: As in Besley and Case (2003). The Governor's characteristics are from the *Book of the States*.

Notes: Data is only for the 48 continental US. The time period is 1950–2000.

the vector Δ_{st} we include the growth in state taxes per capita in the past two years, the growth in state spending per capita in the past two years and the change in (log) income per capita in the same window. The means for these variables are in Table 3.1.

The results are in Table 3.2. We present two sets of results which vary slightly in the sample of governors that we look at. In the first instance (columns 1 and 3 of Table 3.2), we look at all governors who are eligible to stand for re-election regardless of whether they did. In effect, this is treating a decision not to run as a defeat. The second sample considers only those governors who actually ran again for office (columns 2 and 4). In columns 1 and 2, we do not control for the governor's personal characteristics—these are introduced in columns 3 and 4. One finding from the data is that governors who put up taxes are significantly less likely to win in all specifications. There is also evidence that the economic growth rate within the state is related to the election chances of the governor (contrary to earlier results by Adams and Kenny (1986) and Peltzman (1987)). By contrast, spending growth is not correlated with re-election chances.

Table 3.2 Accountability

	(1) Governor re-elected	(2) Governor re-elected	(3) Governor re-elected	(4) Governor re-elected
Growth in real taxes per capita	−0.704 (2.49)*	−0.734 (2.29)*	−0.932 (3.22)**	−0.873 (2.76)**
Growth in real income per capita	1.808 (3.05)**	2.501 (4.73)**	1.475 (2.54)*	2.350 (4.82)**
Growth in real expenditure per capita	0.132 (0.37)	−0.013 (0.03)	−0.035 (0.10)	−0.258 (0.71)
Log of state population	−0.001 (0.00)	0.230 (1.43)	0.025 (0.15)	0.241 (1.53)
Vote share in last election	0.004 (1.04)	0.010 (2.87)**	−0.001 (0.17)	0.006 (2.09)*
Governor's age			−0.017 (5.08)**	−0.013 (2.77)**
Governor is trained as a lawyer			0.021 (0.38)	0.007 (0.13)
Years of work experience before governorship			0.018 (5.58)**	0.016 (3.95)**
Fraction of previous experience in politics			0.636 (5.48)**	0.775 (6.85)**
Years of education			0.003 (0.35)	0.003 (0.38)
Constant	−1.983 (0.90)	−3.131 (1.31)	−1.856 (0.87)	−4.186 (1.76)
Observations	485	381	475	372
R-squared	0.17	0.26	0.31	0.41

Note: Robust t statistics in parentheses (* denotes significant at 5%; ** denotes significant at 1%). Data sources are given in Note to Table 3.1.

Across the board, having an older governor is associated with a lower re-election probability. Years of experience before governorship is positively correlated with election success and this is particularly true if this is years of political experience. The vote share at the last election is positively correlated with being re-elected for governors who choose to stand again.

In Table 3.3 we look at the votes that the governor received if he/she was re-elected, denoted by v_{gst}, as a function of the same set of right

Table 3.3 Votes if re-elected

	(1) % vote captured by the winner	(2) % vote captured by the winner
Growth in real taxes per capita	−13.288 (2.50)*	−11.901 (2.18)*
Growth in real income per capita	9.452 (1.10)	7.275 (0.82)
Growth in real expenditure per capita	4.945 (0.85)	5.068 (0.83)
Log of state population	−0.126 (0.28)	−0.175 (0.36)
Vote share in last election	0.432 (4.94)**	0.424 (4.84)**
Governor's age		−0.110 (0.66)
Governor is trained as a lawyer		1.592 (1.18)
Years of experience before governorship		−0.010 (0.07)
Fraction of experience in politics		2.479 (0.97)
Years of education		0.147 (0.44)
Constant	36.291 (3.98)**	38.904 (3.12)**
Observations	268	261
R-squared	0.18	0.22

Note: Robust t statistics in parentheses (* denotes significant at 5%; **
denotes significant at 1%). Data sources are given in Note to Table 3.1.

hand side variables. Specifically, we run:

$$v_{gst} = \rho x_{st} + \gamma z_{gt} + \theta \Delta_{st} + \lambda v_{gst-1} + \eta_{st}.$$

These results parallel those from the previous table—we find that
the governor has fewer votes if he/she puts up taxes. Put together,
this evidence confirms the relevance of retrospective voting based on
policy and economic concerns for US governors.

The Term-Limit Effect

There are a number of previous contributions that have looked at term limit effects. One way to examine term limits is cross-sectionally, looking at the permanent differences in policies in those states that have such limits. This is the approach in early work on the topic by Crain and Tollison (1977, 1993) and Crain and Oakley (1995). Crain and Tollison (1977) make the interesting and important point that if political office is a productive asset, i.e. one used to produce political outcomes, then candidates for the office should be willing to pay more for the opportunity to serve in states with longer terms and in states without term limits. They find, using cross-sectional data for races run in 1970, that challengers spend less money when running for two two-year terms than do those running for one four-year term. In addition, challengers spend less in states with term limits than in states without term limits. Crain and Oakley (1995) examine whether states that allow governors to succeed themselves indefinitely have different public capital stocks and flows than do states where governors are restricted by some sort of term limit. They find, using data from the 1980s, and controlling for a number of state institutions, that the stock of state government capital per capita, the change in the stock, and the percentage change in the stock, are all lower in states with term limits. Bails and Tieslau (2000) argue that term limits should lower the rate of growth of spending, by making policy makers more responsive to citizens' preferences (the premise being that voters want smaller government). They test for this using a random effects model for the period 1969–94, and confirm a negative coefficient on state expenditures. All of these results raise the usual issue of whether such limits are merely proxying for omitted state level characteristics. State income per capita and state population are significantly lower in states with term limits, to name but two important differences between states with and without term limits (Besley and Case 1995b: Table III, p. 778).

Besley and Case (1995b) identify the effect of a term limit from the difference between first and second terms in office for incumbents who face term limits. Controlling for state fixed effects and year effects, and using annual data from the 48 continental US states from 1950 to 1986, they find that a variety of policy measures are affected by term limits. Specifically, state taxes and spending are higher in the second term when term limits bind in states that have them. Such limits tend to induce a fiscal cycle with states having lower taxes and spending in the first gubernatorial term compared to the second.

List and Sturm (2001) apply a similar methodology to cross-state variation in environmental policy. They find that governors in their last term in office are significantly more likely to spend resources on environmental protection using data for the period 1960–99. However, this term limit effect is muted in states where a larger fraction of citizens belong to environmental organizations. They also show that their term limit effect varies according to the margin of victory in the Gubernatorial race going into the last term in office—with term limit effects being attenuated when the margin of victory is larger.

The empirical framework that we use here is as follows: suppose that there is a policy that can be chosen in state s at time t denoted by p_{st}, then we model this as

$$p_{st} = \alpha_s + \beta_t + \gamma t_{st} + \theta y_{st} + \varepsilon_{st}$$

where α_s is a state fixed effect and β_t is year dummy variable. The variable t_{st} is one in years in which there is a binding term limit and zero otherwise. The term limit effect is then estimated from γ. The control variables y_{st} that we use are log of real per capita income, log of state population, proportion aged over 65, proportion under the age of 18, whether the governor is a democrat, whether the democrats hold a majority of the seats in the House and Senate of the state government and whether there is divided control of the House/Senate and the governor's chair. To interpret this equation, note that all governors who are facing a term limit are being compared to all those governors who are unconstrained.

The means of the raw data are in Table 3.4.

Results from running a specification of this form are given in Table 3.5. In the first column we look at real government spending per capita. This shows that there is a term limit effect with states that have a term limited governor spending significantly more. There is a weak effect of a similar kind for total taxes (column 2). When taxes are disaggregated, we find a significant effect for both personal income and corporate income taxes (columns 4 and 5).[21] The consistent effect of term limits can be contrasted with the patchy significance of the

---

[21] In both cases, we make the condition that the state has a personal income tax and a corporate income tax, i.e. we only consider states who permit such a tax.

Table 3.4 Means of variables used in term-limit regressions

Variable Name	Mean	Standard Deviation
Real government spending per capita (thousands $ 1982)	1.04	0.50
Real government taxes per capita (thousands $ 1982)	0.49	0.25
Real government sales taxes per capita (thousands $ 1982)	0.31	0.14
Real government income taxes per capita (thousands $ 1982)	0.14	0.14
Real government corporate taxes per capita (thousands $ 1982)	0.04	0.03
Congruence (ADA) [−100 to 0]	−22.09	11.42
Congruence (COPE) [−100 to 0]	−25.22	11.96
Governor cannot run due to term limit	0.29	0.45
Log state income per capita	16.63	1.56
Log state population	14.83	1.01
Proportion of population aged over 65 (%)	10.71	1.01
Proportion of population aged 5–17 (%)	22.41	3.46
Governor is a democrat	0.56	0.50
Democrats are a majority in the state senate	0.65	0.48
Democrats are a majority in the state house	0.67	0.47
Divided government	0.38	0.49

Source: As in Besley and Case (2003).

Note: Data is for the 48 continental states for the period 1950–2000. Nebraska is excluded from political variables as it does not have a two party system.

other political variables. There is some evidence that democrat control in legislatures and the governor's chair raises some kinds of taxes and spending. The evidence of divided government is of reduced taxation, especially of corporate income, but no effect on spending. This is consistent with earlier results by Alt and Lowry (1994) suggesting that a divided government tends to increase state deficits.

Table 3.6 looks at a different aspect of term limits. Instead of using a policy variable on the left hand side, we use a measure of policy congruence between citizens and governors generated by Berry et al.

Table 3.5 Term-limit effects

	(1) Real government spending per capita ($ 1982)	(2) Total taxes per capita ($ 1982)	(3) Sales taxes per capita	(4) Income taxes per capita	(5) Corporate taxes per capita
Governor cannot run	0.034	0.090	0.030	0.116	0.028
	(4.45)**	(1.81)	(0.83)	(3.35)**	(2.76)**
Log of real income	−0.244	1.015	1.522	−0.579	−0.142
per capita ($ 1982)	(4.53)**	(2.59)**	(5.52)**	(1.80)	(1.91)
Log of state	−0.047	−1.570	−0.675	0.184	−0.021
population	(0.84)	(3.80)**	(2.05)*	(0.56)	(0.26)
Population aged 65	−0.851	6.167	9.202	0.155	0.492
and above (%)	(1.97)*	(2.39)*	(4.63)**	(0.06)	(0.93)
Population aged 17	−0.571	6.063	3.328	7.241	−0.051
and below (%)	(1.68)	(2.65)**	(2.20)*	(3.86)**	(0.13)
Governor is a	0.020	0.037	0.033	0.060	−0.000
democrat	(3.36)**	(1.03)	(1.33)	(2.06)*	(0.06)
Democrats control	0.032	0.299	0.099	0.159	0.021
senate	(3.78)**	(5.26)**	(2.15)*	(3.30)**	(1.46)
Democrats control	0.004	0.202	0.049	0.103	0.032
house	(0.39)	(3.39)**	(1.08)	(2.19)*	(2.23)*
Divided government	−0.000	−0.103	−0.039	0.030	−0.032
	(0.03)	(2.68)**	(1.47)	(1.00)	(3.72)**
Constant	7.181	13.813	−16.489	4.798	3.462
	(21.78)**	(4.84)**	(6.36)**	(2.30)*	(4.93)**
Observations	2162	2203	2210	1749	1810
R-squared	0.95	0.91	0.88	0.87	0.79

Note: Robust t statistics in parentheses (* denotes significant at 5%; ** denotes significant at 1%) Data sources are given in notes to Table 3.4. Data is for 47 states for period 1950–97.

(1998). Specifically, we use the absolute difference between the ADA and COPE scores of the governor and the citizens in state s at time t as a measure of congruence. These are ratings of the governors' and voters' ideology by two different groups: Americans for Democratic Action (ADA) and the AFL/CIO's Committee on Political Education (COPE).[22] They are placed on a scale between −100 and 0, where 0 denotes 'perfect' congruence. The empirical results are striking. Governors who cannot run are significantly more congruent than those who can. This is suggestive of a strong selection effect into last periods

---

[22] See Berry et al. (1998) for more detail on these variables.

Table 3.6 Congruence and term limits

	(1) Congruence–ADA	(2) Congruence–COPE
Governor cannot run	1.173 (2.63)**	2.383 (4.40)**
Log of real income per capita ($ 1982)	−29.049 (7.60)**	−22.964 (4.90)**
Log of state population	12.958 (2.88)**	4.569 (0.84)
Population aged 65 and above (%)	−92.096 (3.62)**	−139.090 (4.14)**
Population aged 17 and below (%)	−32.204 (1.20)	−7.249 (0.22)
Governor is a democrat	1.651 (4.68)**	2.104 (4.78)**
Democrats control senate	1.034 (1.93)	−0.818 (1.18)
Democrats control house	−0.113 (0.21)	0.969 (1.41)
Divided government	−3.001 (8.19)**	−3.499 (7.84)**
Constant	343.609 (10.23)**	360.278 (8.41)**
Observations	1632	1632
R-squared	0.72	0.64

Note: Robust t statistics in parentheses (* denotes significant at 5%; ** denotes significant at 1%). Data sources are given in Note to Table 3.4. Data is for 47 states for period 1950–97.

in office where voters get to find incumbents who are more in tune with their preferences.[23]

3.4 Extensions

This section discusses a variety of extensions to the baseline model. As well as increasing the range of issues that can be discussed, it will also

[23] As documented in Besley and Case (1995b: Table II) there were some states that switched from a one-term limit where every new incumbent is term limited. Alt et al. (2006) find that comparing second term lame duck governors with second-termers who can run again (excluding all states that have one term limits) confirms the results in Besley and Case (1995) in a longer sample and in contrast to the results in Besley and Case (2003). This is consistent with selection effects being important as these are absent with one-term limits.

provide a way of locating many of the contributions to the literature that have used a political agency framework.

3.4.1 *Polarization and competition*

In this subsection we discuss three key ideas which affect the way in which elections achieve accountability. First, we consider the implications of randomness in the voting process. This could be interpreted in one of three ways: (i) non-policy relevant factors which shape the popularity of candidates; (ii) lack of information which leads to citizens to vote randomly for one or other candidate; and (iii) voter irrationality. This adds 'noise' to the voting process which weakens the ability of the voting mechanism to hold politicians to account.[24]

Second, we consider the implications of polarization among voters and politicians, in other words, competing views about policy. This could, for example, be based on ideology or ethnicity. Hence, we have in mind a world with two sets of policy issues—partisan issues on which voters disagree and non-partisan (or valence) issues on which they agree. The baseline model considered only a single valence issue. Here we continue to study accountability on the valence dimension. When there is polarization on partisan issues, voters have a reason to like or dislike a candidate on the basis of some reason other than their performance on non-partisan issues. This weakens the extent to which some voters hold politicians to account on the valence dimension.

In this more polarized world the candidates may differ naturally in their electoral strength due to their partisan position—some jurisdictional boundaries may be drawn in favor of one of the candidates. The strength of that advantage is a crude way of thinking about the degree of political competition. Thus, our third extension is to consider how political competition impacts on accountability. It is sometimes suggested that polarized politics is a problem. However, we show that it is the lack of competition, coupled with polarization, rather than the polarization per se that matters to the quality of performance on valence issues.

To examine these issues we extend the basic model above by supposing that the incumbent and challenger have some kind of party

---

[24] The empirical analysis is similar in spirit to Svensson (2000).

affiliation. We label the parties A and B and assume that each party represents a fixed policy position and is associated with a policy agenda which is separable from the valence issues studied in the previous section which we shall now refer to as the *non-partisan issue*. It is clear that this separable approach is artificial. We will relax this when we consider the implications of multiple policy issues below.

We now consider heterogeneous voters. Specifically, voters are of two types: supporters of each party and non-committed voters who vote solely on the basis of the non-partisan issue according to which incumbents are held to account. Let ω be the fraction of partisan voters and $(1 - \omega)$ be the fraction of non-partisan voters. Partisan voters are assumed to get some utility $\phi > 0$ from having their preferred ideology in office. With $\phi = 0$, we are back to the model above. For low levels of ϕ, the non-partisan issue will dominate in voting decisions. However, for large values of ϕ, only the non-partisan voters will vote on the non-partisan issue. This is the case where there is *political polarization* and will be the case studied for the remainder of this section.

Even if there is polarization, there is no necessary reason to expect it to weaken accountability if the two sets of partisan voters' voting intentions simply cancel each other out, as will tend to be the case when they are equal in numbers. Hence suppose that $\frac{1}{2} + \eta$ of the partisan voters prefer party A.

We assume that there is some noise in the votes of non-partisan voters. We will model this within a simple probabilistic voting framework of the kind used extensively by Persson and Tabellini (2000). There is an idiosyncratic shock ι which is uniformly distributed on $[-\frac{1}{2}, \frac{1}{2}]$ and an aggregate popularity shock δ which is uniformly distributed on the interval $[-\frac{1}{2\xi}, \frac{1}{2\xi}]$.

Suppose that the incumbent is of type A. It is now straightforward to see that the incumbent beats the randomly selected challenger if and only if

$$\omega\eta + (1 - \omega)[\Delta[\Pi - \pi] + \delta] > 0$$

where Π is the posterior probability that the incumbent is congruent. The term $\Delta[\Pi - \pi]$ is the reputational advantage of the incumbent while η is the natural advantage and δ the advantage from the popularity shock.

So now the probability that the incumbent wins if he/she takes the congruent action is:

$$
\sigma(\theta + \Delta[\Pi - \pi]) = \begin{cases} 1 & \text{if } \theta + \Delta[\Pi - \pi] > \frac{1}{2\xi} \\ \frac{1}{2} + \xi[\theta + \Delta[\Pi - \pi]] & \text{otherwise} \\ 0 & \text{if } \theta + \Delta[\Pi - \pi] < -\frac{1}{2\xi}. \end{cases}
$$

$$(3.4)$$

where $\theta = \frac{\omega}{(1-\omega)}\eta$. This equation makes transparent how noise, polarization, and competition drive accountability. We can interpret the parameter θ as a measure of pro-incumbent bias driven by whether the incumbent or challenger enjoys an advantage in terms of partisan supporters and how prevalent are partisan supporters in the population. On average we would expect incumbents to have a positive θ given that they have already been elected once in order to be incumbents.

The baseline model is a special case of this model where $\xi \to \infty$, $\omega \to 0$ and/or $\eta \to 0$. If there are sufficiently many partisan voters ($\omega \to 1$), then there is no effective accountability since $\sigma(\theta + \Delta[\Pi - \pi]) \to 1$ or 0 depending on whether η is positive or negative. Lack of competition (high η) is only important when there is sufficient polarization (i.e., when ϕ is above $\Delta[\Pi - \pi]$). Thus, low levels of political competition require sufficient polarization if they are to affect the extent of electoral accountability.

Suppose we are in the case where the probability of winning lies between zero and one. Then, it is straightforward to see that he/she will choose the congruent action if and only if:

$$
r_1 \leq [\sigma(\theta + \Delta[\Pi - \pi]) - \sigma(\theta)]\beta(\mu + E)
$$
$$
= \xi[\Delta[\Pi - \pi]]\beta(\mu + E).
$$

The term $\sigma(\theta + \Delta[\Pi - \pi]) - \sigma(\theta)$ represents the *gain* in the probability of winning if he/she produces Δ for the voters. Then the probability that the dissonant politician takes the congruent action is characterized by

$$
\lambda = G\left(\xi\left[\Delta\pi\left[\frac{(1-\pi)(1-\lambda)}{\pi + (1-\pi)\lambda}\right]\right]\beta(\mu + E)\right).
$$

One key observation with this is that an increase in electoral uncertainty (lower ξ) reduces discipline by dissonant politicians. This makes sense—voters are no longer able to credibly commit to vote for the incumbent even if he/she provides the congruent action. Thus, the greater the noise in the voting mechanism the less likely it is that a dissonant politician will behave in a congruent fashion in the first period.

The assumption of uniformity in the popularity shocks means that θ does not affect the rent-seeking decision of the incumbent on the margin. This is clearly quite special. Suppose instead that the shock δ has a general distribution function $H(\delta)$ which is symmetric around zero (its mean). Then (3.4) needs to be modified to:

$$\sigma(\theta + \Delta[\Pi - \pi]) = \begin{cases} 1 & \text{if } \theta + \Delta[\Pi - \pi] > \frac{1}{2\xi} \\ H(\theta + \Delta[\Pi - \pi]) & \text{otherwise} \\ 0 & \text{if } \theta + \Delta[\Pi - \pi] < -\frac{1}{2\xi}. \end{cases}$$
(3.5)

Clearly this implies that the level of congruent behavior depends on θ. Specifically,

$$\lambda = G(\sigma(\theta + \Delta[\Pi - \pi]) - \sigma(\theta))\beta(\mu + E)$$

We show that in the most natural case, where $h(\delta)$ is unimodal and $\theta > 0$, this results in an incumbent having a smaller incentive to take the congruent action. Then,

$$\frac{\partial \sigma(\theta + \Delta[\Pi - \pi]) - \sigma(\theta)}{\partial \theta} = h(\theta + \Delta[\Pi - \pi]) - h(\theta) < 0$$

if $\theta > 0$. Thus, an increase in pro-incumbent bias as measured by θ reduces the incentive of the incumbent to produce the congruent action.[25] In the case where $0 > \theta + \Delta[\Pi - \pi] > -\frac{1}{2\xi}$, the comparative static on the effect of θ goes the other way. This is the case where an incumbent has a very low chance of being re-elected. However, we do expect incumbents on average to have a positive θ given that they were elected in the first place.

Thus, we have:

Proposition 2: *Suppose that the incumbent enjoys an advantage. Then, an increase in the incumbent's advantage will reduce the congruence of first period actions among dissonant incumbents. This reduces the welfare of non-partisan voters.*

---

[25] Clearly, in the limiting case where $H(\theta + \Delta[\Pi - \pi]) = H(\theta) = 1$ and there is no incentive for dissonant politicians to undertake congruent actions.

In summary, this analysis gives reasons for believing that electoral accountability will be more effective in shaping incumbent's actions when (i) there is less noise voting, (ii) there is less polarization among voters; and (iii) there is evenly balanced political competition.[26]

This theoretical finding echoes a widespread sentiment linking political competition and policy outcomes. This is often argued by political scientists in quite broad terms. For example, in his classic book, Schattschneider (1960) suggests that 'the people are powerless if the political enterprise is not competitive. It is the competition of political organizations that provides people with opportunity to make a choice. Without this opportunity popular sovereignty amounts to nothing' (Schattschneider 1960: 140).

There is a certain amount of suggestive empirical support for this proposition. List and Sturm (2001) observe that the Gubernatorial term limit effect for environmental policy depends on the margin with which the governor was originally elected which could be thought of as a measure of θ. Besley and Preston (2004) use data from UK local governments to argue that local authorities, where the pattern of districting favors one party over another, tend to have higher taxes and spending as well as large public employment. In a similar vein, Besley and Burgess (2002) find that Indian states where the legislature has a tighter margin (in terms of the seats difference between the two major party coalitions) are more responsive in term of providing food aid when there are droughts and floods.

Having introduced heterogeneous voters, it becomes somewhat more difficult to make unequivocal statements about the quality of government. While it is clear that increases in λ still have favorable consequences for the non-partisan voters, whether the incumbent survives or not has a different welfare impact on the partisan voters who are happy to trade reduced accountability for a more favorable partisan bias in policy in their own direction. A welfare calculus would now require taking a stance on which of these groups is more deserving.

3.4.2 *Information and accountability*

The political agency model is a natural vehicle for thinking about the role of information in achieving political accountability. This is

---

[26] These results are similar to those derived in the more standard career concerns setting by Ashworth and Bueno de Mesquita (2005b).

because it focuses on the use that voters make of information that they acquire about politicians and policy. In turn, we have seen that incumbents respond to this information when choosing their actions. This means that the political equilibrium is likely to be affected by the information that voters have. In this section, we explore how information structures affect political accountability through the lens of the agency model.[27]

In practice voters have many different sources of information provision such as the media, think-tanks, and academics. Information may also be part and parcel of political campaigns. Below, we will discuss how these specific sources of information can feed into the model.

The basic model supposed that the consequences of the policy choices of incumbents become known immediately since the voters observe Δ. However, this is very strong and unrealistic. The political agency model frequently assumes that information about the quality of policy becomes known only after the election, even if the incumbent's action is observed. This seems natural in the case of building a highway whose quality and location is difficult to gauge, or fighting a war, the consequences of which may not be felt until far into the future. Obviously the world contains a whole range of actions by politicians, some of which may have immediate consequences and others for which it will take a while for information to be revealed.

Suppose then that with probability χ voters observe Δ after the politician has chosen e. We assume that this probability is the same whether or not the politician is congruent. Hence, there is no information from observing nothing. In addition to the possibility of observing Δ, we also suppose that there is some other source of information about the incumbent's type which does not come from their policy choice. Specifically, the incumbent's type becomes known to the voters with probability τ some time after they have made their policy decision (e) but before the election is held. Everything else about the structure of the basic model is maintained. If no information is revealed, we assume that voters re-elect the incumbent.

Nothing is changed in Period 2. In Period 1, we need to modify the condition for the dissonant incumbent to be willing to do what voters want. If the bad politician does not do this, voters will observe that he is dissonant with probability $\tau + (1 - \tau)\chi$. Thus, he/she will

---

[27] In a related analysis, Ferejohn (1999) considers the possibility that politicians choose an information structure for voters which will act as a restraint on their own behavior.

be re-elected with probability $(1 - \tau)(1 - \chi)$. However, if he/she takes the action that voters prefer, then he/she will be re-elected unless the voters get direct information about his/her type, which occurs with probability τ. Thus, weighing up these re-election benefits against the forgone rent from taking the dissonant action, the probability that a dissonant politician will behave in a disciplined way is:

$$\lambda = G((1 - \tau)\chi[\beta(\mu + E)]).$$

Inspecting this equation, it is clear that increasing χ, the policy relevant information, increases the quality of the incumbent's Period 1 action and hence voter welfare in Period 1. However, increasing the probability that a dissonant incumbent will be found out for non-policy reasons reduces Period 1 discipline. This is because the gain from taking the action that voters like is lower if he/she is not re-elected. In the limiting case where τ equals one, the incumbent has no advantage from doing what voters want in Period 1.

We now ask how increasing information (measured either by higher χ or higher τ) affects voter welfare. It is straightforward to see that voter welfare is:

$$W(\lambda; \tau, \chi) = \{\pi + (1 - \pi)\lambda + \beta\pi[1 + (1 - \pi)[1 - (1 - \tau)$$
$$\times [1 - \chi(1 - \lambda)]]]\}\Delta.$$

Observe that τ and χ enter this formula directly while also affecting the incumbent's actions (as measured by λ). It is straightforward to see that the direct effect of an increase in τ or χ is positive since there is an improvement in the selection of politicians.

As in the baseline case, an increase in λ raises voter welfare. Although the sign of the effect on Period 2 welfare is the opposite of that on Period 1 welfare, the order of the Period 2 effect is smaller. Since λ is increasing in χ an improvement in the observability of policy actions unambiguously raises voter welfare.

The effect of an increase in τ is, however, ambiguous. There is a positive effect on voter welfare in Period 2, since the improved information increases the chances of sorting in congruent politicians in Period 2. However, as we observed above, this comes at the price of reduced Period 1 discipline—lower λ.

Differentiating our expression for voter welfare with respect to τ, the overall effect is:

$$(1 - \pi)[[1 - \beta\pi(1 - \tau)\chi]\frac{\partial\lambda}{\partial\tau} + \beta\pi[1 - \chi(1 - \lambda)]\lambda].$$

This expression is clearly negative for small enough π. In other words, better (non-policy based) information about incumbents reduces welfare when the fraction of dissonant incumbents is sufficiently large. This is true because the selection benefits of better information are negligible in this case—it is highly likely that one dissonant incumbent will be replaced by another—and yet there is a negative discipline effect.[28] We summarize this as:

Proposition 3: *Improving information about which policy choice the incumbent has taken (i.e. higher χ) raises voter welfare. Improving information that is not directly related to the policy action but which reveals the incumbent's type (higher τ) need not raise voter welfare and will reduce it when there are sufficiently few congruent types in the pool of potential politicians.*

These results show that claims about the effect of information in politics must be treated carefully.[29] In the next chapter we consider a number of applications of these ideas in a public finance setting. Underlying this observation is the fact that we are in a second-best setting where voters imperfectly discipline politicians with highly incomplete incentives.

Whether these results should lead us to question the wisdom of providing better information about political behavior to voters is moot. On the whole we might expect this to yield an improvement in accountability. But there is clearly no formal result to support this unequivocally. The specific applications in a public finance model in the next section underline this.

What does appear general is the observation that to evaluate the effects of informational improvements, both discipline and selection effects should be weighed up. In cases where the political class is of low quality (as represented here by low π), the impact on discipline will be key. However, high π polities may yield different conclusions given the importance of selection. The models certainly cast light on the importance of the quality of the political class in thinking about these issues.

---

[28] We shall see other applications of this result in the next section. There, the information structure that achieves this is slightly different—there is some action that only a congruent incumbent is willing to take in equilibrium. The key thing is that there be something that can happen which reveals for sure that an incumbent is good. I thank Michael Smart for helpful discussions on this point.

[29] In a related contribution, Prat (2005) considers a model where the action taken by an agent may not be observed and shows that this may sometimes be a good thing.

The ideas in this section are particularly relevant in thinking about the role of the media in achieving accountability. Besley and Burgess (2002) and Besley and Prat (2006) have used these models to look at the role of the media. Besley and Prat (2006) use a model where improving the role of the media is very similar to an increase in χ in this simple model. They use the model to derive observable implications for the effect of the media on turnover of incumbents. To see how this plays out, note that the probability that the incumbent is defeated in Period 1 is:

$$(1 - \pi)[1 - (1 - \tau)[1 - \chi(1 - \lambda)]].$$

First observe that, for fixed λ, turnover is increasing in both τ and χ. Thus, we would expect this effect of increased media activism to be associated with more short-lived politicians. As is observed by Besley and Prat (2006), the effect operating through λ does lend some ambiguity to this proposition—if media activism raises λ then this will tend to dampen (and may even offset) the direct effect. Note, however, that if media activism raises τ then both of its effects (direct and operating through λ) will increase political turnover.

In Besley and Prat (2006), the information provided by the media is endogenous. This requires a model of the media sector and the possible implications of attempts by incumbent politicians to silence the media. They assume that the media are motivated to reach the largest possible audience. Thus, competition for audience pushes the media to look for interesting news and to establish a reputation for reliability. For simplicity, we focus in on the implications of χ and set $\tau = 0$. Suppose that in the absence of media, $\chi = 0$. In this case, $\lambda = 0$. Voters receive no information and re-elect all politicians as $\tau = 0$.

The media industry is made up of n identical outlets. Assume that they all receive verifiable news on the voter's payoff with probability χ and that this can be reported to the public (for simplicity, we assume that they are either all informed or all uninformed). We assume that a media outlet cannot fabricate news and that an outlet that reports informative news has a higher audience than one that reports no news. Moreover, the audience share of an outlet that reports news is decreasing in the number of other outlets that report news. The best case for an outlet is to be the only one to break news. In this world, news can only be bad for a dissonant incumbent. The important assumption is that news cannot be fabricated. Then, the only situation in which the voters' behavior is affected by news is when the news media report that $e \neq s$.

Suppose that the media market comprises a potential audience of a which is divided up among the number of media outlets who print news. The incumbent is assumed to be willing/able to bribe the media in exchange for silence if the media have news that the voter's payoff is zero. Assume that there is a transactions cost so that out of any bribe to the media they receive only $1/v$ of the payment. The timing of the game is as follows: (1) the media outlets receive or do not receive verifiable information about the incumbent; (2) the incumbent knows what information the media got and makes them transfer offers; (3) each outlet chooses whether to accept or reject the offer; (4) the outlets that accept the offer suppress their information, the ones that reject it report their information to voters; (5) voters re-elect the incumbent or replace him/her with a challenger.

In searching for the equilibrium of this game, the main question is whether the incumbent finds it profitable to buy off the media industry or not. If an outlet thinks that all the other outlets are going to be quiet, then its incentive to reject the incumbent's offer goes up because it would be the only one to break news to voters and it would gain a large audience. This means that, in an equilibrium in which all media sell out, the incumbent must pay each outlet as if it were the only one who could break news. Even if we keep the total industry potential revenues constant, increasing the number of media outlets makes it more expensive for the incumbent to buy their silence. This is the sense in which media pluralism is good for media independence.

Adapting the main result of Besley and Prat (2006) to our setting, whether or not the media is free depends on a comparison of $(v \times a \times n)$[30]—the cost of silencing the media—with $\beta(\mu + E)$ the benefits to a dissonant politician of being re-elected. From this it is clear that besides the number of outlets, the other parameters that determine whether media are captured or not in equilibrium are transaction costs and the amount of audience related revenues. Both n and a decrease the likelihood that the incumbent manages to silence the media. Instead, the probability that the media are informed does not affect media capture but of course it increases the probability that voters are informed.

---

[30] This is equal to the number of media times the amount that has to be paid to them to prevent them from running the story times the size of the transaction cost.

The Besley–Prat model links three key endogenous variables—whether the media operates freely, the turnover among politicians (higher with media freedom), and the quality of government policy (here measured by the probability that voters receive Δ). While it is hard to look at this empirically, it is interesting to look at the core correlations between these three variables. To measure quality of government we use cross-country data on corruption. Clearly this is only suggestive and there are many issues with such data. However, it is notable that in Table 3.7 that these correlations come out exactly in the way in which the agency model suggests. Turnover is higher with more print freedom and lower where there is more corruption. Corruption and print freedom are also negatively related. While only suggestive, it is hard to think of other simple models that would so readily provide a parsimonious account of these basic facts.[31]

Table 3.7 Correlations between print freedom, corruption, and political longevity

	Print freedom	Corruption (ICRG)	Corruption (*Transparency International*)	Corruption (Kaufmann et al.)	Years in office (party)	Years in office (chief executive)
Print freedom	1.000 187					
Corruption (ICRG)	−0.7034 (0.000) 91	1.000 91				
Corruption (*Transparency International*)	−0.6974 (0.000) 89	0.8261 (0.000) 74	1.000 90			
Corruption (Kaufmann et al.)	−0.6750 (0.000) 153	0.8253 (0.000) 91	0.9688 (0.000) 156	1.000 90		
Years in office (party)	−0.2656 (0.001) 148	0.2990 (0.008) 78	0.1095 (0.3246) 83	0.0822 (0.357) 148	1.000 156	
Years in office (chief executive)	−0.3466 (0.000) 172	0.1963 (0.062) 91	0.1630 (0.127) 89	0.1407 (0.086) 150	0.5018 (0.000) 148	1.000 172

Source: Besley and Prat (2006).

Note: p-values in parentheses. Third row is number of observations. Bold face denotes significant at a 10% level.

[31] Besley and Prat (2006) argue that the degree of media freedom could be reflected in the structure of media ownership, within a country using data from Djankov et al. (2003b).

Besley and Burgess (2002) also invoke a political agency model in studying the media, which has a slightly different focus. Here the issue is whether a politician is responsive to a particular vulnerable group of citizens that has been hit by a shock. The context they have in mind for this is India where state governments have to decide whether or not to respond to droughts or floods through public food distribution or organizing public works. They consider a two period model where the responsiveness decision of the politician must be made in each period. Vulnerable voters care about electing responsive politicians—those who will act to protect the vulnerable apart from the electoral gain that it generates. They must infer responsiveness from the observed policy choices. In this model the media can expand the scope for reputation formation by informing a larger group of voters about the politician's Period 1 actions. Besley and Burgess (2002) assume that the vulnerable are a geographically dispersed group and hence they can only see whether or not the incumbent has helped their group if they are subject to a shock. However, if some other vulnerable group experiences a shock, they may not see. Whether the incumbent responds to that group is relevant to learning the politician's type. Media provide that information and this can enhance the incentive that an incumbent has to respond. Thus, the presence of active media can enhance the role of re-election incentives and hence increase government responsiveness.

Besley and Burgess (2002) look at the association between public food distribution and food production in Indian states over the period 1958–92. They find that states that have more newspapers per capita tend to have higher levels of food distribution and are more responsive on the margin to food production. They find similar evidence for the responsiveness of calamity relief expenditures to floods.

Media is clearly only one source of information provided in a democracy. The model could also be used to think about whether better information as provided via an electoral campaign yields welfare improving discipline and selection. The results that we have found do suggest that all information may not be equal in this regard.

When looking cross-sectionally at the quality of government with relatively similar electoral institutions, the provision of information

They find a robust correlation between state and foreign media ownership, concentration in ownership and corruption levels. They argue that these variables capture the underlying parameters that the agency model suggests are important.

could be an important source of heterogeneity in government per-formance.[32] We will discuss application of these ideas to fiscal transperency in greater detail in the next chapter.[33] The agency model is a natural vehicle for thinking about this.

3.4.3 *The nature of the distortion*

In the first generation models of Barro (1973) and Ferejohn (1986) the focus of the agency problem is on politicians who 'shirk'. There are two main varieties of shirking—reduced effort below what voters would like, and diverting resources towards private ends. The latter could be interpreted as straightforward corruption or just rewarding cronies for political favors. What is key in both cases is that there is an undersupply of something which is valuable to voters. In a broad sense, the non-congruent action of the incumbent in the baseline model developed here could be interpreted as a form of shirking. In this setting, the role of election incentives is to promote greater levels of 'good behavior' and reduce shirking. The analysis then examines how far the threat of not being re-elected can sustain outcomes that voters desire.

In this world, faithful politicians continue to deliver goods even in the face of re-election. Elections improve the behavior of the way-ward without damaging the behavior of the well-intentioned. A small emerging literature, however, is concerned with the possibility that agency can lead to poorer quality social decisions because politicians tend to choose outcomes that are too close to what voters want. This is most relevant when politicians have better information than voters. A conflict arises when this information goes against what voters would most likely think to be optimal. Re-election incentives may then lead to politicians to choose excessively popular policies.

To introduce these ideas into our setting we change the model slightly to create incentives for a congruent politician to pick an action in Period 1 that is not in line with what voters want. We assume now that dissonant politicians are biased towards picking one partic-ular action by supposing that the rent is attached solely to the policy

---

[32] For example, Ferraz and Finan (2005) use an agency model to interpret their empir-ical results on the effect of audits on electoral outcomes in Brazil. They find that such audits have a significant effect on election rates of incumbents, reducing them by around 27%.

[33] Alt and Dreyer Lassen (2002) and Alt et al. (2002) argue that fiscal transparency has an impact of fiscal policy both in the OECD and in the US respectively.

choice $e = 1$ regardless of the state of the world. By choosing $e = 0$, regardless of the state, he/she earns no rent. We also assume that the payoff from the politician's action is only observed after the election (equivalent to $\chi = 0$) in the information model of the last section. We continue to assume that each state occurs with equal probability.

The analysis of Period 2 behavior is now changed somewhat even though each type of politician still picks his/her preferred action. Now a dissonant politician will pick $e = 1$ regardless of the state while a congruent politician continues to do what voters would like. Hence $e_2(s, d) = 1$ and $e_2(s, c) = s_2$.

Turning to Period 1, we are interested in characterizing the behavior of both kinds of incumbents. There are a number of possibilities. However, we focus on a situation where (i) a congruent politician picks $e = 0$ in Period 1 and is re-elected for sure; (ii) a dissonant politician also picks $e = 0$ when his/her rent from choosing $e = 1$ is low (less than $\beta(E + \mu)$ and is re-elected for doing so; (iii) a dissonant politician picks $e = 1$ when his/her rent is above $\beta(E + \mu)$ and is removed from office by the voters.

To see when an equilibrium of this form exists, we need to check that voters and politicians are optimizing. Observe that the probability that a dissonant incumbent picks $e = 0$ is now:

$$\lambda = G(\beta(\mu + E)).$$

The logic for a dissonant incumbent being willing to do this is exactly that encountered in the baseline model—weighing up his/her Period 1 rent from $e = 1$ against his/her future payoff from being re-elected. We now show that any incumbent picking $e = 0$ will be re-elected. By Bayes rule, the probability that an incumbent is congruent conditional on having picked $e = 0$ in Period 1 is:

$$\frac{\pi}{\pi + (1 - \pi)\lambda} > \pi.$$

Hence, voters re-elect for sure. Finally, we need to consider the incentives of congruent politicians. So far, we have not been very specific about their payoffs except to say that they are inclined towards doing what voters want. We suppose now that they receive a payoff of E from holding office and care directly about voter welfare too. Then in each period that they are in office they receive:

$$\Delta(es + (1 - e)(1 - s)) + E.$$

Political agency and accountability

These payoffs would lead them to (optimally) behave as we have assumed so far. We also suppose that they care about voters whether or not they are actually in office. Thus, they might sometimes be willing to sacrifice their position in public life 'for the good of the voters'.

In state $s = 0$, a congruent politician faces no dilemma since he/she can pick $e = 0$ and still be re-elected—his/her private payoff and voters' payoffs move in the same way. In $s = 1$, he/she weighs up picking $e = 1$ and being voted out of office in which case his/her payoff is:

$$\Delta + \beta\pi\Delta$$

or picking $e = 0$ and getting an expected payoff of:

$$\beta[E + \Delta].$$

The equilibrium where the congruent incumbent always chooses $e = 0$ in Period 1 is possible when:

$$\frac{\Delta}{E + \Delta} < \frac{\beta}{1 + \beta\pi}.$$

It is clear that a necessary condition for this is that $E > 0$, there is some private utility from holding office. Moreover, this condition will always hold when the private rents from holding office are large enough. The condition is also more likely to hold when π is close to zero. This is because then a congruent incumbent knows it is very likely that he/she would be replace by a dissonant incumbent in Period 2 and he/she is making a bad policy choice today in order to protect the voters in Period 2. For this same reason, the equilibrium where $e = 0$ is always chosen in Period 1 is also more likely when the incumbent is patient. Relating this back to the discussion in Chapter 2, this constitutes another example of political failure (in the Pareto sense) due to a political linkage.

In this equilibrium, the congruent incumbent is 'timid' to use a phrase from Smart and Sturm (2004). While he/she knows that he/she is picking something that is bad for voters, he/she is not courageous enough to do so if the price is to lose the election. The key thing here is the fact that dissonant politicians are biased towards one particular action. Congruent politicians cannot take that action without being mistaken for being dissonant themselves.[34]

[34] Leon (2004) applies this kind of logic to the issue of why governments may be deterred from pursuing long-term projects in the development process when dissonant incumbents are biased towards picking long-term projects.

This equilibrium is also related to the idea that politicians sometimes pander to the voters. This idea is developed in Morris (2001) and Maskin and Tirole (2004) using a somewhat different, but related, model.[35] There are two time periods with an election between them. Suppose that there is a single social decision to be taken in each period which can take on one of two values denoted by $x \in \{a, b\}$. There are two kinds of politicians—those whose preferences are congruent with the electorate and those that are not; this is not observed by the voters. The incumbent politician knows the true state of the world. Voters do not observe this, but have a prior belief that action a is more likely optimal than b. A good example would be a politician who sees that a tax increase is necessary to stave off a fiscal crisis. However, the voters' prior belief is that tax increases are more likely to enhance opportunities for rent-seeking and hence do not look favorably on it.

While good politicians care about making good decisions they also get some kind of personal return from holding office. It is the latter that creates the crucial agency problem. If he/she cares sufficiently about staying in office, a good politician can be induced to take the action that the voters believe to be optimal (action a) even if his/her information says that action b is optimal for voters. This is the pandering effect of political agency modeling. Voters now learn nothing from seeing the action a being taken and so they re-elect. By contrast, when re-election incentives are weak, good politicians choose the unpopular action even when it is known that they will be fired for doing so—Maskin and Tirole (2004) refer to this as the courageous equilibrium. Voters fire them because they believe that such actions are more likely to come from a bad politician than a good one. This is very similar to what we have described above. As observed by Canes-Wrone et al. (2001), there are good examples of pandering in real political behavior.

As with many of the results discussed here, pandering hinges critically on the ultimate success of the action taken not being observed before the election. To the extent that information is revealed throughout a term in office, we would expect political courage to be shown earlier in an election term, while pandering is more

---

[35] Pandering is also modeled by Canes-Wrone et al. (2001). They have a slightly different set up from Maskin and Tirole (2004)—their politicians are not differentiated by their motivation, but by whether or not they know which is the optimal action. However, the definition of pandering is the same—a politician fails to follow information about the optimal action for fear of its electoral consequences.

likely when an election looms. This would give rise to a pandering cycle which is parallel to Rogoff's (1990) equilibrium political budget cycle, which we discuss further below.

When distortions affect the behavior of congruent politicians, there is a question of whether subjecting individuals to re-election is a good idea at all. While periodic election is a cornerstone idea in representative democracy, there are limits to the kind of offices that we require periodic election for. In the UK, the House of Lords comprises individuals who are not subject to re-election concerns. Many systems of government do not use elected judges or elected regulators. One argument for this is that even good politicians are induced to distort their behavior. In similar vein, Smart and Sturm (2004) argue that timidity among politicians could yield an argument in favor of term limits.

Here let's illustrate this by contrasting voter welfare over the two period horizon with and without an election between.[36] In the case studied so far, it will typically be optimal to hold an election. However, this need no longer be true. Observe that the payoff with a 'life term' for the incumbent, i.e. no re-election, is:

$$\pi(1 + \beta)\Delta$$

while with an intermediate election it is:

$$\left[\pi \left(\frac{1}{2} + \beta \right) + (1 - \pi) \left(\frac{1 + \lambda}{2} + \pi(1 - \lambda) \right) \right] \Delta.$$

Thus an election is optimal if

$$(1 - \pi) \left[\frac{1 + \lambda}{2} + \pi(1 - \lambda) \right] > \frac{1}{2}\pi.$$

This is always the case as π tends to zero and never the case as π tends to one. This makes sense—if you can guarantee a congruent politician

---

[36] Maskin and Tirole (2004) contrast three possibilities in their model: representative democracy, direct democracy, and judicial decisions. The latter differs from representative democracy since the judge does not face re-election. In the simple set-up described above, representative democracy is never optimal if there is pandering. In the absence of pandering, representative democracy dominates the other two possibilities if π (the probability of congruent politicians) is relatively large. This is because a large π means that selection is more important than discipline (as discussed in Section 4.2).

from the start, then an electoral mechanism is now purely a source of distortion. Equally, if the politician is certain to be bad some discipline is achieved by having an election.

This section has reinforced the point that political agency is not solely about the problem of underachievement by dissonant politicians. It may also have to deal with electoral distortions among broadly well-meaning politicians. However, this does require that congruent politicians have some reward from holding office. The model suggests that crude efficiency wage arguments need not apply in politics since they may induce distortions of the kind discussed here.

3.4.4 *Within-term cycles*

A stock idea in political economy is that politicians behave differently when elections loom. The agency model provides a natural way of thinking about such issues in general and it is useful to see how the baseline model can be amended to handle them. One simple way to do this is by supposing that the quality of policy choices is most visible the longer the voters have had to assess their consequences and hence there is a difference between actions taken close to an election and those that are further from one.

Suppose then that we augment our model by having three time periods—two before the election and one afterwards. This is artificial, but serves to illustrate our points. We label these three periods 1, 2, and 3. We assume that the rent from taking the dissonant action is drawn afresh each period and draws from the distribution $G(r)$ are independent. Suppose also that the payoff of voters is only observable with a one period lag. Thus, the payoff from the Period 1 action of incumbents is observed by voters only in Period 2 and the payoff from Period 2's action is only observed in Period 3 after the election has been held. We show that this will lead to different incentives for dissonant politicians to do what voters want in Periods 1 and 2. Let λ_1 and λ_2 denote the probability that the dissonant incumbent will take the action that voters desire in Periods 1 and 2 respectively.

The voters now condition their voting decisions on the action taken in both periods and any payoff information that he/she has. It is easiest to begin with Period 2 which follows the case from the model of Section 3.4.2 with $\chi = 0$ and $\tau = 0$. Hence, $\lambda_2 = 0$—the dissonant politician will take whatever rent is on offer and voters get no information on the action taken by the incumbent.

The Period 1 action adds in the fact that the payoff information will be available to evaluate the incumbent by the time that the election comes around. Hence, when the incumbent weighs up the benefit of taking the rent in Period 1 and waiting to collect the full rent in Period 3, the probability that he/she gives up the rent in Period 1 is

$$\lambda_1 = G(\beta^2(\mu + E)).$$

This is basically the same as the baseline model but for the fact that the agent now waits for two periods and hence the discount factor is β^2.

It is now clear that the model generates different payoffs to voters depending on whether an election is close or not. Moreover, this is fully consistent with voter and incumbent rationality. The expected payoff to a voter in Period 1 is $(\pi + (1 - \pi)\lambda_1)\Delta$ while in Period 2 it is $\pi\Delta$. In this model, pre-election government behavior (Period 2) is more ill-disciplined than that at the beginning of the term (Period 1) which seems to parallel the conventional wisdom on political cycles.

The classic instance of election cycles is the macro-economic political business cycle. Early interest in this idea was sparked by contributions by Nordhaus (1975) and Hibbs (1977). However, suspicion was cast over their claims since they seemed inconsistent with rational behavior by voters. Rogoff and Siebert (1988) and Rogoff (1990) developed these ideas using an agency model in which both politicians and voters are rational.

Rogoff (1990) reformulated the model in a political agency model as follows. The model is an infinite horizon where an incumbent politician must choose levels of public goods, taxes, and public investment. The level of public investment is observable with a lag while taxes and public goods are observable immediately. An election takes place every other period, but in each period there is a shock to competence observed only by the incumbent. High competence means that an incumbent can produce a higher level of public goods for a given tax revenue. The competence level in any given period is a moving average of the shocks at dates t and $t - 1$. The value of this shock becomes known to voters with a one period lag. Hence when an election comes, they observe the 'off-year' competence shock but not the election year value.

Rogoff assumes that politicians share voters' concerns about taxing and spending. However, they get some independent level of utility from holding office (ego rents). These drive the agency problem as incompetent politicians will not be willing to voluntarily step down from office, even though doing so would do a favor to voters. Moreover, there is greater uncertainty about more recent shocks than those that occurred earlier in the politician's term. Faced with this, the onus on competent politicians is to find some way of revealing to voters that they are good. This signaling is what generates the equilibrium budget cycle.

The signaling process works as follows. A competent incumbent finds it less costly to choose higher levels of public goods provision than an incompetent one as the latter has to give up more public investment to finance a given level of public goods provision than the former (holding taxes fixed). For some level of public goods provision, therefore, an incompetent incumbent would rather choose a lower level of such spending and be defeated for sure.

In this model, the competent incumbents are responsible for the electoral cycle in taxes and spending. If there were no re-election possible, then no cycle would occur. Moreover, in this kind of model, a higher level of public goods spending and a lower level of taxes are associated with improved electoral chances. Le Borgne and Lockwood (2001a,b) consider the possibility that politicians are chosen endogenously. They find that the argument for cycles is muted by this.

Robust evidence of the political business cycle has been remarkably hard to find. For example, the survey by Alesina and Roubini (1992) is decidedly equivocal on whether such cycles are in the data. However, most have not made direct use of the agency framework in looking at the data. An important exception is Pettersson-Lidbom (2003) who tests Rogoff's electoral cycle model on Swedish data. He finds that spending is raised and taxes are cut in the election year. Moreover, in the election year, spending is higher for a government that will be re-elected as compared to one that will not be re-elected. He also finds that, in the post-election year, spending is higher and taxes are lower for re-elected governments compared to newly elected ones. Re-elected governments appear to spend less and tax more in the post-election year as compared to the election year. These findings are all broadly consistent with Rogoff's equilibrium budget cycle model. The political agency model has also been used in the empirical tests of Shi and Svensson (2002), who look at cross-country data and finds evidence of significant spending increases before elections, which is consistent with the Rogoff model.

3.4.5 *Multiple issues*

The baseline model assumes that there is a single valence issue. In our discussion of polarization, we introduced some separable partisan issues. However, they were not directly linked to the agency problems facing voters. In this section, we will introduce multiple issues in a way that interacts with agency problems. This serves to ask questions about the distortion of policy priorities in the face of agency problems.

There are a number of papers in the literature that have studied the way in which agency affects the choices across policy instruments. Harrington (1993) develops an agency model in which the extent of voter uncertainty about the optimal policy reduces the incentives of politicians to manipulate policies for electoral purposes. This is because the value of the signal created is less useful to voters. Mukand and Majumdar (2004) look at the incentives of politicians to experiment in the face of re-election concerns and investigate how this may lead to either excessive or insufficient experimentation. In a more practical setting, Besley and Burgess (2002) argue that the media can change the salience of issues and lead to more resources being targeted to disadvantaged groups in India. List and Sturm (2001) consider a model where the issue is whether US governors will respond to environmental groups. The importance of environmental issues is endogenous and affected by the extent to which these issues are electorally salient compared to others. Greater political competition will tend to yield greater attention to issues in which agency is important.

Here we consider two applications of multiple issues in a little more detail. First, we consider what happens when politicians can target particular groups of voters. Second, we consider when the incumbent will pick the most efficient policies from the view point of the voters.

CLIENTELISM AND TARGETED POLICIES

We supposed in the model above that all voters receive Δ, i.e. there is no way of targeting specific groups of voters. Suppose instead that there are three groups of voters of equal size (each comprising one third of the population). Each group is labelled $j \in \{A, B, C\}$. The incumbent can now decide whether to pick $e_t^j \in \{0, 1\}$ for each group j at each date t. We assume that the state of the world is common for all three groups. If a dissonant politician picks $e_t^j = (1 - s_t)$ then he gets $\frac{1}{3}$ of the rent on offer. Hence, a politician can now decided to please only a subset of voters. We begin by assuming that the voters only observe their own Δ—they know whether the politician has taken the action that they like, but nothing about what the politician has done for other voters.

In this simple example, a dissonant incumbent need now only do what a majority of voters want which here means targeting two of the groups. Hence, he/she can consume the policy rent for one of the groups and still get re-elected. The probability that he/she chooses to do what a majority (here two-thirds) of the voters wants is:

$$\lambda = G\left(\frac{3}{2}\beta[\mu + E]\right)$$

which means that the probability of some discipline is increased in the targeted case.[37] If we assume that the incumbent picks two of three groups to favor at random then the probability that an incumbent who produces Δ is congruent is:

$$\frac{\pi}{\pi + (1 - \pi)\lambda\frac{2}{3}}$$

which exceeds π. Whether targeting increases discipline from an ex ante point of view depends on whether:

$$\frac{2}{3}G\left(\frac{3}{2}\beta[\mu + E]\right) \underset{<}{\overset{>}{}} G(\beta[\mu + E]).$$

In the case of a uniform distribution $G(R)$, these probabilities are equal.

If the incumbent has even a small preference towards pleasing a particular group of voters, then the model delivers a kind of clientelistic politics in which the politician always serves that group of voters ahead of any others when assembling the majority that he/she needs to be re-elected. In that case, dissonant politicians (but not congruent ones) will use clientelism to get re-elected.

The result shown here depends crucially on voters only seeing what the politician has done for them rather than voters at large. If the entire vector of decisions made by the incumbent could be observed then it would be possible to spot the difference between a dissonant politician and congruent politician if the politician fails to produce Δ for *any* group of voters. If we thought that media was a vehicle for doing this, then this again provides a possible role for how information provision changes politics and policies. However, whether this

---

[37] It is now possible to have $\lambda = 1$.

increases or decreases the likelihood that all voters get what they want is unclear ex ante.

THE CHOICE BETWEEN EFFICIENT AND INEFFICIENT POLICIES

One abiding issue in political economy concerns whether incumbent politicians pursue their ends efficiently. Conditional on having a rent-seeking incumbent, voters would prefer that they take their tributes in the way that imposes least burden on themselves. The notion that rent-seeking will be efficient is a key component of the Chicago school of political economy associated with Becker, Stigler, and Peltzman.

In a world of full information, there is little reason for incumbents to behave inefficiently—even if voters do not like what politicians are doing, they would still prefer that they pursue their agenda efficiently. However, in a political agency model where information is imperfect, Coate and Morris (1995) show why governments may choose to hand out political favors in an inefficient way. This is because politicians may wish to disguise the fact that they like making such transfers.

They use a two period agency model with an election at the end of Period 1. The main social decision to be taken is whether to construct a project. Incumbents also have the technology to make a cash transfer to a special interest group. For concreteness sake, let us describe the project as building a road. There are four key assumptions about road building. First, it benefits the special interest. Second, it may or may not benefit voters.[38] Third, politicians know better than voters whether the road is worthwhile. Fourth, citizens do not learn ex post (at least before the Period 1 election) whether the road is worthwhile even if it is built.

The decision to build the road is made in Period 1 and voters observe whether it has been built. There are two kinds of politicians. Good ones care solely about voter welfare whereas bad ones also care about the income received by the special interest. The voters care about having a good politician in office in Period 2 since a bad incumbent will make a transfer to the special interest group in that period.

The initial electoral mechanism does not screen between the two types perfectly and there is some chance that a bad incumbent holds office in Period 1. If a bad incumbent is in office, then voters would

---

[38] This differentiates this policy example from something like a tariff policy which harms voters relative to a combination of a production subsidy and consumption tax for sure and hence can never be in the voters' interest.

prefer that he/she makes a cash transfer to the contractor rather than allowing him/her to build a road that is not worthwhile to the voters. However, such cash transfers would be observable to the voters and would lead them not to re-elect the incumbent. This leaves a bad incumbent an incentive to hide his/her type by mimicking a good incumbent. However, by building the road even if it is not worthwhile for the voters, this creates a disguised transfer to the special interest.

There are both pooling and separating equilibria. In the separating case, the bad incumbent makes a transfer to the special interest and is not re-elected for sure. In the pooling equilibrium, he/she makes the transfer via building the road. For this to be worthwhile to him/her, it must be the case that he/she is re-elected. This will happen if the voters think that it is sufficiently likely that the building decision is generated by a good incumbent who has seen that its construction is a good idea. Coate and Morris (1995) show that there are parameter values of their model which make this true.[39]

Thus, a political agency model can explain why an inefficient project is chosen in a way that is consistent with rational forward looking behavior by voters and incumbents. The model speaks to debates about whether democracy produces efficient results in general (see Wittman (1989)). It emphasizes the importance of intertemporal distortions created by the re-election mechanism (see also Besley and Coate (1998)).

An important feature of this result is that both moral hazard and adverse selection are necessary to explain such behavior. If incumbents were known to be bad, then the voters would prefer that any transfer that they make to the special interest be made efficiently. There would certainly be no electoral gain from disguising transfers. The only issue would be (as in moral hazard models) whether the electoral mechanism could be used to curb bad incumbent's inclinations to make transfers to special interests.

A nice application of the Coate and Morris framework is Sturm (2006) who tackles the case of 'green' protectionism, invoking trade sanctions against products that are deemed to be damaging to the environment. He argues that this is best explained by the fact that voters are very poorly informed about whether or not such protection

---

[39] Unlike much of the literature, Coate and Morris (1995) also consider whether a good incumbent will have an incentive to distort his/her behavior to try to separate from a bad incumbent. They show that, under reasonable assumptions, this will not happen.

is justified. This gives extensive leeway to politicians to engage in such protection in order to favor some domestic firms.

The main idea of the Coate–Morris model can be seen using the set-up from Section 3.4.3. Suppose that $E = 0$ so that the congruent politician always picks the correct policy. We look for an equilibrium in which the dissonant politician always picks $e = 1$ (i.e. building a road) regardless of the state when the rent from this action is high and picks $e = 0$ regardless of the state when the rent is low. Incumbents who pick $e = 0$ are re-elected and incumbents who pick $e = 1$ are voted out of office. The probability that $e = 0$ is now:

$$\lambda = G(\beta\mu).$$

Using Bayes rule, an incumbent who picks $e = 0$ will be re-elected for sure if:

$$\frac{\pi\frac{1}{2}}{\pi\frac{1}{2} + (1 - \pi)G(\beta\mu)} > \pi$$

or $G(\beta\mu) < \frac{1}{2}$.

The inefficiency arises because the dissonant incumbent does not index his/her action to the state of the world. If the state is $s = 1$ and $r < \beta\mu$, then voters would prefer to write a contract with the incumbent which would allow him/her to keep the rent r in Period 1 and μ in Period 2 in exchange for the action $e = 1$ in Period 1. This would make everyone (including the politician) better off. The informational structure precludes this since s and r are not observable to voters and hence not contractible. Moreover, clearly it would require contracts of a kind that we do not see in representative democracies. The incumbent is picking an action which could come from a congruent incumbent even though it is inferior for voters. They do so to enhance their reputation and hence to earn rents in Period 2.

3.4.6 *Multiple two-period terms*

The baseline model assumed that time ends after the second period. In this section, we investigate what aspects of this are artificial by extending the model to consider a potentially infinite number of two-term incumbents. We show how this model can be used to gain insights into what happens when there is an endogenous pool of politicians.

This model also eliminates a very artificial feature of the two-period model—in the two-period model, any politician who is elected will be a lame duck in Period 2. It would be less artificial to allow the voters to choose between a fresh politician with a two-period time horizon and re-electing the incumbent for a final term. Intuitively, we would expect this possibility to make voters more choosy when deciding whether to re-elect an incumbent since first period politicians tend to behave in a more disciplined manner.

Suppose now that time is infinite, but that politicians can serve at most two terms in office with each term lasting one period. Thus, let $t = 1, \ldots$ and let $j \in \{1, 2\}$ denote the term in which the politician is currently serving. There is an infinite pool of potential politicians. A politician can serve only once after which he/she returns to the pool. We now index politician behavior by time and by the term that they are serving: $e_t(s, i, j)$. We will work with stationary solutions, i.e. those in which these strategies are not time-dependent.

Congruent politicians always choose the outcome that voters prefer in both terms in office, i.e. $e(s, c, j) = s$ for $j \in \{1, 2\}$. The decision of the dissonant politician is exactly the same as in the baseline case, provided that it is optimal for the voters to re-elect a politician for delivering Δ. In order to check this, let $V^N(\pi)$ be the value to the voter of starting over with a new politician and let Π be the probability that the incumbent is congruent conditional on him/her generating a benefit of Δ in his/her first term. Using Bayes rule, Π is the same as in the baseline model and is equal to $\frac{\pi}{\pi + (1-\pi)\lambda}$. Let $\phi(\pi) = \pi + (1-\pi)\lambda$ be the probability that a first term incumbent generates the good action for voters. Then, the value of a newly elected politician under this strategy is:

$$V^N(\pi) = \phi(\pi)[\Delta + \beta \Pi \Delta + \beta^2 V^N(\pi)] + (1 - \phi(\pi))\beta V^N(\pi).$$

This has two parts. The first is the case in which the politician in Period 1 does what voters want. In this case he/she is re-elected for one period after which a new politician comes in. The second term is for the case where the politician does not produce a Period 1 benefit in which case, there is a random selection from the pool. Thus voter welfare viewed from Period 1 is

$$V^N(\pi) = \frac{\Delta}{(1 - \beta)} \cdot \frac{\phi(\pi)(1 + \beta \Pi)}{[1 + \beta \phi(\pi)]} = \frac{\Delta}{(1 - \beta)} \cdot \frac{\phi(\pi) + \pi \beta}{[1 + \beta \phi(\pi)]}.$$

This has a nice interpretation. The first term is the discounted value of voter welfare if everyone behaved like congruent politicians. The second term (multiplying this) is less than one and represents the reduction in voter welfare due to the selection and discipline problems in political life.

Using this expression, we now check whether re-electing an incumbent who has produced Δ is optimal for the voters. This will be true if and only if:

$$\Pi\Delta + \beta V^N(\pi) \geq V^N(\pi)$$

which is equivalent to $\Pi \geq \phi(\pi)$ or

$$\pi \geq \left(\frac{\lambda}{(1-\lambda)}\right)^2.$$

Intuitively, this condition says that re-election is worthwhile if and only if the conditional probability that the incumbent will make the right choice for voters exceeds the probability that a new incumbent will.

In the case where $\pi < \left(\frac{\lambda}{(1-\lambda)}\right)^2$, there is no equilibrium in which voters re-elect politicians who yield a payoff of Δ with probability one. This is because this strategy yields too much restraint by dissonant incumbents, reducing the importance of selection to a point where it would always be optimal to fire the incumbent.[40] In this situation, there is a mixed strategy by voters. Let σ be the probability that an incumbent is re-elected when he/she generates Δ for the voters. Then in a mixed strategy this must make the voters indifferent between re-electing and not re-electing the incumbent. This will happen when:

$$\lambda = G(\sigma\beta(\mu + E)) = \frac{\sqrt{\pi}}{1 + \sqrt{\pi}}.$$

This can be summarized as:

Proposition 4: *Congruent politicians always set $e = s$. Dissonant politicians always set $e = (1 - s)$ in their second term in office. First period*

[40] It is clear that there is no equilibrium in which voters always fire politicians for generating Δ. All bad incumbents would then take the dissonant action. But then, observing a payoff of Δ would (using Bayes rule) lead the voters to update that the incumbent was good with probability one and hence re-elect them—a contradiction.

behavior among dissonant politicians falls in one of two cases:

1. *If $\pi \geq (G(\beta(\mu + E))/(1 - G(\beta(\mu + E))))^2$, then dissonant politicians deliver what voters want in Period one with probability $G(\beta(\mu+E))$ and are re-elected for doing so.*
2. *If $\pi < (G(\beta(\mu+E))/(1 - G(\beta(\mu+E))))^2$, then voters re-elect politicians who deliver Δ with probability σ where σ solves*

$$G(\sigma\beta(\mu + E)) = \frac{\sqrt{\pi}}{1 + \sqrt{\pi}}$$

and dissonant politicians deliver what voters want in Period one with probability $G(\sigma\beta(\mu + E))$.

The first of these outcomes replicates the behavioral pattern of the baseline model. This will happen only if λ is sufficiently *low*. While this may seem paradoxical, it reflects the fact that seeing Δ must make voters sufficiently confident that the incumbent is congruent, otherwise, they would prefer to return to the pool and pick a fresh incumbent. This condition has the best chance of being satisfied when π is high since then it is mostly likely that Δ has been generated by a congruent incumbent rather than a dissonant behaving in a disciplined fashion.

The second case occurs when π is very low. In this case, voters prefer to try their chances with a new politician when the strategy of the baseline model is followed. To make their signal more credible, dissonant politicians have to choose what voters want less of the time. Voters create this incentive by re-electing only some fraction of the time when the incumbent delivers Δ. Thus, even some congruent incumbents are removed from office as part of an optimal voting strategy.

Extending the time horizon of the model without changing the time horizon of politicians actually reduces the probability that a dissonant incumbent does what voters want. Hence, it worsens discipline and improves selection.

This model has a striking implication for the sign of the term-limit effect. Since voters only re-elect incumbents if they are better than a first term incumbent would be, the politicians must perform better than average in their second term than in the first. This reveals the power of the selection effect in agency models with adverse selection.

151

To summarize, this section has extended the two-period model with adverse selection and moral hazard to a multi-period setting while retaining the assumption that politicians can serve only two terms in office. This yields some qualitatively similar findings to the two-period model. However, there are some important differences in the logic due to the fact that voters can always pick a fresh incumbent at any time. This implies that any politician going into his/her last term in office must be *better* on average than a randomly selected politician from the pool.

STANDING FOR POLITICAL OFFICE

The model with an indefinite number of finite terms is a natural vehicle for looking at some factors that make the choice of the pool of politicians endogenous. This is because it lends itself to a steady state analysis where the value of any two-period experience as a politician can be computed. The baseline set-up would give a different value to being a politician in the first and second period for highly artificial reasons.

Here, we look at this issue very crudely—the winning politician is a random selection from among those willing to serve. This abstracts from many institutions that affect candidate selection such as campaigning, party selection and voting. We suppose that there is a continuum of potential politicians with outside per period wages $w \in [0, W^i]$ with $i \in \{c, d\}$. We assume that this is uniformly distributed, with the support of the distributions differing for the two groups of politicians. Suppose that the probability that a candidate is of the congruent type in the entire pool of possible politicians is γ.

For congruent politicians, recruitment implies retention. A politician will stay in office for a second term if $E \geq w$. Since he/she is re-elected for sure, he/she will also enter in Period 1 if $E \geq w$.[41] Thus, the fraction of congruent citizens who will be willing to enter politics is $\frac{E}{W^c}$.

We now turn to the dissonant citizens and their decision to run as candidates. Adding in the outside option will now lead to a slight modification of the model above as the optimal action of dissonant politicians now depends upon their private sector wage rate.

---

[41] Two interesting possibilities are seniority premia for being in office (in the private sector) and a risk of not being re-elected in which case retention can be a problem.

Specifically,

$$e(s, d, 1, w) = \begin{cases} s & \text{if } r_1 \leq \beta([\mu + E] - w) \\ (1 - s) & \text{otherwise.} \end{cases}$$

Thus, politicians with more generous outside opportunities are less likely to take the congruent action. This is because their rent from holding political office compared to the private sector is smaller. Let $\bar{w}$ be the maximal private sector wage that a dissonant politician will forego in order to become a politician. Then the probability of congruent behavior by a randomly selected dissonant politician who is willing to serve is now

$$\Lambda(E, \bar{w}) = \int_0^{\bar{w}} G(\beta([E + \mu] - w)) \frac{dw}{\bar{w}}.$$

Dissonant politicians are willing to serve if they are re-elected if $\mu + E \geq w$. We now look at recruitment on the assumption that this holds. If a politician stays in the private sector, he/she will make a stream of utility $v(w) = \frac{w}{(1-\beta)}$. Then, the value from entering politics when the private sector option is w is:

$$P(E + \mu, w) = E + \left(\int_{\beta[(E+\mu)-w]}^{R} (r + \beta v(w)) dG(r) \right)$$
$$+ G(\beta[E + \mu - w])(\beta(E + \mu) + \beta^2 v(w)).$$

The dissonant politicians who participate in politics are those for which $v(w) \leq P(E + \mu, w)$. Solving this yields:

$$w \leq (E + \mu) + \psi(E + \mu - w)$$

where $\psi(x) = \frac{-\int_0^{\beta x} r dG(r)}{1 + G(\beta x)\beta} < 0$ and $\psi'(x) < 0$. The last term on the right hand side of this expression is the expected forgone rent (i.e. below μ) due to behaving well in the first period. Thus, the critical wage below which dissonant politicians will put themselves forward for office is defined by

$$\bar{w}(E, \mu) \equiv (E + \mu) + \psi(E + \mu - \bar{w}((E, \mu))).$$

We assume that there is a unique solution to this equation.[42] It is clear that $\bar{w}(E, \mu) < E + \mu$. Hence, consistent with what we assumed above,

---

[42] The possibility of multiple equilibria is intriguiging. The mechanism is as follows. There can be a high reservation wage option where a significant fraction of dissonant

dissonant politicians who are willing to enter are also willing to serve a second term if they are re-elected. This implies that the fraction of dissonant politicians who are willing to become politicians is:

$$\frac{\bar{w}(E, \mu)}{W^d}.$$

Using this, the fraction of congruent politicians in the pool of candidates available for public office is:

$$\pi(E) = \frac{\gamma}{\gamma + (1 - \gamma) \left[\frac{\bar{w}(E, \mu)}{E} \cdot \frac{W^c}{W^d} \right]}.$$

This depends upon the relative returns to politics of dissonant and congruent types and their relative private sector options. The additional rents (over and above E) earned by dissonant politicians make them more eager to enter politics than congruent ones and raising wages redresses the balance. Thus, the model predicts that, in addition to discipline effects, raising the rents earned by politicians (as measured by E) improves the pool of politicians who are willing to serve if $\bar{w}(E, \mu) > E$.[43] The size of this effect depends on the ratio $(1 - \gamma)/\gamma$. Thus, the effect is larger if there is a relative dearth of congruent individuals.

While simple, this does provide a way of closing the model in a way that does not require us to treat π as exogenous. However, the model basically predicts that the underlying character of the population (as represented by γ) is important. But so too are the relative rewards of public and private life $\bar{w}(E, \mu)/E$ to congruent and dissonant politicians.

3.4.7 *Indefinite terms*

While the previous model relaxed the two-period structure, it continued to assume that each politician has only a two-period horizon. With some investment in notation, the model could straightforwardly

politicians enter and expected rents are high since these politicians are less likely to be tempted to pick the congruent action. In the low reservation wage equilibrium, expected rents are low since dissonant politicians who enter are more likely to pick the dissonant action.

[43] Observe that

$$\frac{\partial \bar{w}(E, \mu)}{\partial E} = 1.$$

be extended to consider finite terms of any length. However, any such model would have the feature that eventually some term would be known to be the last. In this section, we extend the model to lose this feature and consider a model where politicians do not face a known terminal date. Hence, we consider what would happen if politicians faced no finite horizon, i.e. could stay in office forever.[44] We will characterize a stationary strategy for a dissonant politician in which voters re-elect politicians who produce Δ in any period. In this equilibrium, any politician who is fired will be replaced by another politician who also has an infinite horizon. Arguably this kind of model makes more sense for considering reputation formation by a long-lived entity like a political party rather than a single individual.

A dissonant politician will use a cut-off rule such that he/she picks what voters want if and only if the return to the dissonant action is less than or equal to $\hat{r}$.[45] He/she will be prepared to do so provided that this rent is less than what he/she will look forward to getting in the next period. To characterize this, it is necessary to compare the value of earning a rent today and being removed from office with the continuation value of being re-elected. The continuation value is equal to:

$$W(\hat{r}) = E + \left[\int_{\hat{r}}^{R} r dG(r) + \beta G(\hat{r}) W(\hat{r}) \right].$$

Solving yields:

$$W(\hat{r}) = \frac{E + \int_{\hat{r}}^{R} r dG(r)}{1 - \beta G(\hat{r})}.$$

The critical value is now characterized by $\hat{r} = \beta W(\hat{r})$. This yields:

$$\hat{r} = \frac{\beta [E + \int_{\hat{r}}^{R} r dG(r)]}{[1 - \beta G(\hat{r})]}.$$

Let

$$\hat{\lambda} = G(\hat{r})$$

[44] This section is inspired by Smart and Sturm (2004) who pose this question in a more sophisticated setting where there is no stationary equilibrium in the infinite horizon model.

[45] The solution in this simple setting is stationary. This is because the politician's reputation does not affect his/her incentive to do what the voters want. In general this will not be true and it is this feature of the infinite horizon model that makes it tricky to characterize equilibria in this setting.

be the probability that a dissonant incumbent does what voters want in any time period. It is clear that compared to the term limited case, there is more congruence along the equilibrium path than in the first period of a term limited spell. Let $\hat{\phi}(\pi) = \pi + (1 - \pi)\hat{\lambda}$ be the extent of congruence along the stationary equilibrium path.

Proposition 5: *Suppose that a politician faces an infinite horizon model, then dissonant politicians are more disciplined than in Period 1 when they face a binding term limit i.e. $\hat{\phi}(\pi) > \phi(\pi)$.*

Proof Define:

$$\kappa(x) = \frac{\beta[E + \int_x^R rdG(r)]}{[1 - \beta G(x)]}.$$

It is straightforward to check that this is a strictly quasi-concave function which reaches a maximum at $\kappa(x) = x$. To see this, observe that:

$$\kappa'(x) = (1 - G(x)\beta)^{-1}\beta g(x)[\kappa(x) - x].$$

Moreover, $\kappa(0) = \beta(E + \mu)$. Thus, $\kappa(\hat{r}) > \kappa(0)$ implying that $\lambda < \hat{\lambda}$. QED. □

This makes sense. Dissonant politicians now face the possibility of earning rents in many future periods in office and hence behave better. As the dissonant politician becomes more patient, then he/she may be willing to take the congruent action in every period, sustained only by the legitimate rent from holding public office. We record this as:

Proposition 6: *Suppose that politicians are sufficiently patient and/or office holding rents are sufficiently strong (specifically $\beta E/(1 - \beta) > R$) then $\hat{r} > R$, all politicians do what voters want.*

Thus with sufficiently patient politicians, a high enough legitimate office holding rent and a long enough time horizon, the political agency problem can be solved completely.

It is now straightforward to work out the welfare of voters along this path. First, observe that electing a congruent politician is an absorbing state—he/she always does what voters want and hence is re-elected forever. Let

$$V^* = \frac{\Delta}{(1 - \beta)}$$

be the value to the voter from this. Second, observe that any incumbent who produces Δ will be re-elected as the probability that he/she is congruent is strictly higher than a randomly selected incumbent from the pool. Now consider, the value to the voter at time zero. This is:

$$\hat{V}_0 = \hat{\phi}(\pi)\Delta + \beta\pi V^* + (\hat{\phi}(\pi) - \pi)\beta\hat{V}_0 + (1 - \hat{\phi}(\pi))\beta\hat{V}_0$$

$$= \hat{\phi}(\pi)\Delta + \beta\pi V^* + (1 - \pi)\beta\hat{V}_0.$$

Thus:

$$\hat{V}_0 = \frac{\Delta}{1 - \beta} \left[\frac{(1 - \beta)\hat{\phi}(\pi) + \pi\beta}{1 - \beta(1 - \pi)} \right].$$

Observe that $\hat{V}_0 \to V^*$ as $\hat{\phi}(\pi) \to 1$. It is clear from this that politicians behave better when the value of holding office is greater.

This logic suggests that it will never be a good idea to impose terms limits on politicians since it worsens their behavior and means that periodically good politicians must be removed from office. This can be seen here by comparing $\hat{V}_0$ with $V^N(\pi)$ in Section 3.4.6. A term limit is a good idea if

$$\frac{\hat{\phi}(\pi) - \beta(\hat{\phi}(\pi) - \pi)}{1 - \beta(1 - \pi)} < \frac{\phi(\pi) + \pi\beta}{[1 + \beta\phi(\pi)]}$$

It is clear that in the case where the dissonant politician always takes the congruent action, then voters are strictly better off without term limits.

However, the conclusion that term limits are bad is not general. Smart and Sturm (2004) focus on the case of timid equilibrium along the lines discussed in Section 3.4.3. The equilibrium, as we saw, leads to distortions in behavior by congruent politicians. Moreover, it gets more likely when E is high. In this case, a term limit provides a way of inducing congruent politicians to behave in a congruent way—since they know that they cannot be re-elected. Smart and Sturm (2004) show that a two-term term limit can sometimes be an optimal institution in that setting.

3.4.8 *Multiple agents*

So far, we have considered a situation where there is a single agent responsible for all aspects of policy. This is far from the setting in which many policy decisions are made where many agents have some input into the policy process. We now consider the simplest extension which allows for multiple agents. These could be legislators who jointly pass legislation in a legislature or they could be thought of as the acts of a bicameral legislature, with agents located in each chamber. The latter provides a way into thinking about the welfare consequences of the separation of powers in this setting. It is this example which motivates the work of Persson et al. (1997, 2000) which uses the agency model to think about these issues. We discuss their work in detail below.

From a modeling point of view, introducing multiple agents is interesting since the policy process now has to resolve externalities between the agents if they face a conflict of interest in their policy decisions. For example, when a congruent and a dissonant agent have to make policy together, this may affect rent extraction possibilities open to the latter. The interesting issue is whether these externalities between policy makers work for or against the voters. The analysis here confirms the idea that a multiple agents setting reduces rent extraction possibilities. However, this may also reduce the Period 1 discipline of dissonant incumbents, creating a trade-off for voters.

Suppose then that there are now two politicians labelled $\ell \in \{1, 2\}$. Each politician is directly elected and accountable to the same set of voters. We work with the case where $E = 0$. This washes out the possibility that having two politicians is beneficial because that generates twice the ego rent to discipline politicians. Politicians' types are independent draws from the same distribution comprising dissonant and congruent politicians exactly as in the baseline model—so each is congruent with probability π.

As in the baseline model, there is a single policy decision to be made in each period. We denote this by $e_t \in \{0, 1\}$. Voters receive Δ if $e_t = s_t$ and zero otherwise. The policy outcome is now dependent on the actions of the two agents. We denote these actions by $a_t^\ell (\in \{0, 1\})$ for politician ℓ at time t where the action can be interpreted as a vote in favor of e_t being zero or one. These actions are observed by voters in each time period.[46] We suppose that there is an initial policy $e_0 \in \{0, 1\}$ in place which will remain the same unless the agents who control the policy process decide to change it.

---

[46] Thus this differs from the previous sections where observing the action is equivalent to observing the policy outcome.

There is a fixed pot of rent, denoted by r_t, that is available to politicians who choose the policy $e_t \neq s_t$. This is shared equally between any agents who pick the action $a_t^\ell = (1 - s_t)$, but only if the outcome is $e_t = (1 - s_t)$. In the event that both politicians pick $a_t^\ell = (1 - s_t)$, the rent is shared equally. If only one politician sets $a_t^\ell = (1 - s_t)$ and the outcome is $e_t = (1 - s_t)$, then he/she captures the full rent. The best way to think about this is as bribery by a special interest which is paid only if the policy turns out as the special interest would like. Thus, rents attach to policies not actions.

The two agents determine policy in the shadow of constitutional rules that determine the policy outcome as a function of their individual actions. Suppose that these rules can be described by a mapping from the actions of the two politicians and the status quo policy into a new policy outcome denoted by:

$$e_t = \Gamma(a_t^1, a_t^2, e_{t-1}).$$

We assume that this constitutional rule satisfies unanimity, i.e.,

$$\Gamma(a_t^1, a_t^2, e_{t-1}) = \begin{cases} 1 & \text{if } a_t^1 = a_t^2 = 1 \\ 0 & \text{if } a_t^1 = a_t^2 = 0. \end{cases}$$

Thus, both policy makers must agree to change the policy outcome from the status quo. Otherwise, we suppose that the constitutional rule favors the *status quo* in the sense that:

$$\Gamma(1, 0, e_{t-1}) = \Gamma(0, 1, e_{t-1}) = e_{t-1}.$$

Thus, the policy does not change if the two agents cannot agree to do so.

To model the game played between the politicians, we suppose that the politicians do not know each other's type. We assume that the agents behave non-cooperatively and hence look for a Bayes–Nash equilibrium.

PERIOD 2 POLICY

In Period 2, congruent politicians will do what voters want and dissonant politicians pick $a_t^\ell = (1 - s_2)$. The policy outcome is $e_2 = (1 - s_2)$ if there are two dissonant incumbents. With two congruent incumbents, the outcome is $e_2 = s_2$ in which case voters get Δ in Period 2.

With one dissonant and one congruent incumbent, the outcome depends on whether or not the state matches the status quo policy. If $s_2 = e_1$, then the congruent incumbent can ensure that the status quo prevails and $e_2 = s_2 = e_1$. Voters then receive Δ. If the status quo policy does not agree with the state, i.e., $(1 - s_2) = e_1$, then the dissonant incumbent can preserve the status quo and earn a rent. A key observation is that, unlike the single agent model, voters get Δ some of the time when only one of the incumbents is dissonant. Thus, congruent incumbents can impose an externality on dissonant ones in Period 2 which works to the voters' advantage. Recalling that each of the states is equally likely, the voters get Δ with probability $1/2$ in this case.

It is clear from this that voters always gain from re-electing congruent incumbents in Period 1. Hence, as in the baseline model, incumbents who acquire a reputation for being congruent in Period 1 may be re-elected.

Using this, we can compute the expected rent of a dissonant politician if he/she is re-elected. Let π_2 be the probability that the other politician is congruent. Then he/she obtains:

$$\left[\frac{1}{2} \left(\pi_2 + \frac{(1 - \pi_2)}{2} \right) + \frac{1}{2} \left(\frac{(1 - \pi_2)}{2} \right) \right] \beta\mu = \frac{1}{2} \beta\mu.$$

To see this, observe that the first term is what happens when $e_1 \neq s_2$. In this case, the dissonant incumbent gets all the rent when he/she is with a congruent incumbent and half the rent when he/she is with a dissonant one. The second term is for when $e_1 = s_2$ in which case he/she gets half the rent if the other politician is dissonant.

PERIOD 1 POLICY

Suppose that voters use the following re-elected strategies. Re-elect both politicians if $a_1^1 = a_1^2$ and they receive a payoff of Δ. Otherwise fire any politician whose action is not in favor of a policy that yields Δ. Below we will show that these strategies are consistent with Bayes rule.

We now consider the behavior of the incumbents. The congruent politicians have a dominant strategy to pick $a_1^\ell = s_1$. Thus, the only interesting issue is how a dissonant politician behaves. This will depend on whether or not $e_0 = s_1$. We consider each case in turn.

GOOD STATUS QUO POLICY: $e_0 = s_1$

In this case a dissonant politician knows that he/she can earn a rent only if he/she is with a dissonant politician who decides to take the rent so his/her expected payoff is $\frac{r}{2}(1 - \pi)$ which he/she compares to $\frac{1}{2}\beta\mu$. Thus, in this case he/she sets:

$$\bar{\lambda} = G\left(\frac{\beta\mu}{(1 - \pi)}\right).$$

So in this case, there is strictly more discipline than in the single agent case. As $\pi \to 1$, the dissonant agent knows that he/she cannot extract any rents and will do what voters want in the hope of capturing some rent in Period 2.

BAD STATUS QUO POLICY: $e_0 = (1 - s_1)$

In this case, a dissonant incumbent has more chance to earn a short-term rent. However, he/she will have to share it if the other incumbent is also dissonant. Hence he/she is actually better off with a congruent incumbent in this case. Thus expected rent from taking the dissonant action is now $\frac{r}{2}(1 + \pi)$. This yields discipline of:

$$\underline{\lambda} = G\left(\frac{\beta\mu}{(1 + \pi)}\right)$$

which is strictly less discipline than in the case of a single agent.

Thus, $\bar{\lambda} > \lambda > \underline{\lambda}$ if $\pi > 0$. And $\underline{\lambda} = \bar{\lambda} = \lambda$ if $\pi = 0$, i.e. all politicians are dissonant. In this case, there is no effect on discipline in this model. In this sense it raises rather different issues from the analysis of Persson et al. (1997, 2000) whose contributions are discussed below. Here, the entire issue is how congruent and dissonant incumbents collectively create externalities for one another in the policy process.

Proposition 7: *Congruent politicians always set $e = s$. Dissonant politicians choose $e = (1 - s)$ in Period 2 and will choose $e = s$ in Period 1 if they earn sufficiently small rents from being dissonant. Dissonant politicians exercise more discipline in Period one if $e_0 = s_1$ than when $e_0 = (1 - s_1)$.*

Thus, having two agents creates negative and positive externalities. In the case where $e_0 = s_1$, a dissonant agent must rely on the other agent to be dissonant if he/she is to earn a rent in Period 1 and hence it reduces the marginal benefit from taking the dissonant action in

Period 1. However, if $e_0 = (1-s_1)$, he/she can unilaterally earn the rent and would prefer that the other politician were congruent as that way, he/she earns a larger share of the rent. This encourages ill-discipline on the part of a dissonant politician.

WELFARE CONSEQUENCES

To explore the welfare consequences of the two agent setting in more detail we derive the expressions for voter welfare in each period. In Period 1, the expression is:

$$\hat{V}_1(\lambda^*) = [\pi^2 + (1 - \pi^2)\lambda^*]\Delta \qquad (3.6)$$

where $\lambda^* = \frac{\bar{\lambda}+\underline{\lambda}}{2}$. This is exactly as if there was a single agent who is good with probability π^2 and the dissonant agent exercises discipline in Period 1 with probability λ^*. Period 2 welfare is equal to:

$$\hat{V}_2(\lambda^*) = \pi[1 + (1 - \pi)(1 - \lambda^*)]\Delta. \qquad (3.7)$$

Let

$$\hat{W}(\lambda^*) = \hat{V}_1(\lambda^*) + \beta\hat{V}_2(\lambda^*)$$

be overall voter welfare. As with (3.3), an increase in discipline (as measured by λ^*) is good for voters even though it lowers welfare in Period 2 since selection is worse.

Comparing this with (3.3), we find that:

$$\hat{W}(\lambda^*) - W(\lambda) = [-\pi(1 - \pi) + \pi\lambda - \pi^2\lambda^* + [1 - \beta(1 - \pi)\pi](\lambda^* - \lambda)]\Delta.$$

The first term represents the fact that in Period 1, it is now necessary to have two congruent incumbents to have a *guarantee* that the right policy is enacted for the voters. (In general, this is a cost of our two agent set-up.) Thus, a *necessary* condition for a two person decision making process to be better for voter welfare is that $\lambda^* > \lambda$, i.e. it improves discipline among dissonant agents.

As we have seen from this example, when there are two agents making policy then they need to bargain somehow to bring about a policy outcome. This outcome can change political incentives and either raise or lower discipline. This insight underpins the analysis of Persson et al. (1997, 2000) who model the separation of powers in a political agency framework with moral hazard by considering bargaining between two agents. However, in their setting all agents care only about rents—there is no equivalent of the congruent agents modeled here. They suppose that all incumbents desire to extract rent from voters with their actions being only imperfectly observable. They then compare a situation in which one politician (or a single chamber of a legislature) is given authority to make all policy decisions versus one in which there are two. In the latter case, both authorities are required to reach agreement before a policy is implemented. In that sense, their set-up is quite similar to what we have proposed here.

Persson et al. (1997) lay down an infinite horizon model with each period corresponding to a term in office where the incumbents may choose how much to divert to private use in each period and how much to spend on public goods valued by voters. Each period also yields an unobservable shock to the productivity of providing public services, after which an election occurs. There is an infinite number of potential identical challengers, one of whom may be selected to face the incumbent in an election. Consider first the case of single authority. This follows the analysis of Ferejohn (1986) quite closely. The voters determine a cut-off level of public goods spending below which the incumbent is replaced.

Now suppose that there are two authorities who must agree before any policy outcome can be implemented. Persson et al. (1997) observe that unless mutual agreement is insisted upon, then voters lose. In effect, there is a common pool problem in which both incumbents get to extract rents from the voters in an uncoordinated way. Under mutual agreement, they specify a bargaining game with one player having agenda setting powers. They show that if there are no productivity shocks, then voters are as well off as they were under a single policy maker—the rents are simply shared between the two politicians.

To get a strict benefit for the voters Persson et al. (1997) show that a conflict of interest between the two politicians must be created. They do so by supposing that in the first stage an authority chooses the total budget while the authority that moves second chooses the division of resources between the authorities. The first stage player now has a stronger incentive to propose something that pleases the voters—since it loses out in the second stage rent division game.

In the presence of productivity shocks, the presence of two political agents who know the level of the shock makes it possible to glean better information about such shocks. This parallels well-known results in implementation theory (such as Maskin (1999)) which suggest that better information revelation is generally possible when more than one agent have the same information about some unobservable variable. Each authority can be asked to announce the value of the shock with punishments for equilibrium disagreements. Voters now gain from having more information entering the political process as they use a more exacting re-election rule.

Persson et al. (2000) is concerned with the difference between parliamentary and presidential regimes. In the latter, the executive is directly elected, whereas a parliamentary regime has the executive being subordinated to the legislature. The key issue that they examine is the allocation of resources between political rents and public goods. They develop a model of legislature in which there is a legislature comprising three districts each of which can receive a transfer. In common with political agency models the voters use retrospective voting strategies defining a cut-off level to re-elect incumbents.

The characteristic difference between the modeling of parliamentary and presidential systems is the nature of the agenda setting power. A parliamentary system unifies agenda setting powers while a presidential system diversifies it. The latter tends to reduce rent extraction and tends towards smaller government.[47]

Developing multi-agent extensions of the agency model is a useful step in the direction of realism. It is also an important step in understanding political organization which frequently involves multi-agent settings. However, our understanding of these issues is far from complete and developing it further remains a major challenge for the future.[48]

---

[47] Testa (2002) applies a similar logic to the comparison of a bi-cameral and a uni-cameral legislature and shows when the former can reduce rent extraction by politicians.

[48] Myerson (2000) suggests the following interesting possibility where the separation of powers is dysfunctional. Suppose that an important observable outcome of government (like the inflation rate) depends on the efforts and the skill of two different elected officials, but the voters cannot directly monitor these officials' separate activities that influence this outcome. Suppose also that the politicians A and B who currently hold these two offices are political rivals, expected to run against each other in the near future, but A's office is more powerful and so has more effect on the observable outcome. Then voters should assume that the observed outcome is more an indication of the skills and efforts of politician A. In this situation, politician B may have an incentive to use his/her power counterproductively, in the hope of generating a bad outcome that would make A look inept to the voters. If the voters anticipate such secret sabotage by B then B's incentive to sabotage becomes even stronger, because the voters could rationally infer from a bad

3.5 Discussion

Our study of accountability and agency is useful if it assists us in understanding better how the world works and specifically ways of improving the functioning of democratic systems. In this section, I discuss the implications of the model for two areas. First, we discuss how the model casts light on the link between civic virtue and the quality of government, following on from the influential work of Putnam (1993). Second, we discuss the implications of the models for debates about the optimal degree of decentralization in the policy sphere.

3.5.1 *Civic virtue and the quality of government*

In his celebrated book on politics in Italy, Putnam (1993) argues that civic virtue is a key value that affects the quality of democracy. The centerpiece of the analysis is the observed correlations between measures of civic virtue and the quality of government.[49] His measures of civic virtue are participation in associations, the extent to which voters vote on the basis of preference for one candidate rather than on the basis of clientelistic relationships, and newspaper readership. There is plenty of interesting discussion in the book. But it is not entirely clear how to locate Putnam's ideas in the context of political economy models.

The agency approach gives a persuasive way of thinking about the theory that underpins these ideas. Civic virtue in general could be thought of as an index of π—the probability that any politician elected to office is congruent and hence will pursue what voters want. Societies with a greater commitment to civic virtue will likely have a higher quality political class and hence higher quality government. Since a higher π may also create an increase in private voluntarism, we might expect Putnam's observed correlation.

This observation is a point of departure between the first generation political agency models of Barro (1973) and Ferejohn (1986) with their exclusive focus on moral hazard which cannot give expression to Putnam's ideas. The idea that there are civic minded types

outcome that B is a particularly capable manipulator of government who would be a more effective leader in a higher office.

[49] Putnam uses a 12-dimensional measure of government quality which he analyzes by means of principal components.

is however a key theme of Putnam's discussion, which fits with the broader intellectual focus of this book.

The agency model also fits Putnam's observation that less clientelistic voting improves the quality of government. This can be seen using the analysis in Section 3.4.1 where we observed that accountability is likely to be enhanced when there are fewer voters with entrenched attachments to the incumbent. In this case, even dissonant politicians will likely behave in a more disciplined fashion which increases voter welfare.

His third correlation concerns newspaper readership and the quality of government. Here, we can appeal to the results in Section 3.4.2 on information which create a presumption that improving voter information would improve political discipline and raise the quality of government.

Making democracy work in the context of the agency models means finding effective accountability that improves discipline and selection. All three factors that Putnam correlates with quality of government are factors that affect the performance of politics as an accountability system holding fixed the formal political institutions and hence can explain why the same formal institutions can yield a very different political outcome. Putnam's way of thinking about the quality of government sits naturally with the kind of agency model that we have studied in this chapter.

3.5.2 *Decentralization versus centralization*

One of the key questions in choosing the tier of government at which certain goods and services should be provided is the extent to which government can be held accountable for its actions. The recent push towards the greater use of decentralized provision is built to a significant degree on the notion that having government closer to the people will lead to better governance. Political agency models are a good framework to think about these issues.

One of the key arguments for decentralization is often that it allows citizens to exercise 'voice' more effectively. The latter is often interpreted as providing better information about policies and politicians to the voters. This has been the thrust of work by Bardhan and Mookherjee (2000). Our baseline model can be used to cast light on the issues. Using the model of Section 3.4.2, we would expect a difference between centralized and decentralized government if χ (the probability that Δ becomes known) was higher under decentralization. There are clearly policies for which this is true. Suppose that one task of government is the removal of graffiti. Then voters can see whether this has been successful in their own location, but may have a poor sense of whether this has been done in a larger jurisdiction.

But our model also reminds us that there are other preconditions for successful decentralization. The analysis of Section 3.4.1 suggests that decentralized government will work less well if there is more polarization and less political competition in some jurisdictions. This is a real issue for the working of decentralized governments in regions with strong ethnic conflict or areas that are dominated by one particular group. It may be that at the national level these things aggregate to give much less bias for the incumbent than they would for any local incumbent. This line of argument suggests a more equivocal answer to whether decentralization necessarily improves accountability.[50]

Decentralization may also be important because of the way that it induces competition between governments. One particular aspect of this concerns whether the electoral mechanism works better when voters can make yardstick comparisons between jurisdictions. We explore this in greater detail in the next chapter. The basic idea behind this comes from the literature on moral hazard in teams developed in Holmstrom (1982). A group of agents are asked to perform tasks where the outcome depends on some unobserved variable which is common to all. Effort put into making the outcome successful is not observable. It then becomes optimal to condition the incentives given to one agent on the outcomes achieved by others. This has applications in a number of areas, crucial to the regulation of firms with unknown costs.[51] Yardstick competition can be thought of broadly as improving the information that voters have. Hence, our analysis from Section 3.4.2 is once again relevant in thinking about it.

[50] Bardhan and Mookherjee (2000) argue that another key issue is the propensity of government to be captured by special interests which may vary at the national and local levels.
[51] Besley and Case (1995a) and Salmon (1987) observed that this kind of mechanism could have value in the context of decentralized political competition where a number of local or regional governments are being asked to perform a similar task against a backdrop of correlated private information. For example, the cost of building roads may be similar in jurisdictions that have similar topography. The theory of yardstick political competition is studied in Besley and Case (1995a); Bodenstein and Ursprung (2001); Bordignon et al. (2001); Hindriks and Belleflamme (2001) and Besley and Smart (2007). We discuss these ideas in greater detail in the next chapter.

The empirical relevance of these ideas was formulated in Besley and Case (1995a) which considered interdependent tax setting for states in using geographically neighboring states as a benchmark. They find that there is positive co-movement in the tax rates across state boundaries. Consistent with the agency model, this positive co-movement is not found among governors who are not eligible for re-election. Similar co-movement results for European countries are found in Bordignon et al. (2001) (Italy), Revelli (2001) (UK), and Schaltegger and Küttel (2001) (Switzerland).

Decentralization can also be important because of the constraints placed on politicians by resource mobility. Brennan and Buchanan (1980) ventured the idea that competition for resources among governments would place a desirable constraint on the power to tax given the tendencies towards revenue maximizing Leviathan governments. From a normative perspective this claim is puzzling since the externalities due to tax competition tend to reduce the efficiency of revenue collection and hence enhance the possibilities for welfare improving collusion among governments.

Besley and Smart (2007) consider this argument in a political agency model and their analysis is discussed in greater detail in the next chapter. They point out that an apparently second-best policy of inducing tax competition can be welfare improving for voters because it induces a favorable change in the political equilibrium. This is because the initial outcome that voters can achieve is second-best—some dissonant politicians are ill-disciplined and others are re-elected. Hence, as in the general theory of the second best, a further distortion can be welfare improving.

Hindriks and Lockwood (2005) look at centralization versus decentralization in a political agency framework similar to the one that we use in the next chapter. They model centralization as a situation in which a politician is answerable to multiple constituencies subject to a common budget constraint. They show that in a model where politicians differ in competence, then decentralization unambiguously dominates, whereas when politicians differ in their honesty the outcome is ambiguous.

Myerson (2005) also studies decentralization issues in a agency model. He argues that the value of decentralization is that local leaders have incentives to cultivate reputations before succeeding to national office. Decentralization is then worthwhile because it improves political selection at the national level.

3.5.3 *Autocracy versus democracy*

The structure studied can provide a useful framework for thinking through some basic differences between political accountability in autocratic and democratic regimes. While autocracies do not have elections to determine who will hold office, incumbents do typically rely on the support of particular groups in society to remain in office. In principle, some aspects of the agency model could be applied to thinking about an autocracy where a decisive group (such as the military) rather than the voters have to decide whether to keep an incumbent in power at the end of Period 1.[52] It also seems consistent with standard discussions that there is a mixture of good and bad autocrats in the world. Notwithstanding, it is perhaps reasonable to suppose that π is lower under autocracy because there is more limited entry of congruent candidates.

In situations where the decisive group has the broad interest of citizens at heart, the model suggests that there could be little difference between accountability under democratic and non-democratic systems of government. The distortions may come in models such as that studied in Section 3.4.5 where the autocratic incumbent targets a specific group (the decisive group for keeping him/her in power) at the expense of voters at large.

Autocracies and democracies may also differ because the decisive group is informed about the incumbent's type and may therefore have an interest in keeping $\pi = 0$ if that is a guarantee of future rents. There are also issues of what kind of contracts between decisive voters and autocrats are feasible and whether this is broader than what we allow in stylized representations of representative democracy.

Clearly, a complete account of these issues goes well beyond the analysis here. But the basic structure of agency models is a fruitful framework for thinking through the differences. Moreover, it will likely provide an understanding of what contributes towards 'making autocracy work', to paraphrase Putnam.

3.5.4 *Accountability to whom?*

Throughout the analysis, we have assumed that accountability is to the voters. Our discussion of the last section suggested that there is no

[52] An example of this approach to studying autocracy is Gallego and Pitchik (2004). However, their focus is on turnover rather than accountability issues.

particular reason to think that the ideas apply solely in this context. One of the classic critiques of representative democracy by thinkers of the left is that some types of voters are systematically ignored. Our model of multiple issues illustrated this idea in a very limited way. One important ground for ignoring some voters is that they are ignorant about policy outcomes. If the rich and better educated are better informed then the agency model can rationalize why these groups will tend to get more politicians to make policy choices that reflect their needs.[53]

The model can also be extended to think about the possibility that politicians gain rewards after they have left office—we have so far concentrated on rewards that accrue while in office. In the spirit of the original career concerns model, the outside option may be indexed to behavior in office. If this outside option is strong enough and rewards politicians for producing Δ for voters, then this could reinforce good behavior and may even induce politicians to produce Δ in the second period. In such cases, outside options are a complement with achieving accountability. However, one could also imagine a (less agreeable) world in which politicians are rewarded in the future for their rent-seeking behavior while in office, reducing discipline among dissonant politicians. This depends on whether the characteristic of being dissonant or congruent is more valuable in the market place.

Recent important work by Diermeier et al. (2003) has looked at the way in which political careers are valued in the market place, although they are not able to say whether the reward is indexed to behavior while in office. However, they do find an overall positive premium. The agency model leads naturally to thinking about these issues and to the occupational choices that lie behind the profession of politics. We will return to these ideas in Chapter 5.

3.5.5 *Wage policies for politicians*

So far, we have considered only the implications of re-election rules. However, there are other dimensions of the contract that is given to politicians that are potentially important. One key example is the wage. This can be thought of in the model as affecting E—the benefit of holding office. Similarly, perquisites such as free accommodation,

---

[53] See also Stromberg (2004) who gets a result like this by supposing that politicians make ex ante policy commitments to groups of voters.

transportation, and state banquets may be part of it. This raises the question of whether there is an optimal degree of generosity in the package that is offered to politicians.

The framework that we have considered provides an ideal vehicle for exploring this.[54] On the electoral side of the model, as E changes there will be discipline and selection effects. The first order effect is to increase the discipline of incumbents. This can be seen immediately by observing that $\lambda = G(\beta[\mu + E])$ which is increasing in E. This is like a rather standard efficiency wage argument and was observed in Ferejohn (1986). However, in a model of heterogeneous incumbents, this will tend to lead to relatively fewer congruent incumbents being sorted in to serve during the second term. As observed by Gersbach and Liessem (2001), there is a case for setting wages that depend on the seniority of the politician with higher wages in the second period to induce better behavior by incumbents. The conclusion that higher wages always improve political discipline is however fragile. This can be seen from the analysis of Section 3.4.3 where we observed that timid behavior by congruent politicians becomes a possibility for high enough E.[55]

The analysis in Section 3.4.6 suggests that wages may also affect the quality of the pool of politicians. Recall that the equilibrium fraction of congruent politicians as a function of E that we derived there was:

$$\pi(E) = \frac{\gamma}{\gamma + (1 - \gamma)\left[\frac{\bar{w}(E,\mu)}{E} \cdot \frac{W_c}{W_d}\right]}.$$

It is straightforward to see that this is increasing in E so long as $\bar{w}(E, \mu) > E$. This is because standing for political office is more attractive on the margin to the dissonant politicians. It is interesting to note though that if we had added some sufficient public service motivation from holding public office to the congruent politicians this conclusion would be reversed.

Another issue that we have not considered is the possibility of designing incentive contracts that index the pay of politicians explicitly to their performance while in office. This is considered by Gersbach (2003, 2004). While this is an interesting idea, we do not seem to see such schemes in practice. One reason is surely the fact

---

[54] The discussion here is based on Besley (2004). Gersbach (2003, 2004) and Gersbach and Liessem (2001) discuss aspects of incentive contracts in political life.

[55] This point is made in Smart and Sturm (2003).

that, by focusing attention on specific measurable goals, agents will tend to distort their efforts away from socially valuable tasks whose outputs are difficult to measure (Gersbach and Liessem (2001)).

3.5.6 *Behavioral versus rational choice models*

The agency model that we have studied here has rational politicians and rational voters—the latter who use Bayes rule to process information. There is some debate in the political science literature about how far the rationality postulate should be pushed in modeling political behavior. Our baseline model is consistent with voters using a simple behavioral rule where politicians who do something good for them get re-elected. This happens in this case to be consistent with Bayes rule. Thus, there is no difference in the baseline between a rational model of voters and a sensible behavioral model.

More generally, it is interesting to postulate the implications of a behavioral model of accountability in which voters favor politicians who generate some utility for them during their term in office. This will not in general yield any form of 'optimal' accountability of the kind studied here. However, some fraction of the time it will stand the voters in good stead. Going forward it would be interesting to understand better what the differences are between behavioral models of politics and the postulates of the strict rationality supposed here. It would be useful to understand when simple and sensible behavioral rules lead to large policy distortions.

3.6 Concluding comments

Political agency models extend insights from contract theory and information economics to political situations. Their main focus is on how voters hold politicians to account for their actions. In this chapter, we have explored the insights that they offer and discussed a number of applications from the literature. This should give the reader some notion of their potential in explaining real situations. The models also put some structure on the data, in particular with regard to the term-limit effect.

As well as illustrating theoretical issues, we have also developed an empirical application to US governors. The striking thing about that context is how well the basic framework applies. Governors are directly elected chief executives who are directly accountable. Given the murkiness of situations where chief executives are accountable to legislatures or parties, it is much harder to formulate the model's implications. However, doing so constitutes a major challenge for future empirical applications in this area.

But how does all this relate back to the grand themes of Chapter 1? The agency problem is able to formulate the idea of policy in the interests of voters (the case where the voter gets Δ) from that run by individuals with their own agendas. This is a core idea at the heart of the political economy literature. However, the approach for the most part is simplistic. In a multi-issue world congruence is difficult to achieve and even to define. Thus democracy giving voters what they want is complex. As we discussed in the last chapter, then the achievements of democracy need to be judged according to some agreed upon social criterion.

Once this is recognized, the normative significance of congruence becomes problematic. It could well be that the role of politicians is to take unpopular actions for the social good even if they do not result in re-election. This is especially true when voters want inconsistent things. Politicians who simply follow voters' interests may actually be worse for society. Of course, the dangers of populism have always been recognized and this is really only an instance of such concerns in an agency framework.

In the next chapter, I will develop an approach to political agency which is more specific in its ambitions. First, it is applied to public finance questions which means developing a more specific model. Second, we structure the model in a way that makes the normative issues more transparent.

4

Political agency and public finance

with Michael Smart

To make the argument for constitutional constraints, it is
necessary, first of all, to derive the elementary logic of limits or constraints on the exercise of free or voluntary choice,
whether at the level of an individual or a collectivity.

(Buchanan 1999: 111)

4.1 Introduction

The literature on the political economy of public finance falls into
two main camps. On the one hand is the literature which uses the
median voter model as a means of studying how the conflict of interest
between different citizens plays out in the political process. This has
been used to provide insights into the equilibrium level of the income
tax and/or public goods. The main task is to view the political process
as an aggregation mechanism—determining a set of social decisions
from underlying preferences.

The other main tradition in political economy and public finance
recognizes the conflict of interest between governors and the governed, recognizing the possibility that there is a limited ability to
restrain the power of non-benevolent politicians. The political agency
model discussed so far and the Leviathan model of Brennan and
Buchanan (1980) are squarely in this tradition. This chapter tries to

pull together some thinking on this theme using a simple model of public finance with an agency model of politics.[1]

The objectives of the chapter are twofold. First, we seek to provide a textbook level treatment of public finance issues that illuminates many of the ideas of the last chapter in a more concrete policy setting. Second, we will use the model to address some substantive policy concerns. The first is whether there is a case for imposing restraints on government over and above the electoral mechanism. The second is whether there is an advantage in bringing non-governmental organizations to substitute for public provision of goods and services.

The political agency model is a useful starting point for the former exercise as it provides a rigorous underpinning for the view that elections (while important) can serve only a limited role in restraining politicians' behavior. Thus, it is important to think about whether additional constraints above the need to be re-elected are a good idea.

Debates on restraining government bring into sharp relief the core theme of this book. If governments were benevolent then restraints in a fiscal setting would be welfare reducing for voters as they would distort the policy process. Thus, the essence of the reason for considering fiscal restraints has to be that government is imperfect. But to provide a precise account of how restraints will work will inevitably require a model of how well government performs.

One response to imperfections in government resource allocation is to rely more on private organizations—non-governmental organizations (NGOs)—to substitute for government provision. These issues are widely debated. However, there is no generally agreed framework for thinking about this. One context where this has been brought into sharp relief is aid flows to developing countries. The political agency approach is ideally suited to thinking about these issues as it models the capacity of government to deliver services. It is also important to tackle head on the problems of accountability that are likely to arise in NGOs. We extend the model to allow for this.

The analysis developed here builds on a very simple model put forward in Besley and Smart (2007). A government must choose how much to tax and how to spend it. Spending can be either on public goods which are valuable to voters or personal perks which we label generically as 'rent'. We assume that rents are unobservable to voters.

---

[1] See Hettich and Winer (2004) for an overview of approaches to the positive economics of taxation.

In principle, voters should be able to determine them once they know the level of spending and taxes. However, in practice this is difficult for a host of reasons. We capture this idea here in a very simple way by supposing that the 'cost' of providing the kind of public spending that voters like is not observable. Thus taxes and spending levels are an imperfect means of detecting rent extraction.

In the spirit of Chapter 3, types of politicians may also vary between rent-seeking politicians and good politicians who serve the public interest.[2] The role of the electoral process is both to sort in the right types and to discipline the rent seeking politicians if they are elected to office. The agency model developed here studies the role of electoral incentives in affecting public finance decisions—the overall level of taxation and the balance of spending between rent and public spending. We also allow for the government to raise revenues by issuing public debt.

The model has two time periods for policy making with an election occurring between the two. Voters make inferences based on observed policy outcomes and use this information to update their assessments using Bayes rule. Incumbents who displease voters by extracting excessive rents are removed from office.

The setting sometimes yields some surprising insights. For example, some restraints on government are likely to be good for voters only when government is relatively benevolent. This is because these restraints work by improving selection which is most valuable when there is preponderance of good politicians in the population.

Many of the key findings in this chapter rest on the *political theory of the second best*. This was first articulated in Fischer and Summers (1989). This is an exact extension of the economic theory of the second best due to Lipsey and Lancaster (1956). When agency problems generate distortions in political behavior, then there is no guarantee that standard reasoning about how good government should be organized is valid. Measures that would not be sensible in a first best world of benevolent government earn a rationale. When it comes to instruments that restrain government, examples of the political theory of the second best abound.

The chapter is organized as follows. In the next section, Section 4.2, we lay out the basic agency problem and the main assumptions. In

---

[2] Our good politicians are similar to the congruent politicians in the last chapter and our bad politicians are like the dissonant politicians.

Section 4.3, we go through the three basic kinds of agency model. The first has purely hidden type, the second only hidden action and the third both features. In Section 4.4, we draw out some implications of the model for the data—for example, patterns of re-election rates and the impact of term limits. These facts are consistent with the US data.

In Section 4.5, we use the model to discuss a variety of means for restraining government. This allows us to re-examine the theoretical foundations of some ideas that have been central to the public choice approach and to see to what extent they hold up in an explicit agency model. Specifically, we consider a variety of proposals to restrain government—explicit restraints on taxation, tax competition, increased transparency, and yardstick competition. Modeling the micro-foundations of the political agency problem suggests that the issues can be quite subtle. At the heart of the agency problem are two main effects: discipline and selection. Greater discipline here means reduced levels of rent extraction. Changing the environment in which government operates can affect this. Selection refers to the information revealed to the voters to allow them to throw bad politicians out of office. There is a fundamental trade off between these two—greater discipline makes it harder to tell who the bad guys are. The trade off that this creates is important to appraising the effect of greater restraints on government.

The model is then extended to include public debt. If public debt is observable, then the model and its insights remain unchanged. However, difficulties in observing public debt levels do create a rather different spin on the model. This is discussed in Section 4.6. In Section 4.7, we apply the ideas to whether an NGO is a more efficient provider of public spending. In Section 4.8, we look at what happens if it is fiscal competence that is not observed. Section 4.9 concludes.

4.2 The model

GOVERNMENT AND THE ECONOMY

There are two periods. In each period t, the government must decide on three things—the level of 'valuable' public spending G_t, the level of public spending devoted to private ends s_t, and the level of taxation

x_t. We assume that there is a maximal feasible level of government tax collections in any period, thus $x_t \in [0, X]$.

In each period, the unit cost θ of providing a public good is determined randomly by nature. The cost of the public good is independently and identically distributed in each period, with $\theta \in \{L, H\}, H > L$ and $\Pr(\theta = H) = q$. We denote the realized value in period t by θ_t.

For now we assume that tax collections in each period are constrained to equal total government spending. (We consider government debt in Section 4.6.) The government budget constraint in each period t is

$$x_t = \theta_t G_t + s_t.$$

The representative voter derives utility from public goods, net of the cost of government spending. When the politician provides public goods in the amount G and total spending is x, the welfare of the voter is $W(G, x) = G - \mu C(x)$, where C is a strictly convex, increasing function and μ is an exogenous parameter that indexes the marginal cost of public funds in a simple way.

OPTIMAL POLICY

We take as a benchmark the pattern of taxing and spending that would be picked by a benevolent government which cared only about the voter welfare. In this case there will be no diversion of public resources to private ends, i.e., $s_t = 0$ for $t = 1, 2$. First define

$$G_\theta^*(\mu) = \arg\max\{G - \mu C(\theta G)\} \qquad (4.1)$$

and let $x_\theta^* = \theta G_\theta^*$ with $W^g(\theta, \mu)$ being the level of voter welfare at these optimal levels. Finally, let

$$EW^g(\mu) = qW^g(H, \mu) + (1 - q)W^g(L, \mu).$$

We assume that $X > x_L^*$. The fact that $C'(\cdot)$ is increasing implies that $x_L^* > x_H^*$, i.e., government is optimally larger when the cost of public goods is lower. It is clear that $G_\theta^*(\mu)$ and $W^g(\mu)$ are decreasing in μ—citizens are better off when it is less costly to provide public goods.

POLITICS

We study an agency model of elections with two time periods; in each, the politician in office makes decisions about taxation and government spending. Between periods there is an election in which a voter chooses between the incumbent and a challenger. The cost shock, θ, and the amount of rent diverted for private purposes, s, is privately observed by the politician.

Politicians may be one of two types: 'good' or 'bad'. Thus we label the politician's type by $i \in \{b, g\}$. A good politician simply chooses G and x in each period to maximize voter welfare, and places no value on rents diverted from public spending. In other words, he/she will pick the optimal policy bundle outlined in the previous subsection.

In contrast, a bad politician behaves strategically, choosing policies to maximize the expected, discounted sum of rents $s_1 + \beta \sigma s_2$ extracted from government, where $\beta < 1$ is a discount factor, and σ is the probability of re-election to second term. The determination of the re-election rule is discussed below.

The types $i \in \{g, b\}$ of the first period incumbent and challenger are independent draws from an identical distribution with $\Pr(i = g) = \pi$. The incumbent then observes the first period cost shock θ_1 and chooses public goods provision G_1 and rent diversion s_1. The voter then observes G_1 and government spending x_1 prior to the election at the end of the first period. However, the types of incumbent and challenger, the unit cost θ_1, and the level of rent diversion s_1 are unobserved. In the second period, the politician then in office again chooses G_2, x_2, and s_2 given θ_2. There are no further elections; thus even newly elected challengers are 'lame ducks' in the second period. In casting their votes in the election, therefore, the voter must make an inference about the incumbent's type based on observed performance and compare it to prior beliefs about the type of the challenger.

The interesting issues in the model pertain to incumbent behavior in Period 1 and the determinants of electoral success. In the two-period setting, there are no incentive issues to consider in Period 2.

The Leviathan model of government behavior of Brennan and Buchanan (1980) can be thought of as a special case of this model where $\pi = 0$, i.e. all politicians are known to be bad. In their model, as in this one, there are two kinds of public spending—rents to politicians and spending that voters value. Brennan and Buchanan (1980) assumes that these are produced in fixed proportions from any given tax revenue. However, in this model incumbents can choose how they allocate tax revenues between these ends.

179

4.3 Three scenarios

The model can be used to develop three scenarios for the study of political agency problems. In the first, we suppose that incumbents cannot control the amount of the rent that they extract—bad ones take rent and good ones do not. The only problem for voters is then to pick them out. In the second case, we study moral hazard problems. All politicians are bad and re-election is a reward for limiting rent extraction. In the third case, we study the combined effect of adverse selection and moral hazard. We study the possibility that the bad incumbents mimic the good ones to gain re-election. This has short run advantages in curbing rent-seeking but long-run disadvantages in reducing selection.

The model with adverse selection and moral hazard provides some bridge between the full-blown public choice model and the benevolent government model. The only thing that prevents the benevolent outcome is, therefore, the inability of voters to identify who will behave benevolently (the selection problem).

4.3.1 *Pure adverse selection*

We begin with pure adverse selection. This is defined by a case in which politicians have no ability to influence the amount of rents that they take. Good politicians deliver the outcomes preferred by voters while bad ones extract some predetermined amount. We assume that G is fixed at some commonly known level $\overline{G}$. While this model is not at all realistic, it will serve to initiate a discussion of selection problems that will be useful in the ensuing discussion and analysis.

If the levels of public spending chosen by the different types of politicians perfectly revealed their type, then pure adverse selection would be uninteresting. Hence, we assume that a bad politician extracts rents equal to $s = (H - L)\overline{G}$.[3] Obviously this is a very specific assumption. However, it is the simplest way, in a two state model, for there to be one state of the world in which voters are unsure whether their incumbent is good or bad after they have seen the policy outcome. If they observe that public spending is $H\overline{G}$, they are uncertain

---

[3] As we will see below, this level of rent has siginificance even in a model where rents and public spending can be chosen endogenously.

whether it is a good incumbent who has received a cost shock of H or a bad one who has received a cost shock of L.

We can now compute the voting rule used by voters according to Bayes rule. It is clear that since G is fixed at $\overline{G}$, voting depends exclusively on the level of taxation. Given our assumptions, $x \in \{L\overline{G}, H\overline{G}, (2H-L)\overline{G}\}$, two of these tax levels perfectly reveal the incumbent's type. An incumbent that chooses $L\overline{G}$ must be good and one that chooses $(2H - L)\overline{G}$ must be bad. The key question is what inference the voters make when they see $H\overline{G}$. Using Bayes rule, the probability that the politician is good is conditional on seeing $H\overline{G}$ is

$$\frac{q\pi}{q\pi + (1 - q)(1 - \pi)}.$$

To decide whether or not to re-elect the incumbent, they compare this with π, the probability that a randomly selected challenger is good.

It is easy to check that this is greater than π if $q > \frac{1}{2}$. Then re-election is a good idea—it is more likely that the state is H than otherwise and the incumbent is given the benefit of the doubt. If $q < \frac{1}{2}$, then it is always a good idea to remove an incumbent who chooses $H\overline{G}$ even though this will lead to some good incumbents being removed from office. We summarize this as:

Proposition 1: *Under pure adverse selection, there are two possibilities:*

(i) *If $q \geq \frac{1}{2}$, then politicians are re-elected if they set taxes of $L\overline{G}$ or $H\overline{G}$—all good politicians and some bad politicians are re-elected,*

(ii) *If $q < \frac{1}{2}$, then politicians are re-elected only if they set taxes of $L\overline{G}$—all bad politicians are thrown out of office along with some good ones.*

A couple of features of this outcome are worth noting. First, voter behavior does not depend on the distribution of politicians in the population but purely on the likelihood of the state in which good and bad politicians are confused—specifically the likelihood ratio $\frac{q}{(1-q)}$. The model also provides a simple justification for voters being more likely to remove incumbents from office when they charge higher tax rates—which is consistent with both folk wisdom and empirical evidence. We discuss this in greater detail below.

It is clear that under adverse selection voters benefit from having better quality incumbent pools (higher π) and more information about the true state of the world on which they condition their voting decisions. The pure adverse selection model yields some stark insights. However, the idea that incumbents cannot make real choices which affect voters' perception of them is too strong. We now consider models which relax this.

4.3.2 *Pure moral hazard*

As we discussed in the last chapter, the case of pure moral hazard was the subject of the 'first generation' political agency models of Barro (1973) and Ferejohn (1986). We now show how this case can be studied in the framework introduced here.

Suppose then that the type of every politician is known to be bad so that they care primarily about rent extraction with voter welfare as a secondary concern. We allow both G and s to be chosen and assume that only G and x are observable. Voters need make no inference on the incumbent's type. The role of voting is purely to achieve some level of discipline—rewarding politicians for delivering something closer to what voters would like (in this context, lower rent-seeking). We therefore consider a game in which the voter may announce—and commit to—an incentive based re-election rule prior to the incumbent's first period policy being chosen. Let the re-election rule used by voters be denoted by a function $\sigma(G, x)$. Then for fixed G, the incumbent's rent extraction problem is to choose rent diversion in Periods 1 and 2 denoted by (s_1, s_2) to maximize $s_1 + \beta \sigma(G, \theta G + s_1) s_2$.

In Period 2, there are no re-election incentives to restrain rent-seeking and every politician will choose $s_2 = X$. In Period 1, the incumbent can be rewarded for reducing his/her rent-seeking. Voters reason as follows: since incumbents can always extract X today and forego re-election, then they must be offered an incentive to prevent them from doing so. Since all they care about are rents, they are indifferent between all packages which yield them X. Hence, consider the threshold level of rent, $\widehat{s}(\sigma)$, which satisfies

$$\widehat{s}(\sigma) + \sigma \beta X = X.$$

As long as the level of 'permissible' rent satisfies this, the incumbent will choose $\widehat{s}(\sigma)$ and get re-elected with probability σ. However, since the level of Period 1 rent-seeking that satisfies this incentive constraint is decreasing in σ, it is best for voters to set $\sigma = 1$. In the language of the principal—agent literature, we may therefore think of the condition $s_1 \geq (1 - \beta)X$ as the 'participation constraint' that must be satisfied to insure that the incumbent produces the level of public spending desired by voters for each cost level $\theta = L, H$.[4]

The pure moral hazard model is consistent with a term limit effect in politicians' choices of the kind found by Besley and Case (1995b). However, given the choice in reality between a challenger who can serve an extra term in office and an incumbent who will be a lame duck, the model cannot explain why the voters would ever prefer a lame duck.

The model predicts that rent taking is lower by βX when politicians face re-election incentives. The more patient are politicians, the larger the rent improvement for voters. The level of public spending is higher in the first period than the second and the level of taxation is X in Period 2 and less than X in Period 1.

Even though information about θ is imperfect, it is revealed to voters in equilibrium via the choice of G. This is because politicians do not care intrinsically about θ—it does not affect the amount of rent that they can extract.

The model also makes voters indifferent about electing any politician in Period 2. There are no types in the model that make voters intrinsically prefer one kind of politician over another. This is because the model makes the most pessimistic assumptions about the political class—all are out to serve themselves.

Finally, even the pure moral hazard model is more optimistic about the prospects for electoral competition compared with the Leviathan model of Brennan and Buchanan (1980). The promise of future office can restrain rent-seeking.

We now wish to determine the levels of spending and taxes (G_θ, x_θ) that the voter will require from the incumbent in exchange for re-election. This is a 'mechanism design' problem, which involves some technicalities not relevant to most of the material in this chapter. We therefore provide an informal discussion of the problem here, and a more complete treatment in an Appendix to the chapter.

Consider first the case of the high cost level. The incumbent is willing to supply any fiscal policy (G_H, x_H) that satisfies the participation constraint

$$s_H \equiv x_H - HG_H = (1 - \beta)X$$

---

[4] In this section, we ignore mixed strategy mechanisms by voters and incumbents.

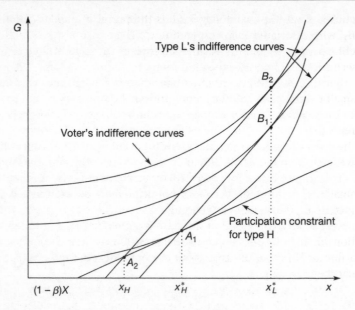

Figure 4.1 Optimal spending with bad politicians

If the cost level were known to the voter, the problem would then be merely to maximize voter welfare $G_H - \mu C(x_H)$ subject to this constraint. This 'first best' choice is depicted in Figure 4.1, as the point of tangency A_1 between the participation constraint for type H, which has slope $1/H$, and an indifference curve for the voter, with a tax level x_H^*. (Observe that voter welfare is increasing in the 'northwesterly' direction in the diagram, while the politician's rents are increasing in the 'southeasterly' direction.)

Figure 4.1 also shows the difficulty with this outcome: if true cost is unobserved by the voter, an incumbent who faces cost $\theta = L$ must be deterred from implementing the high cost fiscal package (G_H, x_H) and obtaining additional rents equal to the true cost difference $(H-L)G_H$. In other words, fiscal policies must also respect an incentive constraint for the low cost type

$$s_L \geq (1 - \beta)X + (H - L)G_H$$

In Figure 4.1, the indifference curves for type L are the straight lines with steeper slope $1/L$. If the first best spending point A_1 for H were

184

chosen, then the best policy for L is the point of tangency labelled B_1, with associated level of spending x_L^*. The L incumbent is indifferent between A_1 and B_1, but the latter gives the voter strictly higher welfare.

But the voter can do strictly better than this outcome. Consider a small reduction in spending along the participation constraint for H, to the point labelled A_2. Since G_H is now smaller, so is the level of rents that L may obtain. The incentive constraint for L is relaxed, and the voter can insist on higher spending from type L, yielding higher welfare (the point labelled B_2).[5]

This model therefore suggests why agency problems may lead to smaller government. Even if all politicians are known to have bad incentives, restrictions on government spending impose limits on the rents politicians can extract through 'cost padding'. The formal solution to this problem, given in the Appendix to this chapter, yields a number of other insights about the optimal levels of spending. In particular, we find:

Proposition 2: *The voter's preferred incentive compatible spending level x_H is smaller:*

1. *When L is smaller;*
2. *When the voter's beliefs about costs are more optimistic (q is lower).*

Thus the proposition states, somewhat counterintuitively, that a reduction in true costs induces a *reduction* in government spending. Thus, reductions in the cost of government services may actually lead to further restrictions on government spending, as they worsen the potential agency problems created by bad politicians.

4.3.3 *Combining moral hazard and adverse selection*

As in Chapter 3, we now have two roles for elections—(i) selecting good politicians as in the adverse selection case and (ii) providing incentives to reduce rent-seeking as in the moral hazard case. The model defines a game of incomplete information between the incumbent politician and the representative voter. We seek to characterize perfect Bayesian equilibria of this game. As usual, the game is most easily solved by applying a type of backward induction. In the second

[5] As voter welfare is quasilinear with respect to G, the equilibrium tax level is the same regardless of the equilibrium level of rent extraction.

period, the politician in office faces no further possibility of electoral discipline. Thus $s_2 = X$ for $i = b$ (bad politicians take maximal rents) while $s_2 = 0$ for $i = g$.

Given that second period strategies are identical for challenger and incumbent, the sequentially rational voting rule for the voter is to re-elect the incumbent if the posterior probability the incumbent is the good type exceeds the prior probability π that the challenger is good. The voter's posterior beliefs depend in turn on the equilibrium strategy of the first period incumbent. Since the good type cares only about voter welfare in the current period, he/she chooses (G_H^*, x_H^*) with probability q and (G_L^*, x_L^*) with probability $1 - q$. It follows that, in any perfect Bayesian equilibrium, the voter's posterior beliefs assign probability zero to the good type at any other information set (G, x). To economize on notation, we therefore write posterior beliefs as a function $\Pr(g|x)$ of first period spending alone.[6]

We confine attention to three possible strategies for the bad incumbent, each associated with one of the three spending levels (x_L^*, x_H^*, X) that are observed with positive probability along the equilibrium path. First, b might choose $s_1 = 0$ or $s_1 = X$. Since future rents are discounted ($\beta < 1$), however, the latter strategy dominates the former.[7] Thus:

$$\Pr(g|x_L^*) = 1$$

in any equilibrium, and the voter always re-elects when first period spending is x_L^*. Beliefs conditional on observing x_H^* are more complicated. A bad politician who faces low true costs may, instead of taking maximal rents, choose to produce G_H^* units of the public good and spend x_H^*, diverting $\hat{s}(\mu) \equiv (H - L)G_H^*(\mu)$ to private rent consumption. This strategy allows type (b, L) to 'pool' with type (g, H), and doing so may be desirable if it brings a positive probability of re-election. Accordingly, let

$$\lambda = \Pr(x = x_H^* | \theta = L, i = b)$$

denote the probability type (b, L) exercises restraint in this sense, and let σ denote the probability of re-election when the voter observes x_H^*.

---

[6] The voters' beliefs are not restricted by Bayes's rule at nodes not reached in equilibrium. Since the good type's actions are pinned down by our preference assumption, we impose the minimal restriction on out of equilibrium beliefs that $\Pr(g|x) = 0$ if $(G, x) \neq (G_\theta^*, x_\theta^*)$ for $\theta \in \{L, H\}$. At any such information set, the voter would elect the challenger in the second period.

[7] Regardless of true costs, $s_1 = 0$ yields a payoff to the bad type of βX if re-elected and zero otherwise, while $s_1 = X$ pays $(1 + \beta)X$ if re-elected and X otherwise.

The posterior probability that spending x_H^* was generated by a good politician is

$$\Pr(g|x_H) = \frac{\pi q}{\pi q + (1 - \pi)(1 - q)\lambda}$$

A best response for the voter is to re-elect with positive probability ($\sigma > 0$) only if $\Pr(g|x_H) \geq \pi$ or, equivalently, $\lambda \leq q/(1 - q)$. If the inequality is strict, then $\sigma = 1$. Further, type (b, L) prefers to exercise restraint instead of diverting maximal rents ($\lambda > 0$), only if $\hat{s}(\mu) + \beta \sigma X \geq X$. When this inequality is strict, then $\lambda = 1$.

Collecting these observations, there are three possible equilibrium configurations. First, the equilibrium may be *pooling*, as type (b, L) chooses $s_1 = \hat{s}(\mu)$ and so is indistinguishable from type (g, H). Second, the equilibrium may be *separating*, as type (b, L) chooses $s_1 = X$ and is revealed *ex post*. Third, the equilibrium may be a *hybrid* one, in which type $(b\ L)$, adopts a strictly mixed strategy on actions $s_1 = \hat{s}(\mu)$ and $s_1 = X$, so that type is revealed with positive probability strictly less than one. The following result fully characterizes the possible configurations.

Proposition 3: *An equilibrium exists for all values of parameters and is generically unique.*

1. *A pooling equilibrium, with $\lambda = \sigma = 1$, exists if and only if*

$$q \geq \frac{1}{2} \quad \& \quad \hat{s}(\mu) \geq (1 - \beta)X$$

2. *A hybrid equilibrium, with $\lambda = q/(1 - q)$ and $\sigma = (X - \hat{s}(\mu))/(\beta X)$, exists if and only if*

$$q < \frac{1}{2} \quad \& \quad \hat{s}(\mu) \geq (1 - \beta)X$$

3. *A separating equilibrium, with $\lambda = 0$ and $\sigma = 1$, exists if and only if*

$$\hat{s}(\mu) \leq (1 - \beta)X$$

For a formal proof of this, the reader is referred to Besley and Smart (2007). Thus, there are three possible kinds of equilibria. In the separating equilibrium, the bad politician takes maximal rents and is detected with certainty and replaced by the challenger. This equilibrium outcome is therefore equivalent to that which would be obtained if voters could observe the cost shock directly. In the pooling and hybrid equilibria, the incumbent is taking less than maximal rents and his/her type is revealed with lower probability.[8] The latter is most likely when $\hat{s}(\mu)$ is high and the incumbent discounts the future heavily so that he/she prizes rents earned in Period 1.

The result has features of the adverse selection and moral hazard models. Like the adverse selection model, there is some possibility that a bad incumbent is re-elected. In the pooling and separating equilibria, there is no chance that a good incumbent is removed from office—it is always optimal to re-elect any incumbent who chooses x_H^*. In line with the moral hazard model, the incumbent also restrains his/her rent-seeking endogenously to get re-elected. However, this is incomplete—when the cost shock is H there is no restraint. This arises because (unlike the pure moral hazard model) the voters are not indifferent between a bad incumbent and a challenger because of the existence of good politicians in the pool of potential politicians. The model also predicts that, even if they exercise restraint, bad incumbents choose a higher level of rents than under pure moral hazard when they face the cost shock H.[9]

4.4 Implications

In this section, we draw out some positive and normative implications of the equilibrium described in Proposition 3.

We begin with some normative implications. We first look at how selection and incentive effects combine to determine voter welfare. We also look at how the model predicts the case for government intervention in the economy as circumscribed by the agency costs implied in the political equilibrium. We also look at the implications of having only a few good politicians available to voters and whether this can be worse than having only bad politicians.

For positive implications, we look first at how the model links taxes, spending, and political turnover. We then look at what the agency model predicts about the existence of fiscal cycles.

---

[8] In the pooling equilibrium, the outcome is similar to that assumed in the Leviathan model where rents are assumed to be positively related to the amount of 'legitimate' public spending.

[9] For bad incumbents with cost shock L, the level of rents may not be higher—it depends on how much the high-cost fiscal policy is distorted under the pure moral hazard model.

4.4.1 *Equilibrium voter welfare*

To understand how the electoral process affects political decision making in the model, it is useful to calculate expected voter welfare in equilibrium. As a benchmark for the analysis, suppose that politicians are removed from office each period with certainty. Expected voter welfare when type g is in office would then be $EW^g(\mu) = qW^g(H, \mu) + (1 - q)W^g(L, \mu)$, whereas welfare with b in office would simply be $W^b(\mu) = -\mu C(X)$, since 'lame-duck' bad politicians divert maximal rents. To simplify notation, let $W^0(\mu) = \pi EW^g(\mu) + (1 - \pi)W^b(\mu)$ be the unconditional expected per period welfare in this case. It follows that the present value of expected welfare is just $(1 + \beta)W^0(\mu)$ when there is no chance of re-election.

Equilibrium welfare in the equilibrium described in Proposition 3 can be written as

$$EW(\lambda, \sigma, \mu) = (1 + \beta)W^0(\mu) + (1 - \pi)(1 - q)\lambda\Delta(\mu) + \beta(\pi_2 - \pi)\Sigma(\mu) \tag{4.2}$$

where:

$$\Delta(\mu) = W^g(H, \mu) - W^b(\mu) \tag{4.3}$$

$$\Sigma(\mu) = EW^g(\mu) - W^b(\mu) \tag{4.4}$$

and

$$\pi_2 - \pi = \pi(1 - \pi)[q\sigma + (1 - q)(1 - \sigma\lambda)]. \tag{4.5}$$

Equation (4.2) has a simple interpretation, as the last two terms represent the deviation from welfare in the absence of re-election possibilities. The term $\Delta(\mu)$ is the discipline effect induced by re-election possibilities—the fact that bad incumbents restrain rent seeking—while $\Sigma(\mu)$ represents selection—the fact that elections improve the quality of Period 2 policy by weeding out bad incumbents. Multiplying each effect is the probability that the relevant events occur and these benefits of elections are reaped. With probability $(1 - \pi)(1 - q)\lambda$, the first period bad incumbent chooses to produce G_H^* of the public good and divert rents $\hat{s}(\mu)$ instead of X, resulting in the welfare gain from 'discipline'. The expression $\pi_2 - \pi$ is in turn the increased confidence that the Period 2 incumbent is good.[10]

---

[10] This is similar to the expression $\Pi - \pi$ in Chapter 3.

Political agency and public finance

In summary, the possibility of re-electing incumbents can increase voter welfare both by improving average quality of office-holders (the 'selection effect') and by offering prospective incentives for low quality incumbents (the 'discipline effect'). To understand the impact of changes in the fiscal regime, the effects on selection and incentives in elections must be understood. This in turn requires understanding how equilibrium political behavior (as represented by λ and σ) is affected.

Differentiating (4.2) with respect to λ yields:[11]

$$\frac{\partial EW(\lambda, \sigma, \mu)}{\partial \lambda} = (1 - q)(1 - \pi)[\Delta(\mu) - \beta \pi \sigma \Sigma(\mu)]. \qquad (4.6)$$

The sign of this depends on the magnitude of the discipline effect $(\Delta(\mu))$ and the selection effect $(\Sigma(\mu))$. A higher λ (more discipline) is good for voters if $\Delta(\mu) > \beta \pi \Sigma(\mu)$.

The formula in (4.2) also gives a precise characterization of agency costs in government. This gives a criterion for government to intervene in the economy which is more conservative than that which is studied by the standard public economics model. As a point of comparison, we take an extreme case where the government does not intervene at all and sets $G = x = 0$. Below, in Section 4.5, we consider more subtle possibilities that restrain government rather than closing it down completely.

A purely benevolent view of government would see the case for intervention in terms of optimal citizen welfare under government intervention. In this case, government is worthwhile if and only if $(1 + \beta)EW^g(\mu) > 0$. A welfare economist operating in a world of benevolent government would advocate this case for government.

The agency model suggests that this is too optimistic. However, the identification of specific agency costs makes this more conservative case for government more precise. For the sake of illustration suppose that the equilibrium being played is separating so that $\sigma = 1$ and

---

[11] Some care is needed in interpreting this heuristic argument. As we have seen, λ is an equilibrium outcome. To have a larger λ, we need to have a lower X, a higher β, a lower μ, a higher H, and a lower L. But a change in these parameters also affects the voter welfare. For example, if λ goes up by lowering X, then the condition for more discipline being better will be weaker than $\Delta(\mu) > \beta \pi \Sigma(\mu)$ because a reduction in X also mitigates the negative effect of re-electing a pooling bad incumbent.

$\lambda = 0$. Then, welfare in the political equilibrium is:

$$(1 + \beta)EW^g(\mu) - [EW^g(\mu) - W^b(\mu)](1 - \pi)(1 + \beta(1 - \pi)). \quad (4.7)$$

The second term in this expression (which is proportional to $(1 - \pi)$) represents the agency cost of running the government. The higher is the cost, the greater is the difference between having a good and bad politician in office. This gives an exact sense of why a political economy approach is less sanguine about the case for government. The criterion $(1 + \beta)EW^g(\mu) > 0$ is too optimistic.

The above expression gives precise content to the public choice critique of welfare economics in this context.[12] This way of thinking is reminiscent of the analysis of Acemoglu and Verdier (2000) which looks at how imperfections in the policy process can militate against government intervention. It gives sense to the idea that failures of government (here due to the existence of rent-seeking politicians and imperfect information) should be weighed up against the positive case for government. This could be thought of in terms of the market failure that underpins the case for having government spending on G in the first place.

The expression in (4.7) also shows how the model that we have laid out here can be thought of as lying between the pure public choice view and the standard benevolent government view. If π tends to one, there are only benevolent politicians and the agency cost goes to zero leaving us with the standard welfare economic criterion for government. As π gets close to zero, then the expression gets close to $(1 + \beta)W^b(\mu) = -(1 + \beta)\mu C(X) < 0$ and it is not worthwhile to have the government. Thus, having the government function depends in a discernible way on the size of agency costs and on whether government operates closer to the benevolent or public choice model.

4.4.2 Are good politicians necessarily good for voters?

Comparing the models in Sections 4.3.2 and 4.3.3, it is interesting to contrast the outcomes in which there are a few good politicians with those that would be obtained were all politicians bad. We will observe in this case that things could actually be better if all politicians were bad. To this end, we will contrast welfare in the pure moral hazard case and that where there is some fraction of good politicians.

---

[12] See Besley and Coate (2003) for a model of the public choice critique.

In both cases, all bad politicians will extract maximal Period 2 rents. However, if there is *any* chance that a good politician will be found, then having some good politicians is clearly better for voters. Now consider Period 1. The bad politician under pure moral hazard takes rents of $(1 - \beta)X$ for sure in Period 1. Suppose that the equilibrium in the combined moral hazard/adverse selection model is separating so that $\lambda = 0$ and $\sigma = 1$. Then the Period 1 rent will be X if there is a bad incumbent and zero if there is a good one. It is now easy to see that the pure moral hazard case can be better.

Voter welfare under pure moral hazard is:

$$q\left[\frac{x_H}{H} - \mu C(x_H)\right] + (1-q)W_L^g - \frac{\hat{s}}{H} - (1-q)\frac{H-L}{HL}x_H + \beta EW^b.$$

where $\psi = q/H + (1 - q)/L$, while under moral hazard and adverse selection, it is (re-writing (4.7)):

$$(1 + \beta)W^b(\mu) + \pi(1 + \beta(2 - \pi))[EW^g(\mu) - W^b(\mu)]$$

in the case of a separating equilibrium. It is now easy to see that, for small enough π, welfare is higher under pure moral hazard. It is also clear that as π tends to one, welfare is unambiguously higher when there is both moral hazard and adverse selection.[13]

This may seem paradoxical. However, the reasoning behind it is clear after a little thought. Once there are good politicians in the population, they create a benchmark against which bad politicians are measured when they seek re-election. Proposition 3 tells us that it is worthwhile to mimic the good types when there is sufficient rent for doing so available to the bad types. Otherwise, they would prefer to take X. Thus, the good types create an externality which affects the bad type's behavior. However if good types are not very numerous, they have a negligible direct effect on the voters' payoffs. Thus, voters are worse off if there are just a few good types in the population.

Another way to look at this is in terms of the voters' ability to commit. With pure moral hazard, voters are indifferent (ex post) between

---

[13] In the case of a pooling equilibrium, the above expression becomes

$$(1 + \beta)W^b(\mu) + \pi(1 + \beta + \beta(1 - \pi)q)[EW^g(\mu) - W^b(\mu)] + (1 - \pi)(1 - q)[W^g(H, \mu) - W^b(\mu)].$$

So for small enough π, welfare under pure moral hazard is very likely to be higher because $W^g(H, \mu)$ is smaller than $EW^g(\mu)$ and because $\psi(1 - \beta)X$ is small due to the condition for a pooling equilibrium. So the same logic basically applies when we compare to a pooling equilibrium.

voting for the incumbent and a randomly selected challenger. Hence, they can pick a standard for incumbents to meet that creates the best possible incentives for incumbents to reduce their rent extraction. Voters cannot commit to this voting rule, however, when the incumbent could be a good type even though they would prefer to commit to the voting rule that is used under moral hazard.

This finding suggests that the pure moral hazard model is rather fragile to a small variation in the model to include some good types of politicians. This is because the strict indifference rule that underpins incentives in that case allows the voters to commit. Once this indifference is broken, then there is actually a constraint on optimal voting strategies which can make things worse.

4.4.3 *Turnover of politicians*

As we discussed in Chapter 3, one of the distinctive features of the political agency model is how it links turnover rates among politicians and government policy. Given the particular economic concerns being studied here, this refers to links between taxes, public spending, and voting behavior. The model can underpin the empirical prediction that higher taxes are bad for re-election chances and can also look at the link between public spending and political turnover.

Using Proposition 3, the model predicts that the retention rate of a randomly selected first period politician is:

$$f(\lambda, \sigma) = 1 - [\pi q(1 - \sigma) + (1 - \pi)(q + (1 - q)(1 - \lambda\sigma))].$$

It is straightforward to verify that the retention rate is increasing in λ and σ.

Empirically, the interesting issue is not how turnover relates to λ and σ since these equilibrium strategies are not observable. Instead, the data come in the form of observations about x and G and how these relate to whether politicians are re-elected. To tease out these empirical implications turns out to be a little complicated since the probability of re-election depends on two variables: total taxation and the amount of valuable public spending undertaken. To summarize the result implied by Proposition 3:

$$\sigma(x_L^*, G_L^*) = 1, \sigma(x_H^*, G_H^*) \in [0, 1], \text{and } \sigma(X, 0) = 0. \qquad (4.8)$$

There is one clear cut prediction—a politician who provides more valuable public spending is always good for re-election chances.

This is rather obvious as higher public spending is always brought forth by good incumbents. In practice, however, testing this would require being able to separate expenditure items into their G and s components which cannot easily be done.

Thus, the more interesting empirical prediction links total taxation with re-election prospects. However, as is plain from (4.8), there is a potential non-monotonicity in the relationship between taxes and re-election if $\sigma(x_H^*, G_H^*) < 1$ since $x_H^* < x_L^*$. This is because the state in which good politicians differentiate themselves from bad ones is when the cost of providing public goods is low ($\theta = L$). The low spending state can be consistent with bad politicians extracting some rent and masquerading as good politicians.

In either a pooling or separating equilibrium, retention probability is constant for low levels of spending—incumbents are re-elected for sure when $x = x_L^*$ or x_H^*. However, for all levels of taxation above x_L^*, the incumbent is removed from office.

In a hybrid equilibrium, $\sigma(x_H^*, G_H^*) = (S - \hat{s}(\mu))/(\beta S) < 1$. In this case, there is a non-monotonicity and while high tax incumbents are still thrown out for sure, the middle range (those who pick x_L^*) are retained more often than those who pick low total taxes x_H^*.

This model gives a more direct underpinning for the empirical results on US governors that we discussed in Chapter 3. There we looked at patterns of taxation and spending and the way in which they drove re-election chances and were subject to term limit effects. The results on re-election as a function of taxes are consistent with this model.

4.4.4 *The spending cycle*

Political agency models predict a spending cycle depending on whether or not politicians are able to stand for re-election. In the current model this comes out only in the comparison between first and second period taxation decisions. It is straightforward to study this in the model. We will show that the sign of the electoral cycle—comparing two incumbents who can and cannot run again—is ambiguous. It depends on the balance of the discipline and selection effects.

Consider, first of all, the difference between the tax policy of second period (term limited) and first period (non-term-limited) incumbent. In a separating equilibrium, expected Period 1 expenditures are:

$$Ex_1 = \pi(qx_H^* + (1-q)x_L^*) + (1-\pi)X$$

while expected Period 2 taxes are:

$$Ex_2 = (\pi + (1 - \pi)\pi)(qx_H^* + (1 - q)x_L^*) + (1 - \pi)^2 X.$$

Comparing the two yields:

$$Ex_1 - Ex_2 = (1 - \pi)\pi(X - (qx_H^* + (1 - q)x_L^*)) > 0.$$

The effect of selection is to reduce the number of bad incumbents and hence to reduce the average level of taxation between the first and second periods of office.

Now we look at what happens in the case of pooling. Using the result in Proposition 3, we have that Period 1 expected taxes are:

$$Ex_1 = \pi(qx_H^* + (1 - q)x_L^*) + (1 - \pi)[(1 - q)x_H^* + qX].$$

In Period 2, expected taxes are:

$$Ex_2 = \pi[1 + (1 - \pi)q](qx_H^* + (1 - q)x_L^*) + (1 - \pi)(1 - q\pi)X.$$

For low enough x_H^* (assuming that the conditions for the equilibrium to be pooling continue to hold), then it is possible to have Period 1 expected taxes being below Period 2 expected taxes.[14] In effect, this is because the gain from having a bad politician exercise discipline in Period 1 is large. This is consistent with the results of Besley and Case (1995b) and the empirical results that we presented in Chapter 3—governors who face a binding term limit seem to spend and tax more.[15]

Even though the sign of the electoral taxation cycle is ambiguous and hence an empirical question, its existence is not. It is central to the agency model that political agents will behave differently depending on whether they face the prospect of being re-elected.

4.5 Restraining government

Advocating methods to restrain government as a means to raising voter welfare is a staple prescription of the public choice approach

[14] It is also straightforward to show that as x_H^* gets close to x_L^*, Period 1 expected taxes are higher than those in Period 2 as the selection effect now dominates.

[15] Taken literally, this empirical result would suggest that, in US states, the equilibrium is not the separating one implying that $\hat{s}(\mu) > (1 - \beta)X$.

to public finance. It has been hugely influential in the policy sphere as well as in the classroom. In a nutshell, the idea is that voters are unable to control the taxing and spending proclivities of incumbent politicians and hence would benefit by developing institutions and constitutional rules that will restrain government further in addition to elections.

In this section, we explore these arguments in the framework developed above. We will exploit the fact that our political economy model has micro-foundations to see how various parameters that affect the workings of the political process impact on policy outcomes.

One general lesson that emerges is that incentives should be thought about in a second-best framework in which the core incentive mechanism is the (highly imperfect) electoral mechanism. In cases where this has no power in achieving improved discipline or better selection of politicians, then the extra-electoral restraints advocated by public choice economists are the only sources of restraint and it is fairly easy to see their implications. At the other extreme, if there are sufficient institutions to completely determine the outcome that voters want, then further incremental constraints have no value. This analysis operates in the middle ground where electoral incentives have some incomplete ability to discipline and select incumbents. Any extra restraints must then be viewed in this kind of second-best context and can have more subtle effects.

We divide our discussion of restraints on government into two parts. We first consider direct restraints—imposing limits on taxing and spending. We then consider a set of more indirect restraints which might serve to make politics work better. We specifically look at measures to increase the cost of taxation. In practice, these come in a variety of forms. One of them is by introducing restrictions on tax bases and tax rates. In the US, these have often been implemented though direct democracy, i.e. citizens' initiatives. Increasing the intensity of tax competition is also a means of raising the marginal cost of public funds.[16] A second class of indirect measures work through increasing the amount of information available to voters. There are two main

---

[16] There is a huge literature on the economics of tax competition surveyed in Wilson (1999). The main focus has been on implications of increased mobility of goods and services for tax setting by governments. The literature shows that allowing competitive determination of taxes will lead to externalities that skew taxes towards immobile factors such as labor and away from mobile factors such as capital. These negative externalities between competing governments lead to an increase in the marginal cost of public funds.

possible sources of this: improvements in budgetary transparency and greater use of yardstick comparisons of politicians.

Measures to restrain the size of government are important in practice. For example, many states in the US have passed restrictions on taxing and spending. These fall into three broad categories: (i) indexed limits on the growth of revenues or expenditures, for example, to the population growth rate; (ii) requirements that voters approve all new taxes; and (iii) supermajority requirements that require anywhere between three-fifths and three-quarters of the legislature to approve tax increases. There are 24 states with indexed limits, 13 of which allow an override with a supermajority vote. Five of these states require a simple majority if the governor has declared a state of emergency. Half the states with indexed limits restrict the growth in state expenditures to the growth rate in personal income averaged over some previous period. Five others restrict the size of appropriations to a specified percentage of state income, while four others restrict growth to an index of population growth and inflation. Three other states restrict the absolute expenditure growth rate. Spending on capital projects is excluded, as are federally funded projects. Half of the limits in place are constitutional, with the remainder being statutory.[17] Most tax and expenditure limitations were introduced in the 1970s, which many believe reflected a general disillusionment with government and a view that spending was out of tune with what a majority of voters preferred. While the institutional detail may be complex, the thrust of such rules is to diminish the discretion that politicians enjoy.

Many tax and expenditure limitations were the result of citizen power exercised through citizens' initiatives. The latter are constitutional rules that allow citizens to place legislation directly on the ballot. At the present time, 23 US states permit an initiative process whereby citizens can place ballot propositions, which are voted on subsequently. Tax and expenditure initiatives are a large fraction of those that are brought.[18] Perhaps the best known example is Proposition 13, passed in California in 1978, which restricted property tax increases for current residents.

---

[17] See Rueben (2000) for a useful overview of the history and content of limitations in category (i) above.
[18] For existing theoretical treatments of initiatives, see Gerber (1996) and Besley and Coate (2001).

Political agency and public finance

The theoretical approach to initiatives suggested by Denzau et al. (1981) is explicitly premised on the idea that they are a discipline device on politicians who do not act as faithful servants of the people. Thus, they stem from a view that the electoral process is insufficient to provide a check on such behavior. There is a good deal of empirical analysis in this spirit. Zax (1989) investigates how access to initiatives affects state expenditures per capita, in a cross-section of 50 states for 1980. Contrary to the idea that initiatives promote smaller government, he finds that state spending is significantly *higher* in states that permit direct statutory initiatives.[19] Farnham (1990) estimates the cross-sectional effect of citizens' initiatives and referenda using data on 735 communities, taking the log of community expenditures as the dependent variable, finding little or no evidence that access to the initiative is important. Matsusaka (1995) regresses government expenditures and revenues in 49 states (Alaska is excluded) on a number of control variables for a panel of states sampled over a 30-year period at 5-year intervals from 1960 to 1990. His main finding is a strong negative effect on expenditures of access to the initiative. He also finds some evidence that the effect is strongest where the signature requirement to hold an initiative is low.[20] This is in tune with the idea that initiatives may have a role to play in reducing agency problems that result in the state being too large.

These findings are consistent with empirical evidence of Knight (2000) and Rueben (2000) which show that tax and expenditure limitations tend to reduce government spending with the presence of citizens' initiatives being used as an instrument to control for the potential endogeneity of such limitations.

Apart from work on the United States, there is extensive work on the consequences of direct democracy in Switzerland. Feld and Kirchgässner (2000) provide an excellent overview of studies that use the cross-canton variation in direct democracy to identify its effects. In similar spirit to the US findings, they argue that the weight of studies find that public expenditure and pubic debt are lower in cantons that make greater use of direct democracy. However, unlike the evidence

[19] This may, of course, be suggestive of reverse causality—states with higher spending also tend to have citizens' initiatives.

[20] To table an initiative requires a minimum number of voters to support it. A low threshold is a situation where this minimum number is low making it easier to get an initiative on the ballot.

above, iniatives are not used to place direct restrictions on politicians. They argue that the mechanism at work is through increasing the supply of information that voters have about policy issues. Thus, their interpretation of the role of iniatives fits better with the discussion of information provision to voters which we discuss below.

However, finding that limitations reduce spending allows us to draw no welfare conclusions. The effect of such limitations may drive out public spending that voters like rather than reducing rent-seeking. Indeed this is bound to be the case when all politicians are good. Hence, the balanced likelihood of good politicians in office will likely be a key factor in determining whether such limitations are valuable.

4.5.1 *A direct restraint on the size of government*

Suppose that the government creates a constitutional restriction on the size of government which lowers X, the maximum tax level that the government can levy. This has the direct advantage of reducing the rent that a bad politician can extract and hence improves voter welfare (assuming that the limitation does not distort the behavior of good politicians). Thus, its direct consequences for voters is favorable: *a tax limitation that leaves the behavior of the good politicians unaltered and does not change the political equilibrium is welfare improving for the voters.*[21]

However, to understand its impact fully, we also need to understand how it affects the political equilibrium. This depends on the balance of discipline and selection effects. Proposition 3 makes clear why lowering X increases the incentive of incumbents to pool, and so to make the political equilibrium less informative. This suggests that a tax limitation will be attractive when selection is less important than discipline. Referring to equation (4.6), this happens when $\beta\pi\Sigma(\mu) < \Delta(\mu)$.[22] Thus, a tax limitation is more likely to be desirable when there is a predominance of self-interested politicians—when π is small. This is in line with the traditional public choice view about the value of tax limitations.

[21] Here we consider only the case where the maximum spending level X remains high enough to leave the behavior of good politicians unchanged.
[22] As pointed out in our discussion of equation (6), this condition is not exact. A change in X also affects $\Sigma(\mu)$ and $\Delta(\mu)$ through $W^b(\mu) = -\mu C(X)$.

Thus, we have:

Proposition 4: (Besley and Smart (2007)) *Suppose that a limit is imposed on the size of government (as measured by X). Then there exists a $\hat{\pi}$ such that voter welfare increases if $\pi < \hat{\pi}$.*

For high values of π, the result may go the other way if it shifts the political equilibrium towards a pooling outcome, since the importance of selection may dominate.

4.5.2 *Indirect restraints*

We now discuss other ways of restraining government that work less directly. We begin by studying the argument that allowing taxes to be collected in a more inefficient manner can actually be good for voters. This argument has been around in various guises. For example, Becker and Mulligan (2003) consider how changing the efficiency of the tax system alters the resources devoted to political influence. If greater deadweight cost in the tax system leads to reductions in influence activities that more than offset the direct costs to taxpayers then it can be good from a societal point of view. Krusell and Rios-Rull (1996) argue that income taxation can be attractive relative to consumption taxation even when the latter has less deadweight loss, since it leads to a lower level of transfer activity in equilibrium.

Raising the marginal cost of public finance could work by constitutional restrictions on the tax bases that can be used. For example, many of the US states did not traditionally allow corporate and personal income taxes. They could also come from specific restrictions on particular taxes implemented via citizens' initiatives. Tax competition is also seen as a way of making it more difficult for governments to raise taxes, and hence as a break on government. This was suggested, for example, by Brennan and Buchanan (1980). Finally, they could come from technological progress in tax collection technologies.[23]

INCREASING THE COST OF TAXATION

In terms of the model, we consider the effect of an increase in the marginal cost of public goods μ. We are interested in when this leads to

---

[23] Peltzman (1980) argues that technological differences in the ability to collect taxes have been important historically and in comparing developed and developing countries.

an increase in voter welfare. It is clear that rent diversion in a pooling or hybrid equilibrium is decreasing in μ.[24] By reducing the level of spending by benevolent governments, increasing inefficiency in the tax system restricts the amount of wasteful spending that can be undertaken by self-interested officials without fear of detection. However, *increased inefficiency in the tax system (as represented by an increase in μ) that leaves the political equilibrium unchanged reduces voter welfare, even if it reduces rent diversion by bad politicians.* This result holds in spite of the fact that increasing inefficiency of the tax system does (sometimes) lower rent extraction by bad incumbents. This fails to deliver a benefit to voters in any of the equilibria described in Proposition 3.

When the equilibrium is separating, rent-seeking is maximal anyway and voters would prefer to be 'robbed' efficiently. Inefficiency in the tax system only increases the costs of venality—even when, as in the pooling or hybrid equilibrium, greater tax inefficiency leads to reduced rent-seeking. To see this, observe that voter welfare in Period 1 in the pooling/hybrid equilibrium is:

$$\pi EW^g(\mu) + (1-\pi)[\{q + (1-q)(1-\lambda)\}W^b(\mu) + (1-q)\lambda W^g(H,\mu).$$

As the political equilibrium is unchanged, this expression falls with μ. The key to understanding the logic is to consider the case where bad incumbents imitate good ones. Although the rent extraction goes down, voter welfare itself does not depend on the amount of rent extracted because the level of welfare is the same as when the good incumbents face a high cost shock, i.e., $W^g(H,\mu)$, which is decreasing with μ.

The key assumption in the above argument is that the political equilibrium remains unchanged. Returning to Proposition 3, it is clear that increasing inefficiencies in the tax system can lead to a move from a pooling or hybrid equilibrium to a separating equilibrium. Specifically, defining $\underline{\mu}$ from $\hat{s}(\underline{\mu}) = (1-\beta)X$, then for all $\mu > \underline{\mu}$, there will be separation between the good and bad incumbents. This occurs because equilibrium rents are proportional to the size of government in the pooling or hybrid cases. As the size of government is reduced by greater inefficiency in the tax system, rent extraction possibilities are limited, making it more likely that a bad incumbent will 'go for broke' and extract maximal rents. In this instance, all equilibrium information (about θ and the type of the politician) is revealed

---

[24] Observe that $\hat{s}(\mu) = (H-L)G_H^*(\mu)$ is decreasing in μ.

in equilibrium. Hence, to ascertain the welfare effects of an increase in the cost of tax collection which increases μ above $\underline{\mu}$, we need to compare full information welfare with that in the equilibrium with $\mu < \underline{\mu}$.

Intuitively, the impact on voter welfare of a move to separation involves a trade off between the short-run costs of reduced discipline, and the long-run benefits that result when bad politicians reveal type and are removed from office. Computing welfare for the two cases from (4.2) shows that the selection effect outweighs the discipline effect, so that welfare is higher in the separating equilibrium only if $\beta \pi \Sigma(\mu) \geq \Delta(\mu)$.

Besley and Smart (2007) derive the following result on the welfare effect of tax inefficiencies:

Proposition 5: (Besley and Smart (2007)) *There exists a $\pi^* > 0$ such that increasing the inefficiency of the tax system (as represented by an increase in μ) unambiguously reduces voter welfare for all $\pi < \pi^*$. For $\pi \geq \pi^*$, an increase in the inefficiency of the tax system may increase voter welfare if it induces a shift from a hybrid or pooling equilibrium towards a separating equilibrium.*

This result says that an increase in the inefficiency of the tax system can enhance voter welfare only if it leads to an increase in the ability of the voter to detect bad incumbents. This leads to some rather paradoxical implications. First, a sufficiently large increase in the cost of public funds may indeed increase equilibrium welfare, but only if the change *increases* the amount of wasteful spending in the first period. Voter welfare will be higher from improved selection when the fraction of good types in the population π is sufficiently high. In other words, raising the marginal cost of funds can increase voter welfare only when the political process is closer to the benevolent government paradigm.

INFORMATION PROVISION

We now discuss means of restraining government by generating better information for voters.

Fiscal transparency

Transparency is fast becoming the motherhood and apple pie of good governance. However, the emerging literature on transparency in government is often quite vague about what exactly is the essence of transparent government. There is actually a long history of discussions related to this. For example, John Adams, the first vice president and second president of the United States, argued that '[l]iberty cannot be preserved without a general knowledge among the people who have a right... and a desire to know... the characters and conduct of their rulers.'[25]

In practice, there is a huge amount of variation in the world in the way that governments allow their citizens to observe the workings of government and the basis of social decisions. Polities also differ in the extent to which there are developed private institutions such as the media and independent watchdogs that are effective sources of commentary and information about the quality of policies and politicians. There seems little doubt that in most developed polities, the rise of mass media has increased the scrutiny to which most governments' fiscal decisions are exposed. However, there remain many countries around the world whose media systems remain closed and repressed.

Given the concerns of this chapter, our main interest is how transparency plays out in the fiscal process. One widely cited definition of transparency in a public finance setting is that of Kopit and Craig who suggest that '[F]iscal transparency is defined... as openness toward the public at large about government structure and functions, fiscal policy intentions, public sector accounts, and projections' (1998: 1). This definition is quite broad—applying to a whole array of fiscal institutions.

However, when transparency is defined in a specific framework or model, it is often required to be more precise about which variables are being varied. Within public finance, one of the primary concerns has been in the accounting procedures used by government. This comes to the fore in many discussions of public deficits. In particular it is possible for the citizens to observe the true fiscal stance being taken by a government from the reporting procedures which it has. This is the focus of contributions by Milesi-Ferretti (2000), Alt et al. (2002), and Alt and Dreyer Lassen (2002). The latter focus on the issue of

---

[25] 'John Adams: A Dissertation on the Canon and Feudal Law', *Oxford Dictionary of Political Quotations* Oxford: Oxford University Press.

how greater transparency affects budget deficits from both theoretical and empirical viewpoints. In both papers, their underlying model is political agency. However, unlike our approach, they use a model where government must make an intertemporal financing decision—tax or debt. We will develop a model that includes public debt in Section 4.6. We will then revisit some of the transparency issues.

In a related contribution, Shi and Svensson (2002) model transparency as reflecting the fraction of the informed voters in the population. They show that a greater degree of transparency will tend to sharpen re-election incentives, making it more likely that an incompetent incumbent will be removed from office. Ferejohn (1999) studies the link between transparency and the size of government. He argues that greater transparency will see voters being willing to put government in charge of a larger amount of tax revenue.

In Chapter 3, we showed that whether more information is good or bad in agency models depends crucially on how that information is modeled. The model of this chapter suggests at least three dimensions of transparency which could be important:

- Information about the past records of candidates which reveals information about their underlying type, permitting voters to 'pre-screen' candidates and leading to an increase in π.
- Information about the fiscal outcomes: better observations of s or, in a more general setting, better information about taxing and spending.
- Information about the cost of public spending (θ)

The only unambiguous case is transparency which raises π—which can be thought of as improvements in public scrutiny, which make it more likely that a politician devoted to serving voters' interests is elected. The reason for this being welfare improving is clear—the equilibrium strategies are unaltered and voters always benefit from having a 'good' politician in office.

Our analysis of discipline and selection effects spelled out so far confirms that, even if voters are provided with better information about s or θ, there is no guarantee that voter welfare will be higher. This will depend upon whether changes in incumbent discipline are more or less important than changes in selection. To model this, suppose that, after the incumbent has chosen s_1 and before the Period 1 election is held, the voter may learn about the true cost of public services θ. Specifically, the true value of θ is revealed with probability ξ; otherwise, no signal is received by the voter. The result in Proposition 3 is now modified. The payoff when a bad politician pools with a good one is $\hat{s}(\mu) + (1 - \xi)\beta X$ while, if he/she chooses to reveal his/her type, it is X. Pooling is now worthwhile if and only if $\hat{s}(\mu) > (1 - (1 - \xi)\beta)X$, a more stringent condition than in the absence of an informative signal (see Proposition 3). Moreover, pooling is less likely to be optimal the closer ξ is to one. Indeed, if $\xi = 1$, then the only possible Period 1 equilibrium is separating.[26]

Better information therefore tends to reduce discipline and increase first term rent seeking. At the same time, however, it improves selection, as bad incumbents are less likely to survive re-election. By evaluating the trade off between agency costs of first term and second-term incumbents, we can assess whether such a change in the political equilibrium is worthwhile. Assume that $q > 1/2$, the only comparison is between pooling ($\lambda = 1$) and separation ($\lambda = 0$). Evaluating welfare from (4.2) gives the difference between separating and pooling equilibrium welfare as:

$$(1 - \pi)(1 - q)(\beta\pi\Sigma(\mu) - \Delta(\mu)).$$

The following result is due to Besley and Smart (2007):

Proposition 6: *Suppose $q > 1/2$ and that the voter receives an informative signal about the cost of providing public goods. The signal improves voter welfare only if the selection effect of elections dominates the discipline effect, i.e. $\beta\pi\Sigma(\mu) \geq \Delta(\mu)$.*

The above expression reveals the determinants of this trade off. The larger is the selection effect, the better is the pool of incumbents (π close to one), and the lower the level of discounting.[27]

This result builds on the findings of Section 3.4.2 in Chapter 3. In political agency models, more information need not be desirable for voters. This is related to the broader theoretical literature on the value of information in agency relationships. In the standard complete contracts model of Holmstrom (1979), more information is better. Dewatripont et al. (1999) show that coarser information may sometimes be better in motivating agents in a career concerns model where

---

[26] A similar argument can be made if we instead supposed that with some probability information about whether s_1 is positive comes to light before the election.

[27] This is also the case the higher is $W^g(L, \mu)$, the lower is q, and the lower is $W^g(H, \mu)$.

incentives are implicit. This reflects a kind of second-best reasoning—with incomplete incentives, an otherwise welfare improving change (more information) may have deleterious effects on equilibrium behavior that more than offset the direct welfare impact. In our model, incentives are incomplete since the threat of not being re-elected is the only mechanism with which the voter may discipline incumbents.

Yardstick competition

The last subsection considered the direct effect of information provision. However, there are also indirect means of generating information about incumbents. One important example of this applies to decentralized governments where intergovernmental yardstick competition can be important.

This idea was first discussed in the context of governments by Salmon (1987) and its empirical relevance established in Besley and Case (1995a).[28] The theory of yardstick competition is also studied in Bodenstein and Ursprung (2001); Bordignon et al. (2001); Hindriks and Belleflamme (2001); and Sand-Zantman (2004). Increasingly, public spending functions in a number of countries are being decentralized to local governments and agencies. Decentralization is motivated in part by a desire to generate performance comparisons among decision makers and so to enhance incentives for efficient provision of public services. If there is a positive correlation in the cost shocks, then this creates an informational externality. However, unlike the pure transparency model, studying this requires a model of equilibrium behavior generating information, i.e. equilibrium in both jurisdictions. Whether such yardstick competition is welfare improving also depends on how it affects the balance of discipline and selection effects in government.

To extend the model to include yardstick comparisons, suppose now that there are two identical jurisdictions, labeled 'domestic' and 'foreign'; variables that apply to the foreign jurisdiction will be denoted by the prime symbol. To focus on symmetric equilibria of the game among incumbents and voters in the two jurisdictions, assume that the joint probability distribution function of cost shocks $\Pr(\theta, \theta')$ is

---

[28] See Revelli (2001) for UK evidence and Shaltegger and Küttel (2001) for Swiss evidence.

symmetric, with:

$$\Pr(H,H) = \Pr(L,L) = \frac{\rho}{2}$$
$$\Pr(H,L) = \Pr(L,H) = \frac{1-\rho}{2}.$$

(4.9)

Moreover, we work with the case where $\rho > 1/2$, so that cost shocks in the two jurisdictions are positively correlated. To further simplify the analysis, we assume that $\hat{s}(\mu) > (1-\beta)X$, so that a separating equilibrium cannot exist. Since the marginal p.d.f. has $q = \Pr(\theta = H) = 1/2$, it follows from Proposition 3 that the unique equilibrium of the game without yardstick competition is one with pooling. We now show that, depending on the value of π, both hybrid and pooling equilibria are possible with yardstick competition.

When performance of foreign as well as domestic officials is observable, voters may base their decision to re-elect the incumbent or not on *relative* performance in the two jurisdictions. Voters will now condition their voting behavior on tax setting in both the domestic and foreign jurisdictions. Accordingly, let the probability of re-election in the domestic jurisdiction be $\sigma(x,x')$ when observed spending levels in the domestic and foreign jurisdictions are x and x' respectively. We say the voter's strategy involves yardstick competition when re-election occurs with positive probability if spending is high in both jurisdictions, but the probability of re-election is zero if domestic spending is high and foreign spending is low. That is, a re-election rule with yardstick competition has $\sigma(x_H, x_H) = \sigma$ for some $\sigma > 0$ and $\sigma(x_H, x_L) = 0$.[29]

As before, let λ denote the probability that type (b,L) chooses $s_1 = \hat{s}(\mu)$. Since we look for an equilibrium in which the strategies adopted by domestic and foreign incumbents are symmetric ($\lambda = \lambda'$), the p.d.f. $\Pr(x,x'|i)$ of domestic and foreign spending conditional on the type of the domestic politician can be calculated as:

$$\Pr(x_H, x_H|g) = \pi\frac{\rho}{2} + (1-\pi)\lambda\frac{1-\rho}{2}$$
$$\Pr(x_H, x_H|b) = \pi\lambda\frac{1-\rho}{2} + (1-\pi)\lambda^2\frac{\rho}{2}.$$

(4.10)

[29] Of course, $\sigma(x_L, x') = 1$ in equilibrium for all x', as in the unilateral model of Section 4.3.

(There are two terms in each probability because $x' = x_H$ might have been generated by a good foreign politician facing high costs or a bad foreign politician facing low costs.) Voters' posterior beliefs about the incumbent can therefore be calculated from Bayes's rule:

$$\Pr(g|x_H, x_H) = \frac{\pi}{\pi + (1 - \pi)\ell(\lambda, \rho, \pi)}$$

where $\ell(\lambda, \rho, \pi) = \Pr(x_H, x_H|b)/\Pr(x_H, x_H|g)$ is the likelihood ratio that (x_H, x_H) was generated by a bad rather than good incumbent. Key to understanding the logic of the ensuing results is the fact that $\ell(\cdot)$ is a decreasing function of π—the worse the initial reputation of the incumbent, the more likely it is that (x_H, x_H) was generated by a bad incumbent. This is because, at low π, (x_H, x_H) is more likely generated by a foreign bad incumbent with cost of L than a foreign good incumbent with a cost of H. But with positive correlation in costs, it is also more likely that the cost at home is L and hence that the domestic incumbent is bad.

A necessary and sufficient condition for an equilibrium with yardstick competition to exist is that $\Pr(g|x_H, x_L) < \pi$, so that the voter prefers to remove the incumbent from office when domestic spending is high and foreign spending is low. Moreover, the equilibrium is pooling if $\Pr(g|x_H, x_H) > \pi$ for $\lambda = 1$, and is hybrid otherwise. After some tedious manipulation, these conditions reduce to a simple one, given in the following result:

Proposition 7: (Besley and Smart (2007)) *Suppose that $\hat{s}(\mu) > (1 - \beta)X$. Then voters use yardstick competition in equilibrium. A pooling equilibrium exists if and only if $\pi \geq 1/2$, and a hybrid equilibrium exists if and only if $\pi < 1/2$.*

To interpret this, recall that, in the absence of yardstick comparisons, the equilibrium would have bad incumbents choosing x_H when the state is $\theta = L$, yielding a pooling equilibrium. Compared to this benchmark, the case of yardstick competition deviates in three ways. First, a bad domestic incumbent may not be re-elected when he/she chooses x_H, if the foreign incumbent is good and gets a low cost draw. Second, a good domestic incumbent is retained in office when costs are high, and the foreign politician chooses maximal rents. These changes to the voter's strategy reflect the clear cut information advantage from yardstick competition. Third, pooling may no longer be optimal for incumbents when the foreign incumbent has a poor initial reputation. To see this, observe that the likelihood ratio $\ell(\lambda, \rho, \pi)$ is decreasing in π, as it depends on the voter's assessment of the quality of the incumbent in the *other* jurisdiction. Thus facing a foreign incumbent with a low reputation makes it relatively less likely that the (x_H, x_H) outcome is generated by a good domestic incumbent, and hence that voters will re-elect an incumbent who picks x_H. The equilibrium now has the bad incumbent reducing the probability that he/she chooses $\hat{s}$ in order to raise the signaling value of the outcome x_H. A foreign incumbent with a poor reputation inflicts a reputational externality on a domestic bad incumbent and reduces his/her incentive to pool with a good incumbent. Moreover, this aspect of yardstick competition increases rent-seeking.

Since improved information available through yardstick comparisons has countervailing effects on incentives and selection of politicians, its net impact on voter welfare is unclear. The following result shows that the reputations of politicians are key to understanding this.

Proposition 8: (Besley and Smart (2007)) *Suppose that $\hat{s}(\mu) > (1 - \beta)X$. Then there exist parameters $0 < \tilde{\pi}_a < \tilde{\pi}_b < 1/2$ such that voter welfare is lower when yardstick comparisons are available than when they are not if $\pi < \tilde{\pi}_a$, and the converse is true if $\pi > \tilde{\pi}_b$.*

This result emphasizes that voters who are better informed about the fiscal environment may be worse off in equilibrium, as bad politicians put less effort into building a reputation when they first take office. This insight explains the above result. In some circumstances (π low), voters would be better off if they could commit to ignoring the fiscal performance in the other jurisdiction in the course of a domestic election.

Yardstick competition is welfare decreasing when politicians' reputations are poor because rents are increased with little advantage from the improved information generated as most politicians who are kicked out are replaced by an incumbent of the same type.

4.5.3 *Summary*

To summarize, the following lessons learned here are central to understanding what follows:

- Improving information about the state of the world need not be welfare improving—selection and discipline effects can work in opposite directions.

- Changing features of the environment in which political agency plays out has direct effects and indirect effects—the latter working through changes in the political equilibrium. These welfare consequences of the direct and indirect effects can work in different directions.

Together these propositions make clear how a micro-founded model of politics is important to understand the economic logic of fiscal restraints.

4.6 Debt and deficits

So far, we have focused on the case where government can only finance public spending through taxation. In this section, we extend the model to allow for public debt. One reason for doing so is simply that debt is an important tool of government and hence it should be considered in a dynamic model of public finance. However, debt plays an especially prominent role in the political economy of public finance. A central theme of the political economy literature is that public debt is unlikely to be chosen optimally from a social point of view.

There are two main arguments around to this effect:

- Strategic use of debt: this has been argued most prominently by Tabellini and Alesina (1990) and Persson and Svensson (1989). They suggest that an incumbent may choose to run a budget deficit in order to constrain the actions of future incumbents. The most popular application of these ideas is to the large Federal budget deficits of the Reagan era which provided a constraint on the spending patterns of future Democratic incumbents. This argument gives a reason for tendency towards excessive budget deficits since it is only putting future pressure on the government budget constraint will it have any effect.
- Fiscal illusion: the other main concern with debt arises from the possibility that it is a less visible means of public finance than raising taxes. One aspect of this argument concerns the complex accounting conventions that surround public debt. Another possibility is that politicians deliberately find ways to cover up their deficits in order to make hay until eventually discipline is required.

The most prominent advocate of the fiscal illusion view of excessive debt finance is Buchanan and Wagner (1977) who argue that 'complex and indirect payment structures create a fiscal illusion that will systematically produce higher levels of public outlay than those that would be observed under simple-payments structures' (1977: 129) and that 'events of fiscal history strongly support the hypothesis that unconstrained access to public borrowing will tend to generate excessive public spending' (1977: 142).

While the first is clearly an important and interesting point, it has no direct bearing on political agency relationships being studied here. This is because Period 1 incumbents in the model studied here derive no utility from Period 2 fiscal policies unless they are re-elected. Fiscal illusion stories are frequently treated with a good deal of suspicion in the modern political economy literature (see, for example, Alesina and Perrotti (1995)). The concern is that it attributes a systematic bias which appears to rest on voter irrationality. The fiscal illusion argument can be interpreted in terms of the information that voters are likely to have on which to base their fiscal decisions.

In this section we explore two things. First, we consider how adding public debt into the model changes the insights in a world where political equilibria balance discipline and selection effects. Second, we investigate the need for a limit on the size of the deficit using this approach.

Debt has a dramatic impact on incentives of bad politicians. If they face no (non-economic) external constraint on debt issuance, they can steal tax revenue in Period 1 and Period 2, and divert it to their own ends. This dramatically reduces their incentive to behave like good politicians in Period 1. This bears out the standard public choice suspicion about debt as an instrument.

PUBLIC FINANCE AND GOVERNMENT DEBT

We begin by outlining a simple extension of our two period model to incorporate government debt. Suppose that, after observing θ_1, the incumbent may issue debt D in Period 1 which is observable to the voter, incurring a gross liability payable in Period 2 for the government of $R(D)$, where $R(D) \geq D$ for $D \geq 0$ and $R(D) < D$ for $D < 0$. We also assume that $R(\cdot)$ is increasing and strictly convex.[30] Furthermore, we will assume that $\beta R'(0) = 1$, so that (as we shall see) the role of debt for a good government is to smooth taxation between periods in view of the shocks to the cost of providing public goods.

In the presence of debt, the government's budget constraints in the two periods become:

$$x_1 = \theta_1 G_1 + s_1 - D$$

and

$$x_2 = \theta_2 G_2 + s_2 + R(D).$$

The optimal fiscal policy may again be solved by backward induction. In Period 2:

$$G_{\theta 2}^* = \arg\max\{G - \mu C(\theta_2 G + R(D))\},$$

which implies that:

$$1 = \theta_2 \mu C'(\theta_2 G_{\theta 2}^* + R(D)).$$

Thus Period 2 taxes will, as in Section 4.2, be equal to x_θ^* with spending equal to $x_\theta^*/\theta - R(D)/\theta$. Thus debt reduces Period 2 resources devoted to valuable public spending but does not affect Period 2 taxation levels. Expected Period 2 welfare is therefore equal to $EW^g(\mu) - \psi R(D)$ where $\psi = q/H + (1-q)/L$ as before.

It is now straightforward to determine the Period 1 optimal policy. The level of public spending will solve:

$$G_{\theta 1}^* = \arg\max\{G - \mu C(\theta_1 G - D)\}.$$

As above, we confirm the principle that the level of Period 1 taxation is set equal to x_θ^* with spending being $G_\theta^* = x_\theta^*/\theta + D/\theta$. So the incidence of debt is purely to increase public spending.

The optimal debt level is used to smooth the cost of public spending across the two periods with taxes remaining constant. At an interior solution, the optimal level of debt, $D(\theta_1)$, satisfies:

$$\frac{1}{\theta_1} = \beta \psi R'(D(\theta_1)).$$

---

[30] The convexity ensures an interior solution for the debt level. For $D > 0$, it crudely captures the possibility of default as perceived by investors. For $D < 0$, it captures the absence of an infinitely elastic supply of quality investment opportunities.

Since $\beta R'(0) = 1$, the model predicts that the government will run a budget surplus when costs are high ($D_H^* < 0$) and a budget deficit when costs are low ($D_L^* > 0$). This is a direct application of the Barro (1979) tax smoothing idea. Compared to the case where $D = 0$, the government runs a deficit when the size of the public sector is large and a surplus when it is small.

THE POLITICS OF DEBT

We turn to characterizing the effect of debt on our political equilibrium. Let $\bar{D}$ be the highest level of debt that can be incurred in Period 1. In the absence of any constitutional restrictions on debt, we will have $R(\bar{D}) = X$; however, we also consider tighter limits below. A bad politician who decides to go for broke in Period 1 will now take rent equal to $X + \bar{D}$. At the same time, the amount of rent that he/she can extract by mimicking a good incumbent with cost shock H is lower in both Periods 1 and 2 than in the case of no debt. This is because he/she will have to repay the debt out of any rents that he/she can capture tomorrow *and* the tax-smoothing argument implies that public spending will be lower today than it would be in the absence of debt (that is, $D_H^* < 0$). Thus, the condition for being willing to exercise restraint is:

$$(H - L)\frac{[x_H^* + D_H^*]}{H} + \beta[X - R(D_H^*)] \geq X + \bar{D}. \qquad (4.11)$$

Comparing this inequality with $\hat{s}(\mu) \geq (1 - \beta)X$ in Proposition 3, it is clear that the condition for incumbent discipline is more difficult to satisfy. Thus we have:

Proposition 9: *Suppose that the government can raise resources though both debt and taxation. Then, public debt reduces incumbent discipline. More specifically, a pooling equilibrium with $\lambda = \sigma = 1$ exists if (4.11) holds. The equilibrium is separating otherwise.*

The fact that debt leads to ill discipline motivates the observation that the citizens would wish to impose a restriction on the deficit that can be raised. If the political equilibrium is pooling, then a relatively weak restriction on debt $\bar{D} > D_L^*$, which does not change the political equilibrium, must improve voter welfare. It leaves equilibrium behavior for good incumbents and bad incumbents in state L unchanged. However, it reduces the long-run harm that bad incumbents can do in state H. If the political equilibrium is separating, then again good incumbent behavior is also unchanged while bad incumbent behavior is now restrained in every state. In all cases, political discipline is improved and the ability of the political process to select good incumbents is unchanged.

Thus, we have

Proposition 10: *A cap on the size of the deficit of $\bar{D}$ which does not change the political equilibrium raises voter welfare.*

If the debt limit is sufficiently tight that the political equilibrium is changed, it is in the direction of increasing incentives for pooling. A switch from separating to pooling reduces the information generated in the political equilibrium and hence is most valuable when selection is not very important (low π). Thus, this view of reducing deficits fits much better with the conventional public choice view that restraining government is important in two senses. First, it is a restraint on bad governments. Second, the resulting changes in political behavior have positive effects so long as the likelihood of a bad government is high.

This focuses on a rather different distortion due to public debt than has been put forward in either the strategic debt model or the fiscal illusion view. The key idea is that debt allows bad politicians not only to extract rent from current taxpayers but also from future ones. Thus, the quality of policy is more susceptible to political opportunism. Without placing a clear restraint on the amount of debt that politicians can run up, there is a risk that ill-discipline will now be much more of a problem.

The result also points to the limitations of elections as a disciplinary device, and so the potential role for fiscal restraints. Unlike the previous results on fiscal restraints, this one does not rest on a balance of selection and incentive effects. Over the range that we considered $(\bar{D} \geq D_L^*)$, the political equilibrium is the same as it would be without the debt restriction—there is a pure discipline effect. Whether further debt restrictions below this level are desirable depends on whether distorting the behavior of good politicians and/or changes in the political equilibrium are desirable.

4.7 Governments versus NGOs

The model so far has assumed that government is the only means of delivering provision of public goods. However, the kind of agency problems studied here are a key motivating force behind efforts to delegate responsibility for public goods provision to non-governmental organizations (NGOs). Indeed pessimism about the state in developing countries has seen increasing amounts of aid assistance being dispersed in this way.

Interest in NGOs versus government provision is not confined to a developing country context. One structural distinction between countries concerns the extent to which private rather than state delivery of services is used. Moreover, there is much debate about where the border should lie. For example, George W. Bush announced a far-reaching proposal to use 'faith-based' organizations in service delivery.

A burning issue in the debate concerns the way in which NGOs are held accountable for the quality of service that they deliver. Unlike (democratic) governments, there is no direct accountability to the beneficiary groups that they help. To understand their role in providing more effective aid provision, it is necessary to understand whether this is an issue. At one extreme, NGOs could be thought of as being free from the kinds of incentive problems that are faced by government. Indeed, the rose-tinted spectacles that have been used to describe NGOs in some quarters perpetuate this characterization. But we need only remind ourselves of the problems that can arise from ignoring incentive problems in government to realize the potential folly of this.

Here, we adopt a level playing field approach. NGOs will be agents just as governments are. We will explore aspects of their behavior as equilibrium phenomena. However, on one hand, we will accept the possibility that there are well meaning NGOs in the world. However, on the other hand, there is a selection problem in identifying them.

We motivate these ideas with the following example. Suppose that an external agency is deciding to fund an increment of public spending and it can do so either by offering resources to a government or via a non-governmental organization. It cares that these resources are turned into public goods that are valued by the citizens.

There are two ways in which NGOs could improve on the outcomes implemented by governments in the kind of setting that we are considering. First, it may be possible to write contracts with NGOs that are more complete than those offered to government. This is because the government is primarily accountable to its citizens via elections. The NGO could, in principle, be subject to all manner of other accountability mechanisms. This should manifest itself in better discipline, i.e. lower rent-seeking.

Second, the outcome could improve if the composition of individuals who work for NGOs is drawn from a better pool. What makes NGOs unique among possible service providers is the idea that they are not merely staffed by self-interested individuals. Working for an NGO is not like working in the private sector. This raises the potential for NGO delivery of services having an advantage over government in that the agents are more likely to be of the 'good type', i.e. maximizing the interests of the beneficiaries. On the downside, it is also pointed out that, unlike governments, NGOs are not accountable to those whom they serve. There are no elections for NGO leaders. This raises the possibility of a trade off between improved selection from having an NGO undertake spending tasks and reduced accountability because there is no electoral mechanism.

We begin by studying the case where the NGO faces the same extent of accountability as does the government. Specifically, the NGO can be fired if it does not do its job properly, but there are no other sanctions available. The NGO accountability mechanism now looks very similar to elections as means of generating incentives.

4.7.1 *Framework*

Suppose that an external organization that cares about G is giving 'aid' to a country. The level of aid is denoted by T. We remain within a two period horizon and the information structure is exactly as above. The decision by the aid provider is whether to give the aid to the NGO or to the government.

We maintain the parallel structure to our model of government by supposing that there are two kinds of NGOs. Good NGOs spend all aid resources on public goods whereas bad NGOs consume the resources privately. We also assume complete symmetry in the technology that governments and NGOs have for producing public goods. Thus each faces the same structure of cost shocks onto the provision of public goods. For simplicity here, we focus on the case where $q > 1/2$. This rules out the hybrid equilibrium in Proposition 3 and allows us to focus on pooling or separation.

The difference between an NGO and a democratic government is that the former is not directly accountable to the people whom it serves. The main incentive that we consider is retaining the right to provide public goods on behalf of the aid provider. Thus, the aid agency cannot commit to an incentive scheme ex ante. It must make a decision whether or not to retain the NGO ex post.

We assume that there is a potential pool of NGOs from which an aid agency can select. The probability that a randomly selected NGO is good is v. Suppose that the aid provider decides to go with an NGO, then the timing of the NGO/aid donor game is as follows.

1. Nature chooses an NGO at random and a cost of public goods provision θ.
2. The NGO decides how much of the aid, T, to spend on public goods and how much on its private interest.
3. The aid agency then decides whether or not to retain the NGO against another randomly selected NGO.
4. The Period 2 value of θ is realized.
5. The incumbent NGO receives T and decides whether or not to spend its resources on public goods or private spending.

This gives rise to a game that is very similar to the one played between a government and its citizens. We now consider the equilibrium policy choice of the NGO.

A good NGO spends T/θ on public goods. Just as in the case of a bad government, a bad NGO can seek to mimic a good one and retain 'its franchise' to provide the public good. In the state where $\theta = L$, it can mimic the good NGO by choosing:

$$G = \frac{T}{H}$$

and collecting a rent of $\left(\frac{H-L}{H}\right) T$. Hence the condition for restraint being optimal (assuming that the NGO is retained) is that:

$$\left(\frac{H - L}{H}\right) T + \beta T > T \text{ or } \beta > \frac{L}{H}.$$

Let λ_n be the probability that a bad NGO picks $G = T/H$ when the state is $\theta = L$ and let σ_n be the probability that the NGO is retained when the observed level of public goods is T/H. We now have the following proposition describing the equilibrium behavior of the NGO.[31]

---

[31] As in our model of government, we assume that an NGO that does anything which could not be generated by a good NGO is assumed to be bad.

Proposition 11: *Suppose that $q > 1/2$. Then an equilibrium exists for all values and is generically unique. There are two cases:*

1. *A pooling equilibrium with $\lambda_n = \sigma_n = 1$ exists if and only if*

$$\beta \geq \frac{L}{H}$$

2. *A separating equilibrium with $\lambda_n = 0$ and $\sigma_n = 1$ exists if and only if*

$$\beta < \frac{L}{H}.$$

The reasoning is exactly the same as for the case of government accountability. Proposition 18 shows that there can be an equilibrium where a bad NGO mimics a good one provided that it is sufficiently patient. The expected discounted level of public goods being provided viewed from the perspective of Period 1 is now easy to calculate for each kind of equilibrium. In a pooling equilibrium this is:

$$T\left[v\psi(1+\beta) + (1-v)\left(\left(\frac{(1-q)}{H}\right) + qv\psi\beta\right)\right]$$

where $\psi = q/H + (1-q)/L$ as before. In a separating equilibrium, it is:

$$T[v\psi(1+\beta) + (1-v)v\psi\beta].$$

Whether, from an ex ante point of view, there are more public goods produced in one case than another is not clear. This is true under pooling if:

$$\frac{1}{H} > v\psi\beta.$$

Since $\frac{1}{H} < \psi$, this can hold only if β and v are low enough. Intuitively, this is clear since pooling is preferable if there is a low level of patience (other things being equal) as the gains from better discipline occur in the short-run. It is also clear that pooling is preferable if the NGO is more likely to be bad.

This analysis shows that the balance of selection and discipline effects are also important in understanding the role of NGOs. Hence the model achieves the level playing field that we desired to investigate the role of NGOs. We now consider what would happen if the aid provider were instead to give the aid to government.

4.7.2 Aid to the government

The alternative to financing an NGO is giving aid directly a government. Thus, suppose instead that the aid donor chooses to give T extra resources to a government. Since it plays no part in the analysis, we set $\mu = 1$. We assume that the level of aid is observable to the citizens/voters and they can condition their voting behavior on it. Let

$$G_\theta^*(T) = \arg \max G - C(\theta G - T)$$

be the level of public goods chosen by a good politician when aid is T. It is clear that if the government acts in the citizens' interests, then this aid will increase in public spending of T/θ—exactly the same amount as a faithful NGO does. Therefore, $\partial G^*/\partial T = 1/\theta$. Modifying the analysis above, the critical rent level at which a bad politician can mimic a good one is now:

$$\hat{s}(T) \equiv (H - L)G_H^*(T).$$

Access to aid resources therefore increases the level of rent extraction that is feasible and consistent with re-election.

The result in Proposition 3 is now modified as follows:[32]

Proposition 12: *An equilibrium exists for all values and is generically unique. There are two cases:*

1. *A pooling equilibrium, with $\lambda = \sigma = 1$, exists if and only if*

$$\hat{s}(T) \geq (1 - \beta)(X + T)$$

2. *A separating equilibrium, with $\lambda = 0$ and $\sigma = 1$, if and only if*

$$\hat{s}(T) < (1 - \beta)(X + T).$$

A bad politician will mimic a good one now if $\hat{s}(T) + \beta(X+T) > X+T$. This result demonstrates an often made claim that aid payments change government incentives and specifically may create worse discipline among incumbents. Aid destroys government incentives to pool in cases where $\beta < \frac{L}{H}$.[33] Thus, a government that is suddenly given a large injection of aid may indeed decide to make hay *even*

---

[32] Recall that we assuming that $q > 1/2$ so that a hybrid equilibrium is ruled out.

[33] This is exactly the condition for a bad NGO to choose separation.

though there may be an electoral penalty from doing so. Such considerations are clearly important when choosing whether or not to run aid programs through governments.

We can now compute the incremental level of public goods spending by government under each kind of equilibrium. Under pooling, it is:

$$T[\pi\psi(1+\beta)+(1-\pi)\left(\left(\frac{(1-q)}{H}\right)+q\pi\psi\beta\right)$$

while in a separating equilibrium it is:

$$T[\pi\psi(1+\beta)+(1-\pi)\pi\psi\beta].$$

Note that both payoffs are identical to what we obtained for the case of an NGO, except that v is replaced by π.

4.7.3 *Comparisons*

Our first observation comes from comparing the expressions for expected additional public good payments by governments and NGOs. Here, we have:

Proposition 13: *Suppose that an external agency wishes to give a transfer to a government or an NGO to promote public spending. Suppose also that the NGO and the government either both pool or both separate, then voter welfare is higher when the transfer is given to an NGO if and only if $v > \pi$.*

This result says that provided that NGOs and government have the same incentives, then whether it is desirable to direct aid via an NGO comes down purely to whether there is a selection advantage.[34] In other words, a preference for NGO provision comes from believing that they have access to a pool of workers who are more likely to run the program in the interest of citizens at large.

A key assumption is that the NGO and the government play the same equilibrium strategy. However, comparing Propositions 11 and 12, it is clear that there is no reason why this should be the case. If it is not, then the result in Proposition 13 needs to be modified. Given that

---

[34] This has a parallel with Besley and Ghatak (2001) who show that NGO provision is preferred to government provision in an incomplete contracting framework with public goods only if the NGO values the welfare of the target group more than does the government.

they are dealing both with taxes and aid payments, it is clear that bad governments may have a larger incentive to pool. The government's 'pooling' condition can be written as:

$$\hat{s}(0) + T\left(1 - \frac{L}{H}\right) > (1 - \beta)(X + T).$$

Hence, in the case where the NGO will pool, this reinforces the incentive of the government to pool. Suppose that the government pools and the NGO separates,[35] then NGO provision is better if pooling is valuable, i.e.

$$(\pi - \nu)\psi(1 + \beta + \beta q(1 - \pi - \nu)) + (1 - q)(1 - \pi)/H > (1 - q)(1 - \nu)\nu\psi\beta.$$

If the quality of government and NGOs is the same, then this condition boils down to:

$$\frac{1}{H} > \pi\psi\beta,$$

in which case then government provision is better if the quality of governmments and NGOs is very low. If NGOs are of better quality than government, then government provision can still be better if the difference in quality is not large and if the quality of government is low.

To summarize, our model makes three key predictions about when NGOs are more likely to be better than government in delivering public goods:

- If NGOs and governments have the same equilibrium strategies then NGOs need to be staffed by individuals who are more motivated towards the public interest (better selection).

- If NGOs separate and governments pool, then we need a large difference in quality between NGOs and government *or* to have a government of good quality.

- If NGOs pool and governments separate, then we need a small difference in the quality of NGOs and government *and* the quality of NGOs to be low.

Obviously the model is simple and stylized. However, it is clear that the model has the key ingredients that are needed to study the issue.

---

[35] This happens only if $\hat{s}(0) > (1 - \beta)X$, i.e. without aid the government would pool.

First, the model models the imperfection in government behavior that generates the case for an NGO endogenously. Second, it models how aid to government changes the incentives of the government. Third, it models the contracting process between the aid agency and the NGO, given the weak accountability that the NGO has.

4.7.4 *Further issues*

There are a number of further issues that could usefully be studied in the framework developed here. In particular, there are a number of asymmetries in the accountability of NGOs and governments that we have set aside.

As noted above, the analysis assumes that the kinds of contracts that can be reached between NGOs and aid providers are exactly the same as those that can be reached between governments, citizens/voters, and NGOs. This facilitated a simple analysis, but it arguably misses an important point. If more sophisticated contracts can be used, then this would enhance the case for NGOs. However, a similar comment applies to government—aid provider relations. We did not allow any direct elements of conditionality into the contracts there and supposed that there was a sovereign political process which governs this. Clearly, meaningful notions of joint accountability to voters and aid providers create some interesting common agency problems which deserve further work and could better illuminate the meaning of conditionality in exchange for aid alongside domestic political processes. This discussion is a first step down this route.

Another feature of the model that could be developed is to suppose that democratic accountability may utilize information about government performance better. We have assumed that aid providers have as much information about how much of the aid finance goes into public goods as do voters. However, it appears more likely that information will be greater among voters. This is particularly true when aid delivery is by local governments. While it might be assumed that this would go in favor of government provision, our observation that better information about the local conditions need not improve voter welfare (see Section 5.2.2) would be an important caveat to the fad for decentralization based on the assertion that this will enhance the use of local information. Developing a model in this direction would cast light on the exact benefit and cost of aid provision through NGOs versus local governments.

Another key difference between NGO and government account-ability concerns the scope of their operations. The government is usually a multi-task agency while NGOs have a more narrow domain of responsibility. This surfaced in a limited way in the analysis so far in the fact that the incentive conditions for NGOs and governments diverged. In general, this observation suggests that it should be easier to design an incentive scheme for NGOs because the specific task that they are engaged in can be written into the contract whereas citizens hold government to account on a wide variety of performance outcomes. The tasks being funded by aid may simply be too small to have a strong impact on government accountability (for better or worse).

4.8 Competence

The model has focused on agency problems due to politicians not serving voters' interest. It is interesting to see how the model might instead be used to study politicians who differ from each other in terms of competence.

To study this, we set up a model where there is an inherent characteristic of politicians which affects the cost of providing public goods. This is similar in spirit to the way that we chose to model competence in Section 2.4.3. If incompetence were the only issue, then incompetent politicians might be happy to fall on their sword and be voted out. To create an agency problem, it must be that incompetents earn a rent. Suppose then that there is an 'ego' rent (i.e. an increment to utility) rather than a monetary payoff which we denote by $\eta > 0$.

To incorporate competence we suppose that the cost of producing public goods depends on θ (a cost shock unobservable to the voter) and also on a competence parameter κ. Specifically, the cost is

$$\theta G \quad \text{if the incumbent is competent}$$
$$\kappa \theta G \quad \kappa > 1: \text{if the incumbent is incompetent.}$$

We assume that an incompetent incumbent can mimic a competent one at a personal cost to himself/herself. This cost is proportional to the amount of cost reducing effort that he/she puts in. To lower costs per unit of public goods by an amount δ requires committing cost reducing effort of $c\delta G$.

The timing of the model is basically the same as in the baseline model. Nature first determines the type of the incumbent and the cost of providing public goods. The incumbent then chooses a level of taxation and public goods and the amount of cost reducing effort to put in. The rest of the game structure is as before.

The features of the story developed in Section 4.3.3 now go through. A competent incumbent will choose $G_\theta^*(\mu)$. An incompetent incumbent observes the cost shock and decides whether to commit cost reducing effort and mimic a competent incumbent or make no such effort. In the latter case voters will observe that they pay taxes of $\kappa\theta G_{\kappa\theta}^*(\mu)$ and will vote the incumbent out of office.

Now consider the incentive of the incumbent to pool. Suppose first that the cost shock is L and let λ be the probability that he/she pools (i.e. picks sufficient effort to mimic the competent incumbent). He/she can pick effort of $(\kappa-1)LG_L^*(\mu)$ or $(\kappa L - H)G_H^*(\mu)$. It is straightforward to check that he/she will always choose to put in effort to mimic the cost shock H. Then he/she can choose the level of public goods $G_H^*(\mu)$ and then 'subsidize' the level of public goods to mask his/her incompetence to the tune of $(\kappa L - H)G_H^*(\mu)$. This is costly today, but if it results in the incumbent being re-elected, this is worthwhile if:

$$\beta\eta - c(\kappa L - H)G_H^*(\mu) > 0.$$

Now consider what happens in the state H. He/she has to commit cost reducing effort of $(\kappa-1)HG_H^*$ to mimic a competent incumbent with a cost shock of H. It is now straightforward to see that the condition required for a pooling equilibrium to exist is:

$$\beta\eta - c(\kappa L - H)G_H^*(\mu) > 0 > \beta\eta - c(\kappa-1)HG_H^*(\mu).$$

Otherwise, the equilibrium will be separating.[36] If $q > 1/2$, then the above condition is both necessary and sufficient for pooling.

The model with competence differences between politicians will exhibit the same selection and incentive issues that we found in the model where the difference between politicians is due to motivational differences.

---

[36] Observe that if the incompetent incumbents always provide G_H^* and $x = HG_H^*$ regardless of the cost shock (i.e., if $\beta\eta - c(\kappa-1)HG_H^*(\mu) > 0$): then the voter ousts any incumbent providing G_H^* and $x = HG_H^*$. In this case, the incompetent incumbents lose an incentive to mimic.

4.9 Conclusions

The main aim of this chapter has been to set the political agency model in a less abstract setting than the previous chapter. Our economic setting has been a simple public finance model where a government must determine a level of public spending and finance this out of taxes and debt. We have presented a simple and stylized political model which determines the equilibrium policy path consistent with voters optimally using re-election incentives.

The core idea, which carries over from Chapter 3, is that the political equilibrium can be understood as the balance of selection and incentive effects in politics. The way in which they interact determines the welfare properties of political equilibria.

Despite being very simple, the model offers some suggestions about the links between re-election and policy outcomes. It also gives some insight into tax and spending cycles when politicians cannot face re-election at the end of the second term.

The main analysis was devoted to studying the implications of the agency model for ways of adding additional constraints on government which affect its ability to tax and spend. We couched this as a kind of political second-best theory. While elections may help to combat agency problems due to information problems, they fall short—some amount of rent-seeking remains along the equilibrium policy path. The problem is then to view additional restraints on government in this second-best context. Restraints can now have two effects—direct effects when the restraint changes the economic constraint set and indirect effects when they lead to politicians changing their political behavior. The latter are mediated through the selection and incentive effects in politics.

We also considered the possibility of chanelling resources through non-governmental organizations. Here, the framework is useful since it allows us to model incentive problems in government and NGOs. The agency model provided some useful insights in this regard.

The model is only illustrative. It is certainly too simple and abstract to provide a guide to the details of policy debates. However, as a way of thinking it provides a balanced perspective, in a public finance setting, on the conflict of interest that arises between voters and government. This is not the only relevant dimension when we think about the political economy of public finance. However, it is an important one and clearly the correct one for addressing policy debates about the need to impose additional constraints on governments. It also has the attraction of being rooted in empirical observations on taxes, spending, and political turnover.

Chapter appendix: Optimal fiscal policy with pure moral hazard

Section 4.3.2 described the voter's optimal fiscal policy in the case of pure moral hazard, in which politicians are known to be the bad type, and the voter can commit to a re-election rule in advance. Here we provide a formal solution of the problem.

The voter's problem is to choose levels of spending and taxation (G_L, x_L) and (G_H, x_H) to maximize expected welfare:

$$q[G_H - \mu C(x_H)] + (1 - q)[G_L - \mu C(x_L)]. \qquad (4.12)$$

subject to the participation constraint guaranteeing that type H prefers to produce (G_H, x_H) to extracting X in rents immediately:

$$s_H = x_H - HG_H \geq (1 - \beta)X \qquad (PC_H)$$

and to the incentive constraint guaranteeing that type L prefers to produce (G_L, x_L) than (G_H, x_H):

$$s_L = x_L - LG_L \geq x_H - LG_H = s_H + (H - L)G_H. \qquad (IC_L)$$

This is the 'relaxed' problem, which ignores the analogous participation constraint for type L and incentive constraint for type H. It is immediately clear however that any solution satisfying the above constraints with $G_H \geq 0$ will also satisfy L's participation constraint (since $L < H$). That H's incentive constraint is also satisfied is less evident, however. Our approach will be to solve the relaxed problem, and then check that H's incentives are also correctly aligned.

Since higher taxation x_θ decreases welfare of the voter but increases rents to the politician, the solution to (4.12) must have both (PC_H) and (IC_L) satisfied as equalities. The first-order conditions for the voter's problem can then be simplified to:

$$\mu C'(x_L) = \frac{1}{L} \tag{13}$$

$$\mu C'(x_H) = \frac{1}{H}\left(1 - \frac{1-q}{q}\frac{H-L}{L}\right) \tag{14}$$

$$x_H = HG_H + (1-\beta)X$$

$$x_L = LG_L + (1-\beta)X + (H-L)G_H.$$

Equation (13) shows that low cost fiscal policies are undistorted: the marginal benefit of spending is set equal to its marginal tax cost, as represented by the point of tangency B_2 in Figure 4.1. Equation (14) shows that spending in the high cost state is distorted downwards: $\mu C'(x_H) < 1/H$.

Note that (14) implies that x_H (and G_H) is an increasing function of L and q. This confirms Proposition 2 in the text that lower costs in the sense of first order stochastic dominance lead to greater spending in the high cost state. Thus, reductions in the cost of government services may actually lead to further restrictions on government spending, as they worsen the potential agency problems created by bad politicians.

To complete the derivation, we must check that a politician facing high costs does not prefer to adopt the fiscal policies intended for the low cost type. The relevant incentive constraint is:

$$s_H = x_H - LG_H \geq x_L - HG_L = s_L - (H-L)G_L. \tag{IC$_H$}$$

Substituting into (IC$_L$), if the two incentive constraints are both two satisfied at any pair of fiscal policies, then we must have:

$$(H-L)(G_L - G_H) \geq 0 \tag{IC$_H$}$$

or simply $G_L - G_H \geq 0$. To verify that this necessary condition for implementation holds, we may invert the first-order conditions (13)–(14) to obtain:

$$L(G_L - G_H) = C'^{-1}\left(\frac{1}{\mu L}\right) - C'^{-1}\left(\frac{1}{\mu H}\left(1 - \frac{1-q}{q}\frac{H-L}{L}\right)\right) \geq 0.$$

5

Final Comments

The main aim of this book has been to look at the problem of good government through the lens of modern political economy. This is an evolving field and much has still to be learned. In this final brief chapter, I will discuss some topics for future research which follow on from the discussions of the previous chapters.

The topic of who chooses to become a politician and how institutional structure shapes this decision is relatively neglected in political economy.[1] However, our analysis has shown that the quality of the political class is an important determinant of good policy. Chapter 2 showed this was a source of political failure. It was also a recurrent theme in agency models with adverse selection and moral hazard in Chapters 3 and 4. Thus, it would be useful to have an understanding of how elections work to select good politicians.

While elections are now accepted as the main vehicle for picking politicians, this was not always for the case. For a period of time ancient Athens filled seats on its legislative council by drawing lots from among its citizens (Manin 1997). Each citizen served for one year and there was a restriction to two terms in a lifetime. The Greeks understood the downside of this method in terms of ensuring good politicians. They did impose safeguards in the form of a kind of confirmation hearing in which the character and competence of the selected candidate was scrutinized. However, the basic premise behind selection by lot is that civic virtue was widely distributed in the population, so that random selection made it relatively unlikely that anyone picked by the lottery would be a bad politician. Selection by lot was deemed preferable to elections for three main reasons.

---

[1] The ensuing discussion of selection is based on Besley (2005).

First, it guaranteed rotation in office, so that politicians were guaranteed to experience both political and everyday life. Second, selection by lot guaranteed the widest possible access to public office and hence was viewed as egalitarian. Third, lots seemed more likely to maintain a unity of purpose in the community, while elections increased the chance that citizens would group into factions.

The use of lottery makes a lot of sense in a relatively homogenous city state such as Athens. For similar reasons, lotteries were also used in the Italian city states of Venice and Florence. However, even political thinkers such as Montesquieu and Rousseau who took the idea of political selection by lot seriously in their writings ultimately favored elections, principally because they believed that elections helped in the selection of a natural aristocracy of the talented and virtuous. After all, selection by lot does not favor those with greater political competence over those with less.

This view heavily influenced the founding fathers of the United States, who similarly saw the task of political selection as selecting a ruling class that was different from the citizens at large—superior in their talents and mental capacities. Indeed the term 'natural aristocracy' originates with Thomas Jefferson (1813), in a letter written to John Adams. Jefferson wrote: 'I agree with you that there is a natural aristocracy among men. The grounds of this are virtue and talents ... May we not even say, that that form of government is the best, which provides the most effectually for a pure selection of these natural aristoi into the offices of government?' Jefferson continues to argue that he favors laws to break up large inheritances and support public education as methods of creating a situation in which the natural aristocracy can rise and be selected.

The idea of a natural aristocracy produced by election contrasts with the prevailing norm in early modern Europe, where many countries still relied heavily on hereditary aristocracy. The idea of selection by blood-line makes sense only if qualities required for making policy are passed between generations, either genetically or by some form of social conditioning, but it offers no safeguards if the transmission of such traits fails. It also has an advantage when it permits the ruling class to take a long-run view. The hereditary aristocracy had some ability to coopt the most talented and successful citizens in any generation—but it was much harder to demote those hereditary aristocrats who lacked political competence. Hereditary aristocracy also has a built in bias towards the interests of the rich. In such a setting, broad-based policy is on the basis of noblesse oblige and/or the threat of revolution.

Some countries, notably the United Kingdom, still have elements of hereditary selection of their political class. Even representative democracies have prominent political dynasties. The Nehru dynasty in India spawned three prime ministers who 'ruled' India between 1947 and 1989 with only a two year hiatus. The current Bush dynasty in the United States appears likely to have held the presidency for 12 out of 20 years. The advantage in name recognition is palpable. But whether politician quality is transmitted intergenerationally is far from clear. Debates about hereditary in politics are reminiscent in this regard to discussions about whether family owned firms have advantages in the market place.

When hereditary aristocracy is considered through the lens of political selection, it is no great surprise that this institution has largely disappeared over time. There is little to commend it as a means of picking the best people to make policy. The principle of heredity was dealt its severest blow by the increasing influence of Enlightenment thinkers, such as John Locke, who championed the idea that government could only gain its legitimacy from consent given freely by the citizens as expressed through the ballot box. This claim about perceived legitimacy has nothing directly to do with whether elections provide incentives to discipline rules; instead, it's a claim about the importance of selection to a well functioning political system.

In the modern world, most autocrats rule by force rather than inheritance. Autocracy's selection rule is to pick those leaders who can muster the greatest loyalty from coercive institutions such as the army and/or police. While autocracies display a fair amount of heterogeneity in their performance, it seems fair to say that the most brutal regimes in human history have typically been of this kind.

Selection by force does not appear to be an effective method either for selecting people who will offer wide-ranging political representation or those who will be the most competent to hold public office. Jones and Olken (2004) offer some evidence that the low quality government under autocracy is rooted in selection problems. They look at economic growth before and after the death in office of world leaders to provide evidence on whether leader quality matters. Their main finding is that the death of an autocrat leads to a change in growth. Democratically elected leaders show no corresponding pattern. This finding is consistent with selection by force having a disadvantage in selecting good leaders compared to democratic selection.

Even though elections are now the most commonly used institution for selecting a political class, there is enormous diversity in institutional structure. There are differences in the wages paid to politicians, the kind of public duties that are required, and the kind of policy discretion that the politician enjoys. There are diverse rules about who can stand for office, such as age, wealth, or literacy requirements. Rules about the conduct of elections also differ across democratic systems, including whether there are primaries for multiple candidates from the same party or runoffs between the top two candidates. Rules also differ with regard to the conduct of campaigns and the kind of financial support that candidates may receive.

For the most part, the political economy model has studied how institutions shape incentives to offer policies either before or after elections have taken place. As a result, our understanding of how electoral institutions shape political selection is in its infancy. Creating a better understanding of this (theoretically and empirically) constitutes a challenge for the future. This requires understanding who to choose to become a politician in the first instance and how this fits into broader career concerns.[2]

The approach throughout most of this book is quite individualistic. But much political activity takes place in collectives such as cabinets, legislatures, parties, interest groups, and NGOs. The dominant tradition in political economy has been to treat them as unitary actors with coherent preferences. But there is much to be done to understand the internal workings of such organizations and the implications for selection and incentives. For example, parties work as filters for picking politicians. Whether this results in the best quality people being picked to run for office is poorly understood.[3] There are also incentive questions concerning how parties form collective reputations and whether they have tools to discipline agents for acting against the collective interest.

There is an extensive literature on cabinets, coalitions, and legislatures. However, this has not yet been embedded in an agency framework. This has a bearing on the optimal structure of decision

---

[2] See Matozzi and Merlo (2005) for an interesting start on such a project.
[3] See Carrillo and Mariotti (2001) for an analysis in this direction.

making rules. A key issue is whether delegating to multiple decision makers worsens or improves the quality of public decision making. The examples discussed in Chapter 3 suggest that this is likely to depend on the details of the institutional structure. Understanding the mapping from institutional structures into policy outcomes in this area presents a challenge for future research.

The analysis above focused mainly on the way in which political processes shape policy. However, political choice is only one dimension of the issue. Policies have to be implemented, typically by bureaucrats. Bureaucrats are typically powerful because they have a lot of information about policy implementation. This creates a multi-layered agency problem between voters, politicians, and bureaucrats which has not been studied extensively in the agency model.[4] Bureaucrat accountability is rather different from politician accountability, in part because bureaucrats can be given more explicit incentives for project delivery and are typically focused on a more narrow set of task than politicians. Bureaucrats may also be more sensitive to market based incentives. Related to the issue of political selection is that of bureaucratic selection. When does a potential public servant choose to become a politician or a bureaucrat?

A more complete book than this would delve into issues of bureaucracy as well as politics in determining good policy. Just as the old style public choice reasoning has now been replaced by more sophisticated models of agency in politics, so there is a need to get beyond the old fashioned budget maximizing models of bureaucracy. A full treatment of these issues would require looking at models which are sensitive to the issues that arise in very different bureaucratic environments— from the armed forces, to schools, to hospitals and town planning. The new literature in political economy still has some way to go to provide a comprehensive approach that covers all these areas.

Another missing element in the discussion above is the exercise of judicial power. As we discussed above, Maskin and Tirole (2004) have used the agency approach to contrast different methods of judicial selection and their consequences for outcomes. It is clear that much important policy making—for example, competition policy— makes extensive use of judicial processes in implementing policy. How far courts (rather than legislatures) can and should be given a policy role raises fascinating questions and one dimension of good

---

[4] See Alesina and Tabellini (2004) for a move in this direction.

government is surely getting the mix of responsibilities right. There is scope for much more work on these issues.

The field of political economy is booming. It is now widely appreciated that incentives in government need to be understood to improve the quality of policy making. The traditional mode of public economics has been to study the pros and cons of different policies. While this has been extremely powerful in shaping policy debates, it is clear that this is only part of the story.

First, we need to understand why good policies are enacted only some of the time. Trade protection based on tariffs is a case in point. It would be useful to understand the source of political failure at work here to see if there is any way to reform the policy process to improve the quality of government policy.

Second, many proposed reforms involve changes in institutional structures. For example, governments wish to understand the pros and cons of decentralizing policy making to lower tiers of government, or of creating an independent agency to carry out policy, or of increasing transparency in policy making. In such cases, it is necessary to work with models of the policy process in which implications for selection and incentives from institutional change can be understood.

In response to both of these cases, the field of political economy is providing the knowledge and tools that are needed to improve the workings of government.

The material in this book shapes broad thinking on the competence of government. We have begun from a position that while markets have their limits in allocating resources, so do governments. It is evident that the economics profession is now providing tools to meet the challenge of deciding where the boundaries lie between public and private responsibility. There is a section of opinion that equates good government to small government. Moreover, this has been a dominant tradition in political economy in the past. However, there is nothing in modern political economics to support this claim even if attitudes towards government intervention are more cautious than in the past. A political economy approach can also fuel optimism—if we can understand the logic of good government, then perhaps this is the first step towards creating it.

References

Acemoglu, D. (2003). 'Why Not a Political Case Theorem?', *Journal of Comparative Economics*, 31: 620–52.
—— (2005). 'Modeling Inefficient Institutions', Paper prepared for the World Congress of the Econometric Society, London.
—— and Robinson, J. (2001). 'Inefficient Redistribution', *American Political Science Review*, 95(3): 649–61.
—— and —— (2003). 'Economic Backwardness in Political Perspective', typescript. MIT: Cambridge, MA.
—— and —— (2005). *Economic Origins of Dictatorship and Democracy*. Cambridge: Cambridge University Press.
—— and Verdier, T. (2000). 'The Choice between Market Failures and Corruption', *American Economic Review*, 90(1): 194–211.
—— Johnson, S., and Robinson, J. A. (2001). 'The Colonial Origins of Comparative Development: An Empirical Investigation', *American Economic Review*, 91(5): 1369–401.
Adams, J. D. and Kenny, L. (1986). 'Optimal Tenure of Elected Public Officials', *Journal of Law and Economics*, 29(2): 303–28.
Ades, A. and Di Tella, R. (1999). 'Rents, Competition, and Corruption', *American Economic Review*, 89: 982–93.
Aghion, P. and Bolton, P. (1990). 'Government Debt and the Risk of Default: A Politico-Economic Model of the Strategic Role of Debt', in R. Dornbusch and M. Draghi (eds.) *Public Debt Management: Theory and History*. Cambridge: Cambridge University Press.
Ahrend, R. (2000). 'Press Freedom, Human Capital and Corruption', typescript. Paris: DELTA.
Aldrich, J. (1997). 'When is it Rational to Vote?' in D. Mueller (ed.) *Perspectives on Public Choice: A Handbook*. Ann Arbor, MI: University of Michigan Press.
Alesina, A. (1988). 'Credibility and Policy Convergence in a Two-Party System with Rational Voters', *American Economic Review*, 78(4): 796–806.
—— and Perrotti, R. (1995). 'The Political Economy of Budget Deficits', *IMF Staff Papers*, 42(1): 1–31.
—— and Roubini, N. (1992). 'Political Cycles in OECD Economies', *Review of Economic Studies*, 59: 663–88.

—— and Tabellini, G. (2004). 'Bureaucrats or Politicians?' CEPR Discussion Papers No. 4252.

Alt, J. E. and Dreyer Lassen, D. (2002). 'Fiscal Transparency and Fiscal Policy Outcomes in OECD Countries', typescript. Harvard University, Cambridge, MA.

—— and Lowry, R. C. (1994). 'Divided Government, Fiscal Institutions and Budget Deficits: Evidence from the States', *American Political Science Review*, 88(4): 811–28.

——, Dreyer Lassen, D. and Skilling, D. (2002). 'Fiscal Transparency, Gubernatorial Popularity, and the Scale of Government: Evidence from the States', *States Politics Quarterly*, 2(3): 230–50.

——, Bueno de Mesquita, E., and Rose, S. (2006). 'Term Limits and Selection Effects in U.S. State Elections'.

Arrow, K. (1951). *Social Choice and Individual Values*. New York: Wiley.

Ashworth, S. (2005). 'Reputational Dynamics and Political Careers', *The Journal of Law, Economics, and Organization* (forthcoming).

—— and Bueno de Mesquita, E. (2005a). 'Delivering the Goods: Legislative Particularism in Different Electoral and Institutional Settings', *Journal of Politics* (forthcoming).

—— and —— (2005b). 'Electoral Selection and the Incumbency Advantage' available at http://www.princeton.edu/~sashwort/inc_adv.pdf

Atkinson, A. B. and Stiglitz, J. E. (1980). *Lectures on Public Economics*. New York: McGraw Hill.

Austen-Smith, D. and Banks, J. (1989). 'Electoral Accountability and Incumbency', in P. Ordeshook (ed.) *Models of Strategic Choice in Politics*. Ann Arbor, MI: University of Michigan Press.

Bails, D. and Tieslau, M. (2000). 'The Impact of Fiscal Constitutions on State and Local Expenditures', *Cato Journal*, 20(2): 255–77.

Banks, Jeffrey and Duggan, J. (1999). 'The Theory of Probabilistic Voting in the Spatial Model of Elections', typescript. University of Rochester, Rochester, NY.

—— and Sundaram, R. (1993). 'Adverse Selection and Moral Hazard in a Repeated Elections Model', in W. Barnett et al. (eds.) *Political Economy: Institutions, Information, Competition and Representation*. New York, NY: Cambridge University Press.

—— and Sundaram, R. (1998). 'Optimal Retention in Agency Problems', *Journal of Economic Theory*, 82(2): 293–323.

Bardhan, P. and Mookherjee, D. (2000). 'Capture and Governance at Local and National Levels', *American Economic Review*, 90(2): 135–9.

Barganza, J. C. (2000). 'Two Roles for Elections: Disciplining the Incumbent and Selecting a Competent Candidate', *Public Choice*, 105(1/2): 165–93.

Barro, R. (1973). 'The Control of Politicians: An Economic Model', *Public Choice*, 14: 19–42.

References

Barro, R. (1979). 'On the Determination of the Public Debt', *Journal of Political Economy*, 87: 940–71.

Bator, F. M. (1958). 'The Anatomy of Market Failure', *Quarterly Journal of Economics*, 72(3): 351–79.

Battaglini, M. and Coate, S. (2005). 'Inefficiency in Legislative Policy Making: A Dynamic Analysis', typesecript. Cornell University, Ithaca, NY.

Baumol, W. J. (1967). 'Macroeconomics of Unbalanced Growth: The Anatomy of Urban Crisis', *American Economic Review*, 57(3): 415–26.

Baye, M., Kovenock, D., and De Vries, C. (1994). 'The Solution to the Tullock Rent-Seeking Game When $R > 2$: Mixed-Strategy Equilibria and Mean Dissipation Rates', *Public Choice*, 81: 363–80.

Becker, G. (1983). 'A Theory of Competition Among Pressure Groups for Political Influence', *Quarterly Journal of Economics*, 98: 371–400.

—— and Mulligan, C. (2003). 'Deadweight Costs and the Size of Government', *Journal of Law and Economics*, 46(2): 293–340.

Bénabou, R. and Tirole, J. (2003): 'Intrinsic and Extrinsic Motivation', *Review of Economic Studies*, 70(3): 489–520.

Bergstrom, T. (1979). 'When Does Majority Rule Supply Public Goods Efficiently?' *Scandinavian Journal of Economics*, 81: 216–26.

Bernheim, B. D. and Whinston, M. (1986). 'Menu Auctions, Resource Allocation, and Economic Influence', *The Quarterly Journal of Economics*, 101(1): 1–31.

Berry, W., Ringquist, E., Fording, R., and Hanson, R. (1998). 'Measuring Citizen and Government ideology in the American States', *American Journal of Political Science*, 42(2): 327–48.

Besley, T. (2004). 'Paying Politicians: Theory and Evidence', Joseph Schumpeter Lecture published in the *Journal of the European Economics Association*, 2(2–3): 193–215.

—— (2005). 'Political Selection', *Journal of Economic Perspectives*, 19(3): 43–60.

—— and Burgess, R. (2002). 'The Political Economy of Government Responsiveness: Theory and Evidence from India', *Quarterly Journal of Economics*, 117(4): 1415–52.

—— and Case, A. (1995a). 'Incumbent Behavior: Vote Seeking, Tax Setting and Yardstick Competition', *American Economic Review*, 85(1): 25–45.

—— and —— (1995b). 'Does Political Accountability Affect Economic Policy Choices? Evidence From Gubernatorial Term Limits', *Quarterly Journal of Economics*, 110(3): 769–98.

—— and —— (2003). 'Political Institutions and Policy Choices: Evidence from the United States', *Journal of Economic Literature*, 41(1): 7–73.

—— and Coate, S. (1997). 'An Economic Model of Representative Democracy', *Quarterly Journal of Economics*, 112(1): 85–114.

—— and —— (1998). 'Sources of Inefficiency in a Representative Democracy: A Dynamic Analysis', *American Economic Review*, 88(1): 139–56.

—— and —— (2001). 'Lobbying and Welfare in a Representative Democracy', *Review of Economic Studies*, 68: 67–82.

—— and —— (2003). 'On the Public Choice Critique of Welfare Economics', *Public Choice*, 114(3): 253–73.

—— and Ghatak, M. (2001). 'Public versus Private Provision of Public Goods', *Quarterly Journal of Economics*, 116(4): 1343–72.

—— and —— (2005). 'Competition and Incentives with Motivated Agents', *American Economic Review*, 95(3): 616–36.

—— and Prat, A. (2006). 'Handcuffs for the Grabbing Hand? Media Capture and Government Accountability', *American Economic Review* (forthcoming).

—— and Preston, I. (2004). 'Electoral Bias and Policy Choice: Theory and Evidence', typescript. London School of Economics, London.

—— and Smart, M. (2007). 'Fiscal Restraints and Voter Welfare', *Journal of Public Economics*, 91(3): 755–73.

Biais, B. and Perotti, E. (2002). 'Machiavellian Underpricing', *American Economic Review*, 92(1): 240–8.

Black, D. (1958). *The Theory of Committees and Elections*. Cambridge: Cambridge University Press.

Bodenstein, M. and Ursprung, H. (2001). 'Political Yardstick Competition, Economic Integration, and Constitutional Choice in a Federation', CESifo Working Paper No. 501.

Boettke, P. J. (2003). 'The New Comparative Political Economy', typescript. George Mason University, Fairfax, VA.

—— and Lopez, E. J. (2002). 'Austrian Economics and Public Choice', *Public Choice*, 15(2/3): 111–19.

Bonaglia, F., Braga de Macedo, J., and Bussolo, M. S. (2001). 'How Globalization Improves Governance' CEPR Discussion Paper No. 2992. http://ssrn.com/abstract=288354.

Bordignon, M., Cerniglia F., and Revelli, F. (2001). 'In Search of Yardstick Competition: Property Tax Rates and Electoral Behavior in Italian Cities', typescript. Universita Catolica di Milano, Milan, Haly.

Borcherding, T. E. (1985). 'The Causes of Government Expenditure Growth: A Survey of the U.S. Evidence', *Journal of Public Economics*, 28: 359–82.

Brennan, G. and Buchanan, J. M. (1980). *The Power to Tax: Analytical Foundations of the Fiscal Constitution*. Cambridge: Cambridge University Press.

—— and —— (1985). *The Reason of Rules: Constitutional Political Economy*. Cambridge: Cambridge University Press.

Brunetti, A. and Weder, B. (2003). 'A Free Press Is Bad News for Corruption', *Journal of Public Economics*, 87(7–8): 1801–24.

Buchanan, J. M. (1967). *Public Finance in Democratic Process*. Chapel Hill: University of North Carolina Press.

References

Buchanan, J. M. (1972). 'Toward an Analysis of Closed Behavioral Systems', in J. Buchanan and R. Tollison (eds.) *Theory of Public Choice*. Ann Arbor: University of Michigan Press.

—— (1989a). 'The Public-Choice Perspective', *Essays on the Political Economy*. Honolulu: University of Hawaii Press.

—— (1989b). 'Constitutional Economics', *Explorations into Constutional Economics*. College Station, TX: Texas A & M University Press.

—— (1999). 'Constraints on Political Action', in J. M. Buchanan and R. A. Musgrave (eds.) *Public Finance and Public Choice: Two Contrasting Visions of the State*. Cambridge, MA: CESifo, MIT Press.

—— and Tullock, G. (1962). *The Calculus of Consent*. Ann Arbor: University of Michigan Press.

—— and R. E. Wagner (1977). *Democracy in Deficit: The Political Legacy of Lord Keynes*. Academic Press.

Calvert, R. L. (1985). 'Robustness of the Multi-dimensional Voting Model: Candidate Motivations, Uncertainty and Convergence', *American Journal of Political Science*, 29: 69–95.

Canes-Wrones, B., Herron, M. C., and Shotts, K. W. (2001). 'Leadership and Pandering: A Theory of Executive Policy Making', *American Journal of Political Science* 45(3): 532–50.

Carrillo, J. and Marriotti, T. (2001). 'Electoral Competition and Politician Turnover', *European Economic Review*, 45(1): 1–26.

Caselli, F. and Morelli, M. (2004). 'Bad Politicians' *Journal of Public Economics*, 88: 759–82.

Cho, I-K. and Kreps, D. (1987). 'Signalling Games and Stable Equilibria', *Quarterly Journal of Economics*, 102: 179–221.

Chubb, J. (1988). 'Institutions, the Economy, and the Dynamics of States Elections', *American Political Science Review*, 82(1): 133–54.

Ciccone, A. (2004). 'Resistance to Reform: Status Quo Bias in the Presence of Individual-Specific Uncertainty: Comment', *American Economic Review*, 94(3): 785–95.

Clarke, E. H. (1971). 'Multipart Pricing of Public Goods', *Public Choice*, 11: 17–33.

Coate, S. (2004a). 'Political Competition with Campaign Contributions and Informative Advertising', *Journal of the European Economic Association*, 2(5): 772–804.

—— (2004b). 'Pareto Improving Campaign Finance Policy', *American Economic Review*, 94(3): 628–55.

—— and Morris, S. (1995). 'On the Form of Transfers to Special Interests', *Journal of Political Economy*, 103: 1210–35.

—— and —— (1999). 'Policy Persistence', *American Economic Review*, 89(5): 1327–36.

Cooter, R. D. (2000). *The Strategic Constitution*. Princeton, NJ: Princeton University Press.

Coughlin, P. (1992). *Probabilistic Voting Theory*. Cambridge: Cambridge University Press.

Crain, W. M. and L. K. Oakley (1995). 'The Politics of Infrastructure', *Journal of Law and Economics*, 38(1): 1–17.

—— and R. D. Tollison (1977). 'Attenuated Property Rights and the Market for Governors', *Journal of Law and Economics*, 20(1): 205–11.

—— and R. D. Tollison (1993). 'Time Inconsistency and Fiscal Policy: Empirical Evidence of U.S. States, 1969–89', *Journal of Public Economics*, 51(2): 153–9.

De Toqueville, A. ([1835] 1994). *Democracy in America*, Everyman's Library Edition. New York: Alfred A. Knopf.

Denzau, A. T., Mackay R. J., and Weaver, C. (1981). 'On the Initiative-Referendum Option and the Control of Monopoly Government', in H. F. Ladd and T. N. Tideman (eds.) *Tax and Expenditure Limitations*. Washington, DC: The Urban Institute.

Dewatripont, M., Jewitt, I., and Tirole, J. (1999). 'The Economics of Career Concerns', *Review of Economic Studies*, 66(1): 189–217.

Diermeier, D., Keane, M., and Merlo, A. (2003). 'A Political Economy Model of Congressional Careers', *American Economic Review* (forthcoming).

Djankov, S., Glaeser, E., LaPorta, R., Lopez-de-Silanes, F., and Shleifer, A. (2003a). 'The New Comparative Economics', *Journal of Comparative Economics*, 31(4): 595–619.

——, McLeish, C., Nenova, T., and Shleifer, A. (2003b). 'Who Owns the Media?' *Journal of Law and Economics*, 46(2): 341–82.

Downs, A. (1957). *An Economic Theory of Democracy*. New York: Harper and Bros.

Farnham, P. G. (1990). 'The Impact of Citizen Influence on Local Government Expenditure', *Public Choice*, 64: 201–21.

Fearon, J. (1999). 'Electoral Accountability and the Control of Politicians: Selecting Good Types verses Sanctioning Poor Performance', in A. Przeworski, S. Stokes and B. Manin (eds.) *Democracy, Accountability and Representation*. Cambridge: Cambridge University Press.

Feddersen, T. and Pesendorfer, W. (1996). 'Abstention in Elections with Asymmetric Information and Diverse Preferences', Discussion Papers 1195. Chicago: Center for Mathematical Studies in Economics and Management Science, Northwestern University.

—— and —— (1997). 'Voting Behavior and Information Aggregation in Elections with Private Information', *Econometrica*, 65(5): 1029–58.

Fehr, E. and Falk, A. (2002). 'Psychological Foundations of Incentives', *European Economic Review*, 46(4–5): 687–724.

Feld, L. P. and Kirchgässner, G. (2000). 'Direct Democracy, Political Culture, and the Outcome of Economic Policy: A Report on the Swiss Experience', *European Journal of Political Economy*, 16: 287–306.

References

Ferejohn, J. (1986). 'Incumbent Performance and Electoral Control', *Public Choice*, 50: 5–25.

—— (1999). 'Accountability and Authority: Toward a Theory of Political Accountability', in A. Przeworski, S. Stokes, and B. Manin (eds.) *Democracy, Accountability and Representation*. Cambridge: Cambridge University Press.

Fernandez, R. and Rodrik, D. (1991). 'Resistance to Reform: Status Quo Bias in the Presence of Individual-Specific Uncertainty', *American Economic Review*, 81(5): 1146–55.

Ferraz, C. and Finan, F. (2005). 'Exposing Corrupt Politicians: The Effect of Brazil's Publicly Released Audits on Electoral Outcomes', typescript. University of California, Berkeley, CA.

Fiorina, M. (1981). *Retrospective Voting in American National Elections*. New Haven, CT: Yale University Press.

Fischer, S. and L. H. Summers (1989). 'Should Governments Learn to Live with Inflation?' *American Economic Review Papers and Proceedings*, 382–7.

Frey, B. S. (1983). *Democratic Economic Policy: A Theoretical Introduction*. Oxford: Basil Blackwell.

—— (1997). *Not Just for the Money: An Economic Theory of Personal Motivation*. Cheltenham: Edward Elgar Publishing.

Gallego, M. and C. Pitchik (2004). 'An Economic Theory of Leadership Turnover', *Journal of Public Economics*, 88: 2361–82.

Gelbach, S. and Sonin, K. (2004). Businessman Candidates: Special Interest Politics in Weakly Institutionalized Environments. University of Wisconsin.

Gerber, E. (1996). 'Legislative Response to Threat of Popular Initiatives', *American Journal of Political Science*, 40(1): 99–128.

Gersbach, H. (2003). 'Incentives and Elections for Politicians and the Down–Up Problem', in M. Sertel and S. Koray (ed.), *Advances in Economic Design*. Berlin-Heidelberg: Springer-Verlag.

—— (2004). 'Competition of Politicians for Incentive Contracts and Elections', *Public Choice*, 12(1): 157–77.

—— and Liessem, V. (2001). 'Incentive Contracts and Elections for Politicians with Multi-Task Problems', CEPR Working Paper No. 4075.

Glazer, A. (1989). 'Politics and the Choice of Durability', *American Economic Review*, 79: 1207–13.

Grossman, G. and Helpman, E. (1994). 'Protection for Sale', *American Economic Review*, 84: 833–50.

—— and —— (1996). 'Electoral Competition and Special Interest Politics', *Review of Economic Studies*, 63(2): 265–86.

Groves, T. (1973). 'Incentives in Teams', *Econometrica*, 41: 617–31.

Hammond, P. (1979). 'Straightforward Incentive Compatibility in Large Economies', *Review of Economic Studies*, 46: 263–82.

Harrington, J. E., Jr. (1993). 'Economic Policy, Economic Performance, and Elections', *American Economic Review*, 83(1): 27–42.

Heal, G., (1973). *The Theory of Economic Planning*. Amsterdam: North-Holland.

Hellman J. S., Jones, G., and Kaufmann, D. (2000). 'Seize the State, Seize the Day: State Capture, Corruption, and Influence in Transition', World Bank Policy Research Working Paper, 2444.

Hettich, W. and Winer, S. (2004). 'The Political Economy of Public Finance: Structure and Application', in D. Wittman and B. Weingast (eds.) *The Oxford Handbook of Political Economy*. Oxford: Oxford University Press.

Hibbs, D. A. (1977). 'Political Parties and Macroeconomic Policy', *American Political Science Review*, 71: 146–87.

Hindriks, J. and Belleflamme, P. (2001). 'Yardstick Competition and Political Agency Problems', Discussion Papers No. 444. London: Department of Economics, Queen Mary and Westfield College. Available at http://www.econ.qmw.ac.uk/papers/ wp444.htm.

——and Lockwood, B. (2005). 'Decentralization and Electoral Accountability: Incentives, Separation and Voter Welfare', typescript. University of Warwick.

Holmstrom, B. (1979). 'Moral Hazard and Observability', *Bell Journal of Economics and Management Science*, 10(1): 74–91.

——(1982). 'Moral Hazard in Teams', *Bell Journal of Economics and Management Science*, 13(2): 324–40.

——(1999). 'Managerial Incentive Problems: A Dynamic Perspective', *Review of Economic Studies*, 66(1): 169–82.

Holsey, C. and Borcherding, T. (1997). 'Why Does Government's Share of National Income Grow? An Assessment of the Recent Literature on the U.S.', in D. Mueller (ed.) *Perspectives on Public Choice*. Cambridge: Cambridge University Press.

Hume, D. (1742). 'Of the Independency of Parliament', in E. F. Miller (ed.) *Essays, Moral Political and Literary*, Liberty Fund, Library of Economics and Liberty. Available at <http://www.econlib.org/library/LFBooks/Hume/hmMPL6.html>. (accessed 5 June 2005).

Jain, S. and Mukand, S. (2003). 'Redistributive Promises and the Adoption of Economic Reform', *American Economic Review*, 94(1): 256–64.

Jefferson, T. (1813). 'The Natural Aristocracy', Letter to John Adams, October 28.

Jones, B. F. and Olken, B. A. (2004). 'Do Leaders Matter? National Leadership and Growth Since World War II', *Quarterly Journal of Economics* (forthcoming).

Kaplow, L. and Shavell, S. (2001). 'Any Non-welfarist Method of Policy Assignment Violates the Pareto Principle', *Journal of Political Economy*, 109(2): 281–6.

Key, V. O. (1956). *American State Politics: An Introduction*. New York: Alfred A. Knopf.

References

Key, V. O. (1966). *The Responsible Electorate: Rationality in Presidential Voting: 1936–60*. Cambridge, MA: Belknap Press.

Keynes, J. N. (1891). *The Scope and Method of Political Economy*. London: Macmillan.

Kopit, G. and Craig, J. (1998). 'Transparency in Government Operations', IMF Occasional Paper 158.

Knight, B. (2000). 'Supermajority Voting Requirements for Tax Increases: Evidence from the States', *Journal of Public Economics*, 76: 41–67.

Krueger, A. (1973). 'The Political Economy of the Rent-Seeking Society', *American Economic Review*, 64: 291–303.

Krusell, P. and Rios-Rull, J.-V. (1996). 'Vested Interests in a Positive Theory of Stagnation and Growth', *Review of Economic Studies*, 63(2): 301–21.

Kydland, F. and Prescott, E. (1977). 'Rules rather than Discretion: The Inconsistency of Optimal Plans', *Journal of Political Economy*, 85: 473–91.

Laffont, J-J. (2000). *Incentives and Political Economy*. Oxford: Oxford University Press.

—— and Maskin, E. (1980). 'A Differential Approach to Dominant Strategy Mechanisms', *Econometrica*, 48(6): 1507–20.

—— and Tirole, J. (1986). 'Using Cost Observation to Regulate Firms', *Journal of Political Economy*, 94(3): 614–41.

—— and —— (1993). *A Theory of Incentives in Procurement and Regulation*. Cambridge: MIT Press.

Lange, O. (1936). 'On the Economic Theory of Socialism, Part I', *Review of Economic Studies*, 4(1): 53–71.

—— (1937). 'On the Economic Theory of Socialism, Part II', *Review of Economic Studies*, 4(2): 123–42.

La Porta, R., Lopez-de-Silanes, F., Shleifer, A. and Vishny, R. W. (1999). 'The Quality of Government', *Journal of Law, Economics and Organization*, 15(1): 222–79.

Le Borgne, E. and Lockwood, B. (2001a). 'Do Elections Always Motivate Incumbents?' Warwick Economic Research Paper No. 580.

—— and —— (2001b). 'Candidate Entry, Screening, and the Political Budget Cycle', typescript. University of Warwick, Kennilworth.

Ledyard, J. O. (1995). 'Public Goods: A Survey of Experimental Research,' in J. H. Kagel and A. E. Roth (eds.) *The Handbook of Experimental Economics*. Princeton: Princeton University Press.

Lee, D. S., Moretti, E., and Butler, M. (2004). Do Voters Affect or Elect Policies? Evidence from the U.S. House, *Quarterly Journal of Economics*, 119(3): 807–60.

Leon, G. (2004). 'Political Considerations and the Implementation of Long Term Projects in the Developing World', unpublished M.Phil Thesis, Oxford University.

Lerner, A. (1944). *The Economics of Control: Principles of Welfare Economics*. New York: Macmillan.

Levi, M. and Stoker, L. (2000). 'Political Trust and Trustworthiness', *Annual Review of Political Science*, 3: 475–507.

Lindbeck, A. and Weibull, J. (1987). 'Balanced Budget Redistribution as the Outcome of Political Competition', *Public Choice*, 52: 273–97.

Lipsey R. G. and Lancaster, K. (1956). 'The general theory of the secondbest', *Review of Economic Studies*, 24: 11–32.

List, J. and Sturm, D. (2001). 'Politics and Environmental Policy: Theory and Evidence from U.S. States', unpublished typescript, University of Maryland and University of Munich.

Lott, J. R., Jr. and Bronars, S. G. (1993). 'Time Series Evidence on Shirking in the U.S. House of Representatives', *Public Choice*, 76: 125–49.

Lowry, R. C., Alt, J. E., and Ferree, K. E. (1998). 'Fiscal Policy Outcomes and Electoral Accountability in American States', *American Political Science Review*, 92(4): 759–74.

McArthur, J. and Marks, S. V. (1988). 'Constituent Interest vs. Legislator Ideology: The Role of Political Opportunity Cost', *Economic Inquiry*, 26(3): 461–70.

Maddison, A. (2001). *The World Economy—A Millennial Perspective*. Paris: OECD Development Centre.

Madison, J. (1788 [1961]). *The Federalist Papers: A Collection of Essays in Support of the Constitution of the United States*. News York: Doubleday.

Manin, B. (1997). *The Principles of Representative Government*. Cambridge: Cambridge University Press.

Maskin, E. (1999). 'Nash Equilibrium and Welfare Optimality', *Review of Economic Studies*, 66: 23–38

—— and Tirole, J. (2004). 'The Politician and the Judge: Accountability in Government', *American Economic Review*, 94(4): 1034–54.

Mattozzi, A. and Merlo, A. (2005). 'Political Careers or Career Politicians', typescript, University of Pennsylvania.

Matsusaka, J. G. (1995). 'Fiscal Effects of the Voter Initiative: Evidence from the Last 30 Years', *Journal of Political Economy*, 103(3): 587–623.

Mauro, P. (1995). 'Corruption and growth', *Quarterly Journal of Economics*, 110: 681–712.

Milesi-Ferreti G.-M. (2000). 'Good, Bad or Ugly? On the Effects of Fiscal Rules with Creative Accounting', IMF Working Paper No. 172.

—— and Spolaore, E. (1994). 'How Cynical Can an Incumbent Be? Strategic Policy in a Model of Government Spending', *Journal of Public Economics*, 55: 121–40.

—— (2003). *Public Choice III*. Cambridge: Cambridge University Press.

Mukand, S. W. and Majumdar, S. (2003). 'Policy Gambles', *American Economic Review* (forthcoming).

Mulligan, C. B., Gil R., and Sala-i-Martin, X. (2004). 'Do Democracies have Different Public Policies than Non-Democracies?' *Journal of Economic Perspectives*, 18(1): 51–74.

Murdock, K. (2002). 'Intrinsic Motivation and Optimal Incentive Contract, ' *Rand Journal of Economics*, 33(4): 650–71.

Murphy, K. M., Shleifer, A., and Vishny, R. W. (1991). 'The Allocation of Talent: Implications for Growth', *Quarterly Journal of Economics*, 106: 503–30.

Musgrave, R. A. (1999). 'The Nature of the Fiscal State: The Roots of My Thinking', in J. M. Buchanan and R. A. Musgrave (eds.) *Public Finance and Public Choice: Two Contrasting Visions of the State*. Cambridge: CESifo, MIT Press.

——and Peacock, A. T. (eds.) (1958). *Classics in the Theory of Public Finance*. London: McMillan.

Myerson, R. B. (1993). 'Incentives to Cultivate Favored Minorities under Alternative Electoral Systems', *American Political Science Review*, 87(4): 856–69.

——(2000). 'Economic Analysis of Constitutions', *University of Chicago Law Review*, 67: 925–40.

——(2005). 'Federalism and the incentives for success of democracy', *Quarterly Review of Political Science* (forthcoming).

Nannestad, P. and Paldam, M. (1994). 'The VP-Function: A Survey of the Literature on Vote and Popularity Functions after 25 Years', *Public Choice*, 79(3–4) (June): 213–45.

Nordhaus, W. D. (1975). 'The Political Business Cycle', *Review of Economic Studies*, 42(2): 169–90.

Osborne, M. J. and Slivinski, A. (1996). 'A Model of Political Competition with Citizen Candidates', *Quarterly Journal of Economics*, 111(1): 65–96.

Ottaviani, M. and Sorensen, P. (2001). 'Professional Advice', unpublished working paper. London Business School, London.

Peltzman, S. (1976). 'Toward a More General Theory of Regulation', *Journal of Law and Economics*, 19: 211–40.

——(1980). 'The Growth of Government', *Journal of Law and Economics*, 23(2): 209–87.

——(1987). 'Economic Conditions and Gubernatorial Elections', *American Economic Review*, 77(2): 293–97.

Persson, T. (2004). 'Forms of democracy, policy and economic development', unpublished typescript, IIES, Stockholm.

——and Svensson, L. (1989). 'Why a Stubborn Conservative Would Run A Deficit: Policy with Time-Inconsistent Preferences', *Quarterly Journal of Economics*, 104: 325–46.

——and Tabellini, G. (2000). *Political Economics: Explaining Economic Policy*. Cambridge: MIT Press.

——and Tabellini, G. (2003). *The Economic Effects of Constitutions*. Cambridge: MIT Press.

——, Roland, G., and Tabellini, G. (1997). 'Separation of Powers and Political Accountability', *Quarterly Journal of Economics*, 112(4): 1163–202.

——, ——, and —— (2000). 'Comparative Politics and Public Finance', *Journal of Political Economy*, 108(6): 1121–61.

——Tabellini, G., and Trebbi, F. (2003). 'Electoral Rules and Corruption', *Journal of the European Ecomomic Association*, 1(4): 958–89.

Pettersson-Lidbom, P. (2003). 'A Test of the Rational Electoral-Cycle Hypothesis', typescript. University of Stockholm, Stockholm.

Pharr, S. J., Putnam, R. D., and Dalton, R. (2000). 'Trouble in the Advanced Democracies? A Quarter-Century of Declining Confidence', *Journal of Democracy*, 11(2): 5–25.

POLITY IV available at http://www. cidcm. umd. edu/inscr/polity/

Pigou, A. (1920). *The Economics of Welfare*. London: McMillan.

Poutvaara, P. and Takalo, T. (2003). 'Candidate Quality', unpublished typescript. University of Helsinki, Helsinki.

Prat, A. (2005). 'The Wrong Kind of Transparency', *American Economic Review*, 95(3): 862–77.

Prendergast, C. (1999). 'The Provision of Incentives in Firms', *Journal of Economic Literature*, 37(1): 7–63.

——and Stole, L. (1996). 'Impetuous Youngsters and Jaded Old-Timers', *Journal of Political Economy*, 104: 1105–34.

Putnam, R. (1993). *Making Democracy Work: Civic Traditions in Modern Italy*. Princeton: Princeton University Press.

Qian, Y. and Roland, G. (1998). 'Federalism and the Soft Budget Constraint', *American Economic Review*, 88(5): 1143–62.

Revelli, F. (2001). 'Local Taxes, National Politics and Spatial Interactions in English District Election Results', *European Journal of Political Economy* (forthcoming).

Robinson, J. A. and Torvik, R. (2005). 'White Elephants', *Journal of Public Economics*, 89: 197–210.

Rodrik, D. (1996). 'Understanding Economic Policy Reform', *Journal of Economic Literature*, 34(1): 9–41.

Roemer, J. (2001). *Political Competition: Theory and Applications*. Cambridge, MA: Harvard University Press.

Rogoff, K. (1990). 'Equilibrium Political Budget Cycles', *American Economic Review*, 80(1): 21–36.

——and Siebert, A. (1988). 'Elections and Macroeconomic Policy Cycles', *Review of Economic Studies*, 55(1): 1–16.

Romer, T. and Rosenthal, H. (1978). 'Political Resource Allocation, Controlled Agendas, and the Status Quo', *Public Choice*, 33(4): 27–43.

Rueben, K. (2000). 'Tax Limitations and Government Growth: The Effect of State Tax and Expenditure Limits on State and Local Government', typescript. San Francisco, CA.

Salmon, P. (1987). 'Decentralization as an Incentive Scheme', *Oxford Review of Economic Policy*, 3(2): 24–43.

Sand-Zantman, W. (2004). 'Economic Integration and Political Accountability', *European Economic Review*, 48(5): 1001–25.

References

Schaltegger, C. A. and Küttel, D. (2002). 'Exit, Voice, and Mimicking Behavior: Evidence from Swiss Cantons', *Public Choice*, 113(1–2): 1–23.

Schattschneider, E. E. (1960). *The Semisovereign People: A Realists View of Democracy in America*. New York: Holt, Rinehart and Winston.

Schumpeter, J. A. (1943). *Capitalism, Socialism and Democracy*. London: Allen & Unwin.

Sen, A. K. (1970). 'The Impossibility of a Paretian liberal', *Journal of Political Economy*, 78: 152–7.

——(1976–77). 'Rational Fools: A Critique of the Behavioural Foundations of Economic Theory', *Philosophy and Public Affairs*, 6: 317–44.

——(1977). 'On Weights and Measures: Informational Constraints in Social Welfare Analysis', *Econometrica*, 45: 1539–72.

Shepsle, K. and Weingast, B. (1981). 'Structure-Induced Equilibria and Legislative Choice', *Public Choice*, 37(3): 503–19.

Shi, M. and Svensson, J. (2002). 'Conditional Political Budget Cycles', CEPR Discussion Paper No. 3352.

Smart, M. and Sturm, D. (2003). 'Does Democracy Work? Estimating Incentive and Selection Effects of U.S. Gubernatorial Elections, 1950–2000', unpublished notes. University of Munich, Munich.

——and——(2004). 'Term Limits and Electoral Accoutability', typescript. University of Munich, Munich.

Smith, A. ([1776] 1976). in R. H. Campbell, A. S. Skinner, and W. B. Todd (eds.) *An Inquiry into the Nature and Causes of the Wealth of Nations*. Oxford: Clarendon Press.

Stigler, G. J. (1971). 'The Theory of Economic Regulation', *Bell Journal of Economics*, 2: 3–21.

Stromberg, D. (2004). 'Radio's Impact on Public Spending, *Quarterly Journal of Economics*, 119(1): 189–221.

Sturm, D. (2006). 'Product Standards, Trade Disputes, and Protectionism', *Canadian Journal of Economics*, 39(2): 564–81.

Svensson, J. (2000). 'Controlling Spending: Electoral Competition, Polarization and Endogenous Platforms', unpublished typescript, IIES, Stockholm.

Tabellini, G. and Alesina, A. (1990). 'Voting on the Budget Deficit', *American Economic Review*, 80: 37–49.

Testa, C. (2002). 'Government Corruption and Legislative Procedures: Is One Chamber Better than Two? Royal Holloway College, University of London. typescript.

Tirole, J. (1996). 'A Theory of Collective Reputations (with Applications to the Persistence of Corruption and to Firm Quality)', *Review of Economic Studies*, 63(1): 1–22.

Treisman, D. (2000). 'The Causes of Corruption: A Cross National Study', *Journal of Public Economics*, 76: 399–457.

Tullock, G. (1959). 'Problems of Majority Voting', *The Journal of Political Economy*, 67: 571–9.

——(1967). 'The Welfare Costs of Tariffs, Monopolies and Theft', *Western Economic Journal*, 5: 224–32.

——(1980). 'Efficient Rent-Seeking', in I. Buchanan, R. Tollison, and G. Tullock (eds.) *Towards a Theory of the Rent-Seeking Society*. College Station, TX: Texas A&M University Press.

Von Hayek, F. ([1944] 1976). *The Road to Serfdom*. Chicago: University of Chicago Press.

——(1948). *Individualism and Economic Order*. Chicago. University of Chicago Press.

Weingast, B., Shepsle, K., and Johnsen, C. (1981). 'The Political Economy of Benefits and Costs: A Neo-classical Approach to Distributive Politics', *Journal of Political Economy*, 89: 642–64.

Weissberg, R. (1976). *Pubic Opinion and Popular Government*. Englewood Cliffs, NJ: Prentice Hall.

Wicksell, K. (1896). 'A New Principle of Just Taxation', in R. A. Musgrave and A. T. Peacock (eds.) *Classics in the Theory of Public Finance*. London: McMillan.

Wilson, J. D. (1999). 'Theories of Tax Competition', *National Tax Journal*, 52(2): 269–304.

Wittman, D. A. (1977). 'Candidates with Policy Preferences: A Dynamic Model', *Journal of Economic Theory*, 14: 180–9.

——(1989). 'Why Democracies Produce Efficient Results', *Journal of Political Economy*, 97: 1395–426.

——(1997). *The Myth of Democratic Failure: Why Political Institutions Are Efficient*. Chicago: University of Chicago Press.

Zax, J. S. (1989). 'Initiatives and Government Expenditures', *Public Choice*, 63: 267–77.

Index

accountability 3, 36, 37, 82, 215, 218
  bureaucrat and politician 232
  political agency and 98–173, 216,
    222–3
accounting conventions 210
Acemoglu, D. 4 n., 8, 15, 16, 35 n., 47 n.,
  67 n., 82, 88, 92, 95 n., 191
ADA (Americans for Democratic Action)
  122
Adams, John 203
Adams, J. D. 115, 116
Ades, A. 12
administrative corruption 10 n.
adverse selection 37, 43, 152
  moral hazard and 108, 147, 180, 185–8,
    192, 228
  power of selection effect in agency
    models with 151
  pure 107, 180–2
affiliation 125
agency costs 190, 191, 205
agency models 39, 51, 61
  see also political agency
agency problems 223
  common 222
  potential, created by bad politicians
    185, 227
agenda setter model 33, 46
Aghion, P. 87
Ahrend, R. 12
aid provision 215–22
Alaska 198
Aldrich, J. 17, 42 n.
Alesina, A. 10 n., 32, 89, 143, 210, 211,
  232 n.
Alt, J. E. 121, 123 n., 136 n., 203–4
altruism 38, 39, 53
ambition 39
aristocracy 229, 230
Arrow, K. J. 21
Ashworth, S. 108, 128 n.

Athens 228, 229
Atkinson, A. B. 1 n., 24, 49, 99 n.
Austen-Smith, D. 107
authoritarianism 14
autocracy 4, 8, 9
  democracy versus 169
  power struggle 84
  selection rule 230
avarice 39

backward induction 185, 212
bad politicians 42, 107, 109, 129, 146,
  147, 176, 188, 191, 195, 228
  dramatic impact of debt on incentives
    of 211
  foreign 208–9
  good ones differentiate themselves from
    194
  lame-duck 189
  less effort into building reputation 209
  masquerading as good politicians 194
  maximal rents taken by 186, 187, 189,
    192
  mimicking good politicians 213, 219
  pooling with good politicians 205
  potential agency problems created by
    185, 227
  re-elected 181, 192
  rent extraction 180, 182, 194, 199, 201,
    213, 214
  strategic behavior 179
  thrown out of office 177, 181, 202
  weeding out 189
Bails, D. 119
Banks, J. 33, 107
Bardhan, P. 166, 167 n.
bargaining 74, 75
  considering 163
  dynamic model of 77 n.
Barganza, J. C. 108 n.

249

Index

Barro, R. 37, 39, 106, 136, 165, 182, 212
Bator, F. M. 47, 97
Battaglini, M. 77 n.
Baumol, W. J. 7
Baye, M. 64, 106
Bayes–Nash equilibrium 159
Bayes rule 148, 149, 150 n., 160, 172, 176, 181, 208
  voters' beliefs not restricted by 186 n.
Becker, Gary 30, 34 n., 146, 200
behavioral models 172
Belleflamme, P. 167 n., 206
Bénabou, R. 41 n.
benevolent government 20, 24, 28, 35, 175, 178, 180, 191, 202
  caring about social surplus 79
  policy achieved is Pareto dominated 81
  pure 63, 190
  reducing the level of spending by 201
  relative 176
  understanding the possibility of 43
Bergstrom, T. 71
Berlin Wall (fall of) 4
Bernheim, B. D. 62
Berry, W. 121–2
Besley, T. 13 n., 32, 34, 41, 42, 43, 49, 62 n., 68 n., 69, 71 n., 82, 85, 86 n., 87, 95 n., 100 n., 107, 119, 123 n., 128, 132, 133, 134, 135, 144, 147, 167 n., 168, 171 n., 175, 183, 187, 191 n., 195, 197 n., 202, 205, 206, 208, 209
Biais, B. 87
  bicameral systems 94, 158, 164 n.
Black, D. 31
black box approaches 34, 82
Bodenstein, M. 167 n., 206
Boettke, P. J. 28 n.
Bolton, P. 87
Bonaglia, F. 12
Borcherding, T. 38
Bordignon, M. 167 n., 168, 206
Brazil 136 n.
Brennan, G. 20 n., 30 n., 51, 168, 174, 179, 183, 200
bribery 2, 61, 62, 63, 68
  avoiding 102
  special interest 159
  transactions cost on 64
Bristol 40 n.
Bronars, S. G. 113
Brunetti, A. 12

Buchanan, J. M. 2 n., 20, 23, 26, 29, 30, 47, 48, 51, 72, 74, 93, 96, 97, 168, 174, 179, 183, 200, 211
budget balance 23
budget constraints 90, 178, 210, 212
budget deficit 210, 213
budget surplus 213
Bueno de Mesquita, E. 108, 128 n.
bureaucracy 232
  corruption 10
Burgess, R. 128, 132, 134, 135, 144
Burke, Edmund 40 n.
Bush, George W. 215, 230

calamity relief expenditures 135
California 197
Calvert, R. L. 33 n., 40 n.
campaign contributions 68
campaigning 43, 94, 135, 152
candidates 22, 32, 34
  assessments based on records of 106
  bad 42–3
  business 42 n.
  corruptible 42
  limited entry of 169
  past records of 204
  quality of 42, 43
  selecting the best 37
  see also re-election
Canes-Wrone, B. 139
capitalism 27
care 40, 41
career concerns model 103, 107, 108, 128 n.
Carillo, J. 231 n.
Case, A. 34 n., 95 n., 107, 119, 123 n., 167 n., 168, 183, 187, 195, 206
Caselli, F. 42
causation 11, 14, 15
Central and Eastern Europe 17
central banks 94
centralized systems 28, 166–8
Chicago School 4, 30
  characteristic of 38
  key component of 146
China 94
Cho, I-K. 111 n.
choices 182
  collective 22
  constitutional 96
  efficient and inefficient policies 146–52
  'first best' 184

institutional 4, 100
occupational 170
political 38
quality of economic policy 96
social 22
see also policy choice; public choice;
    rational choice
Chubb, J. 115
Ciccone, A. 73 n.
citizen–candidate approach 42, 69, 71 n.,
    82, 86 n.
citizens' initiatives 196, 197, 200
    cross-sectional effect of 198
civic virtue 112, 165
civil liberties 95
Clarke, E. H. 46
cleavage 4
clientelism 165, 166
    and targeted policies 144–6
Coase, R. 47 n., 75, 77
Coate, S. 32, 34, 37, 42, 43, 49, 62 n., 68,
    69, 71 n., 77 n., 82, 85, 86 n., 87, 92,
    107, 146, 147, 148, 191 n., 197 n.
coercion 14, 22, 230
common discount factor 109
common good 21, 23, 39
    trying to finds ways of pursuing 22
    very weak and ambiguous idea of 22
common law 11, 94
common pool financing 76, 77, 163
comparative advantage 96
compensation 51
competence 38, 52, 69, 103, 108, 223–4
    firms differ in some core level of 100
    limited 109
    party members 105
    politicians differ in 107
    shock to 142
competition 64
    electoral 68, 183
    limited 1
    polarization and 124–8
    resource 168
    tax 12, 168, 196, 200
    see also political competition
conditionality 222
Condorcet winners 31, 32, 72
conflicts of interest 36, 61, 158, 163
    governors and governed 174
    understanding 43
Congress (US) 113
    empirical evidence from governors
        114–23, 194

congruent politicians 109, 110, 112, 137,
    139, 158, 159–60
    action to enhance reputation 148
    always do what voters want 149, 156
    correct policy picked by 148
    difference between dissonant and 145
    distortions affect behavior of 140
    distortions in behavior by 157
    externalities for dissonant incumbents
        161
    limited entry of 169
    recruitment implies retention 152
    re-elected forever 156
    removed form office 151
    replacement by dissonant incumbents
        138
    rewards to 151, 154
    timid 138, 171
constitutions 36
    checks and controls 38
    fiscal 20, 93
    importance as constraints on
        self-interest 29
    procedural 20, 93
consumption 90, 163
contest function 65
contractarian ideal 60
contracts 148
    incentive 171
    may not be enforced 14
    offering agent a menu of 100
    upholding 14, 15
coordination failure 57, 62, 67
Cooter, R. D. 96 n.
COPE (Committee on Political Education)
    122
corrective policies 24
corruption 10–14, 15, 26, 42, 61–4, 102,
    136
    cross-country data on 134
    foreign media ownership and 134 n.
    opportunity for 104
    reducing 101
'cost padding' 185
cost shocks 180–1, 187, 212, 213, 216
    bad incumbents with 188
    high, good incumbents face 201
    incompetent incumbent observes 224
    joint probability distribution function
        of 206–7
    positive correlation in 206
    privately observed 179
    unobservable to the voter 223

Coughlin, P. 50 n.
courts 1, 232
  constitutional 94
  role of 95
Craig, J. 203
Crain, W. M. 119
cronies 49
  rewarding 104, 136

deadweight loss 63–4, 200
debt 89, 176, 210–14
decentralization 94, 206
  centralization versus 166–8
  important caveat to the fad for 222
decision-making 60, 77, 189, 232
  democratic 71
  private 92
  social 74
  two-person 162
deficits:
  debt and 210–14
  fiscal 89, 95
demand 82, 88
democracy 7, 9, 28, 50, 147
  autocracy versus 169
  direct 94, 140 n., 196, 198
  faith in 10
  key value that affects the quality
    of 165
  making it work in the context of agency
    models 166
  one source of information provided in
    135
  poorly functioning 101
  potential drawbacks of 46
  predictable link between protection of
    property rights and 16
  rejected classical notions of 22
  swing towards 4
  what goes into making it
    work 100
  see also liberal democracy;
    representative democracy
democratic failures 4
democratic structure 93–4
democratization 8, 17
Denzau, A. T. 198
developing countries 175, 215
Dewatripont, M. 205
Di Tella, R. 12
Diermeier, D. 170
disadvantaged groups 144

discipline effect 190, 204, 205, 206, 211
  pure 214
  selection effect outweighs 202
disorder 14
dissonant politicians 109, 111, 137, 144,
    149, 159
  biased 136
  clientelism 145
  congruent action 157
  delivering what voters want 151
  discipline and 112, 113, 126, 130, 156,
    158, 161, 162, 166, 168, 170
  equilibrium always picked by 148
  incentives for 127 n., 141
  maximal private sector wage foregone
    153
  news bad for 132
  optimal action of 110, 152
  randomly selected, congruent behavior
    by 153
  re-elected 129–30, 145, 148, 154, 160,
    168
  rent extraction 154, 156, 161
  replaced 131, 138
  restraint by 150
  standing for political office more
    attractive on the margin to 171
  stationary strategy 155
  underachievement by 141
distribution 1, 22–3, 109, 135
  justice in 53 n.
  undesirable outcome 47
distributional failures 49–52, 56, 81
Djankov, S. 12, 14, 15, 134 n.
Downs, A. 31, 32, 33, 40, 71, 104, 106
Dreyer Lassen, D. 136 n., 203–4
droughts 128, 134
Duggan, J. 33
duty 17, 40, 41, 42 n., 43
  strong sense of 103

economic growth 115, 116, 230
efficiency 23, 24, 47
  information constrained 60
  public service 101
  revenue collection 168
  see also Pareto efficiency
efficiency wage arguments 141, 171
ego rents 40, 104, 109, 143, 158, 223
elections 31, 94, 99, 141–2, 205, 229
  agency model of 178–9

benefits reaped 189
body of law governing conduct of 102
close 34 n.
government incentives to inflate
  economy before 35
how they can motivate politicians 111
mass 17, 42 n.
optimal 140
outcome of 84, 115
periodic 140, 142, 146
politicians' incentive to renege
  after 32
roles of 37, 41, 101
spending raised and taxes cut in year of
  143
trust between 36
turnout 17–18
winning 40
see also candidates; NES; re-election;
  voters/voting electoral cycle model
  143
elites:
  economic 42 n.
  political 42, 51
Enlightenment thinkers 230
entry 42, 43
environmental policy/issues 120, 128,
  144, 147
equilibria 33, 80, 101, 106, 111, 133, 137,
  138, 155, 183, 209
  courageous 139
  deleterious effects on 206
  expected voter welfare in 189
  information revealed in 201–2
  multiple 91
  punishments for disagreements 164
  stationary 156
  strategies unaltered 204
  symmetric 206
  timid 157
  see also hybrid equilibrium; Nash
    equilibrium; perfect Bayesian
    equilibrium; political equilibrium;
    pooling equilibrium; separating
    equilibrium
equilibrium budget cycle 140, 143
equilibrium business cycles 35 n.
equity 47, 53 n.
ethnic conflict 167
ethnicity 124
ethnolinguistic fractionalization 11
exaggerated behavior 107
executive 94–5

directly elected 164
subordinated to legislature 164
expropriation 14, 15
externalities 158, 192, 196 n.
  congruent and dissonant incumbents
    collectively create 161
  due to tax competition 168
  informational 206
  internalized 75
  negative and positive 161
  regulated 1, 14, 93
  reputational 209

fairness 100
faith-based organizations 215
Falk, A. 42
Farnham, P. G. 198
favors 38, 64, 87, 146
  rewarding cronies for 136
Fearon, J. 101 n., 107
feasibility 23, 24
Feddersen, T. 18, 60 n.
Federalist Papers (US) 2, 20, 36–7, 41
Fehr, E. 42
Feld, L. P. 198
Ferejohn, J. 37, 39, 106, 129 n., 136, 163,
  165, 171, 182, 204
Fernandez, R. 72, 73, 87–8
Ferraz, C. 136 n.
fiduciary duty 40, 41, 42 n., 43
Finan, F. 136 n.
Fiorina, M. 106
fiscal illusion 210–11, 214
fiscal policy 183, 184, 188 n.
  optimal 212, 226–7
  transparency impact on 136 n.
Fischer, S. 176
floods 128, 134, 135
Florence 229
franchise 93, 94
free-rider problem 57
freedom:
  calculating the value of 96
  individual 95
  media 12, 134
Frey, B. S. 41 n., 93 n.

gainers 59
  identity of 73
  instruments available to
    compensate 62 n.

gainers (*cont.*):
  losers compensated by 50–1, 72
  trade-offs between payoffs of losers
    and 58
Gallego, M. 619 n.
GDP (gross domestic product) 5, 7
Gehlbach, S. 42 n.
Gersbach, H. 171
Ghatak, M. 41, 100 n.
Glazer, A. 87
global warming 104
good government:
  criteria for 23
  defining 21, 22
  first step towards creating 233
  generating rules for 24
  making sense of 21
good politicians 107, 109, 139, 146, 176,
    179, 199
  bad politicians masquerading as 194
  delivery of outcomes preferred by voters
    180
  differentiating from bad ones 194
  foreign 208
  good for voters 191–3
  mimicked by bad politicians 213, 219
  only a few available to voters 188
  pooling with bad politicians 205
  reduced incentive of bad politicians to
    behave like 211
  re-elected 181
  voters always benefit from 204
governance agenda 11
government:
  and economy 177–9
  expenditure 38, 120
  failure 3, 21, 45–97, 191
  growth 5, 7, 9, 38
  multi-tiered 94
  NGOs versus 214–23
  restraining 190, 195–210
  short-lived 35
  see also benevolent government; good
    government; government
    intervention; government quality
government intervention 24, 54, 188
  case for 26, 45, 58
  conservative way of judging legitimacy
    of 53
  criterion for 190
  economy Pareto efficient without 56
  efficient 55
  gainers and losers from 59

imperfections in policy process militate
    against 191
  motivating 57
  optimal citizen welfare under 190
  possibility of 63
  veto over some aspects of 23
government quality 10, 17, 28, 111–12,
    221
  civic virtue and 165
  key aspect of 14
  link between turnout and 17
  long-lived historical roots 15
  low, under autocracy 230
  measure of 165
  newspaper readership and 166
  unequivocal statements about 128
Grossman, G. 34, 62, 67–8
Groves, T. 46

Hammond, P. 23 n.
Harrington, J. E. 144
Hayek, F. A. von 27, 28, 39, 59
head tax 56, 57, 72
Heal, G. 28 n.
Hellman, J. S. 10 n.
Helpman, E. 34, 62, 68
heredity 229–30
heterogeneity 24, 107 n., 125, 128, 136,
    171
  autocracies display a fair amount of 230
  state-to-state 114
Hettich, W. 175 n.
Hibbs, D. A. 142
Hicks–Kaldor compensation test 50
Hindriks, J. 167 n., 168, 206
holding office:
  benefit of 170
  legitimate rent from 156
  motives for 104–5
  payoff from 137
  personal return from 139
  private utility from 138
  rents from 51, 83, 87, 153
  reward from 40, 141
  rules restricting 94
  selection by force not an effective
    method for 230
  utility independent level from 142–3
  value of 45 n.
  wages from 109
Holmstrom, B. 100, 103, 107, 108,
    167, 205

Holsey, C. 38
House of Lords (UK) 140
House of Representatives (US) 36, 114, 120
human capital 38, 69
human rights 95, 96
Hume, David 38–9
hybrid equilibrium 187, 188, 194, 201, 202, 208, 216
    possible with yardstick competition 207

ICRG (International Country Risk Guide) 11, 15
ideology 40, 122
    conflict 89
    divergences 19
    polarization based on 124
    preferred 125
ignorance 59–61, 170
    rational 104
    veil of 93, 96
illicit returns 10
imperfect information 46, 82, 96, 146, 183
    failures of government due to 191
    stylized model of representative democracy with 100
implementation theory 164
impossibility theorem 21
incentive compatibility 23 n.
incentive constraints 24, 182, 184, 185
incentive effects 188, 214
incentives 2, 3, 17, 35, 81, 96, 99, 196, 222
    best possible for incumbents to reduce rent extraction 193
    building reputations 108
    countervailing effects on 209
    election 136, 176, 196
    good 69
    impact of structural factors on 11
    implicit 206
    incomplete 131, 206
    market based 232
    political 14, 36–43, 87, 162
    private investment 14
    prospective, for low-quality incumbents 190
    restraint 106
    see also re-election

income 56, 91, 116, 120
    government spending of 9
    high 89, 90, 91, 92
    justice in distribution of 53 n.
    low(er) 11, 14, 15, 24, 89–90
    see also national income
income redistribution 55
    acceptable 56
income tax 90, 120, 200
    equilibrium level of 174
    optimal 55, 99
incompetent politicians 100, 143, 204, 223, 224
incumbency advantage 112–13
independent agencies/watchdogs 94, 203
India 128, 135, 144
    Nehru dynasty 230
indifference curves 184, 185
indirect restraints 200–9
individualism 39
inefficiency 56, 148
    private provision of public goods 57
    tax 200, 201, 202
    see also Pareto inefficiency
inequality 22, 213
    aversion 21
    strict 187
infinite horizon model 156, 163
influence 59, 61–8
influence function 34
information:
    and accountability 128–36
    asymmetric 104
    available to voters 196
    eliciting and managing 60
    equilibrium 201–2, 206
    freedom of 95
    full 55, 60, 146
    payoff 142
    provision of 202–9
    revealed 100, 164
    see also imperfect information; private information
information constraints 23, 99, 100
infrastructure 10
injustice 52
institutional failure 96
interpersonal comparisons 21
intertemporal distortions 147
intimidation 101, 102
intuitive criterion 111 n.

investment:
    deterrent effect on 14
    misallocation of 10
    politics and 89–92
    public 142, 143
investment decisions 82, 89, 90
    commitment 78, 79–80
    mobile citizens 91
    no commitment 78, 80–1
    private 92
Italy 165, 168

Jain, S. 73 n., 87
Japan 5
Jefferson, Thomas 229
Jones, B. F. 230
judicial decisions 140
judiciary:
    independence of 15
    role of 94
jurisdictions 206–7
justice 72
    in taxation 53 n.

Kaplow, L. 22
Kenny, L. 115, 116
Key, V. O. 37, 98, 106
Keynes, John Maynard 27
Keynes, John Neville 27, 28 n.
Kirchgässner, G. 198
kleptocracies 39, 50
Knight, B. 198
Kopit, G. 203
Kreps, D. 111 n.
Krueger, Anne 20, 64
Krusell, P. 88, 92 n., 200
Küttel, D. 168, 206 n.
Kydland, F. 35, 78, 80

La Porta, R. 11
labor-intensive services 7
Laffont, J-J. 60–1, 99 n., 100
lame ducks 113–14, 149, 183, 189
Lancaster, K. 176
Lange, O. 28
last period effect 113
laws 10 n.
Le Borgne, E. 143
leadership quality 2, 59, 68–70

Ledyard, J. O. 42
Lee, D. S. 34 n.
'legacy effect' 105
legal systems:
    effective 15
    presupposed existence of 102
legislatures 46, 114, 121
    cabinet members 95
    decision-making 71
    executive subordinated to 164
    policy making 74–7
    responsive in providing food aid 128
    rules within 94
legitimacy 64
Leon, G. 138 n.
Lerner, A. 28
Levi, M. 17 n.
Leviathan model 30 n., 51, 168, 174, 179,
    183, 188 n.
liberal democracy 4, 17
liberty 203
    guarantees of 28
    individual, respect for 22
Liessem, V. 171
likelihood ratio 181, 208, 209
Lindahl–Samuelson rule 24, 46, 49, 57,
    71–2
Lindbeck, A. 33 n.
linkages 78–81, 82, 86–9, 92 n.
Lipsey, R. G. 176
List, J. 120, 128, 144
list systems 94
lobbying 34, 64, 65
    alternative to 42 n.
    coordination failures between lobbyists
    62 n.
Locke, John 29, 230
Lockwood, B. 143, 168
log-rolling 29, 74–7
long-term policy 85
Lopez, E. J. 28 n.
losers 53, 59
    compensated 50–1, 62 n., 72, 88
    identity of 73
    trade-offs between payoffs of gainers
    and 58
Lott, J. R. 113
lottery 228, 229
low-income countries 35
low-quality politicians 43
Lowry, R. C. 115 n., 121
loyalty 40, 41
lump-sum transfers 51, 58–9, 72, 90

McArthur, J. 113–14
Maddison, A. 5
Madison, James 1, 2, 36–7, 38, 39, 40–1
majoritarian systems 9, 94
  less prone to corruption 13
majority rule 72, 90
Majumdar, S. 144
malfeasance 40
Manin, B. 228
Marcos, Ferdinand 50
marginal cost 200, 202
marginal rates 24
Mariotti, T. 231 n.
market failure 24, 46, 48, 57, 191
  defined 49
  fixing 54, 56
  government failures and 45, 67
  main sources of 47
  systematizing the notion of 28
  theory of 93
market power abuses 1
markets:
  attractiveness for resource allocation
    100 n.
  perfect outlet for self-interest 39
  recognizing the role of 28
Marks, S. V. 113–14
Marxist thinkers 27
Maskin, E. 40, 99 n., 105, 139,
    140 n., 164
material gain 104
Matsusaka, J. G. 198
Mattozzi, A. 231 n.
Mauro, P. 11
Meade, James 20
mechanism design problem 183
media 135, 144
  freedom of 12, 134
  mass 203
  news 132–3
  ownership patterns 12–13
median voter outcome 31, 32, 33, 71
menu auction model 62
Merlo, A. 231 n.
Milesi-Ferretti, G-M. 87, 203
Mill, John Stuart 27, 40 n.
Mirrlees, James 20, 23 n.
misallocation 10
mixed economy 4, 28
mobile citizens 46, 90–2
Mobutu, S. 50
monetary policy 94
monitoring 99, 100

monopoly 14, 46, 93
Montesquieu, C. L. de S. 229
Mookherjee, D. 166, 167 n.
moral hazard 37, 43, 100, 106, 152, 163,
    165, 167
  adverse selection and 108, 147, 180,
    185–8, 192, 228
  pure 182–5, 188, 191, 192, 193,
    226–7
  refraining from 41
moral sentiments 39
Morelli, M. 42
Morris, S. 37, 86 n., 87, 92, 107, 139, 146,
    147, 148
motivation 38, 40, 99
  intrinsic 41
  politicians that differ in 107
  public service 171
  uncertainty about 103
Mueller, D. C. 29 n., 31 n., 50, 93 n.
Mugabe, Robert 102
Mukand, S. W. 87, 144
Mulligan, C. B. 8, 30 n., 200
multiple agents 157–64
Murdock, K. 41 n.
Murphy, K. M. 11 n.
Musgrave, R. A. 28 n., 45
mutual agreement 163
Myerson, R. B. 33 n., 164 n., 168

Nannestad, P. 115
narrow self-interest 29, 39, 40, 42
  eschewing 41
Nash equilibrium 57, 65, 66–7
  'good' 58
  private investment decisions 80
  see also Bayes–Nash
national income 7, 91
NES (US National Election Surveys) 20
new democracies 17
news 132–3
newspapers:
  readership 166
  state ownership of 13
NGOs (non-governmental organizations)
    3, 175, 231
  governments versus 214–23, 225
noblesse oblige 230
non-appropriability 47
non-consequentialist criteria 47
non-convexity 47
non-democratic polities 94

Index

non-partisan voters 125, 127
favorable consequences for 128
Nordhaus, W. D. 142
norm of universalism 75, 77

Oakley, L. K. 119
OECD countries 7
fiscal transparency 136 n.
voter turnout 17
Olken, B. A. 230
omniscience 59
openness 203
and corruption 12
opportunism 37, 105, 214
minimizing 99
opportunity cost 52
optimal policy 24, 59, 178
Osborne, M. J. 32, 33, 42
Ottaviani, M. 108 n.
outside options 170

Paldam, M. 115
pandering 139–40
Pareto-dominated outcomes 48, 52, 57,
60, 62 n., 66, 75, 77, 79, 81
Pareto efficiency 22, 49, 56, 57, 72, 73,
75, 85, 97
second-best 24, 54–5
Pareto improvement 46, 51, 52, 54, 66,
68, 70
more difficult to create 69
realized 58
Pareto inefficiency 48–9, 54, 72, 75, 85,
86, 87, 100
government failures based on 53
market resource allocation results in 47
Pareto optimal policy 59
parliamentary government/democracies
9, 16, 164
participation constraint 182, 183, 184,
185
partisan issues 124, 144
payoff function 33 n.
payoffs 57, 58, 62, 65, 78, 137–8, 140,
141–2, 150, 205
congruent politicians 109
future policies 85
maximized 47
negligible direct effect on 192
publicly observable 100
short-run 87

voter 112
zero 110, 133
Peacock, A. T. 28 n.
Peltzman, S. 30, 38, 115, 116, 146, 200 n.
perfect Bayesian equilibrium 110, 185,
186
perfect knowledge 60
perks 104, 109, 170–1, 175
Perrotti, E. 87, 211
Persson, T. 9, 13, 16, 32 n., 33, 34 n.,
35 n., 40 n., 68 n., 89, 95 n., 103, 107,
125, 158,161, 163, 210
Pesendorfer, W. 18, 60 n.
Pettersson-Lidbom, P. 143
Pharr, S. J. 17 n.
Philippines 50
Pigou, Arthur 20, 24, 26, 28
Pitchik, C. 169 n.
planned economies 4, 24, 28
polarization 124–8, 144, 167
policy choice 78, 80, 82, 83, 84, 91,
96, 107
bad 138
community of individuals who have to
make 23
conflict with human rights provisions
95
consequences of 129
equilibrium, NGO 217
evolved 35
improving information about which
taken 131
inferred, responsiveness from 134
mapping into political outcomes 33
maximizes social surplus 50
may be uncertain for a considerable
time 104
Pareto efficient 57, 73, 85
Pareto inefficient 53, 85, 86, 87
particular assumptions shape 36
poor 103
private investment decisions affect 89
quality of 104, 141
reflecting needs 170
strategic 87
term-limited effect on 115
use as signaling device 107
welfare economic model has tended to
say little about 25
policy making 20–6, 33
Buchanan–Tullock critique of 72
consequences for economics 4

legislatures 74–7
  strategic aspects of 84
policy mistakes 59
policy preferences 32, 33 n., 40, 71
  changed once private investment
    decisions made 81
  differences in 75
  heterogeneous 24
  opposite 43
  policy maker succeeded by someone
    with same 83
  strong 104
political agency 3, 12, 13, 14, 82, 96
  and accountability 98–173
  and public finance 174–227
political business cycle 35
  macro-economic 142
  robust evidence hard to find 143
political competition 3, 30, 32, 33, 71
  candidate centered view of 34
  citizen–candidate model of 69
  crude way of thinking about degree of
    124
  decentralized 167 n.
  distributional conflict implicit in 50 n.
  evenly balanced 128
  greater 144
  parties play an important role in 105
  widespread sentiment linking policy
    outcomes and 128
  yardstick 167, 206–9
political corruption 10, 42
political equilibrium 49, 55, 72, 87, 89,
    95 n., 129, 188, 190
  change in 168, 205, 210, 214
  characterizing the effect of debt on 213
  discipline and selection effects 211
  future 88
  made less informative 199
  pooling behavior may or may not be
    optimal in 107
  shift towards pooling outcome 200
  social welfare functions maximized in
    50 n.
  unchanged 201
  welfare in 191
political failure 45–6, 63, 92
  due to political linkage 138
  sources of 70–7
  why deficit finance can be subject
    to 95
political office 152–60, 171
  see also holding office

political resource allocation 31, 36, 57, 93
  basis of 71
  inegalitarian 47
  shaped by rules 93
  tendency to authorize too many
    projects 77
political turnover 13, 14, 112, 188
  link between public spending and
    193–4
politics 30, 178–9
  debt 213–14
  distributive 71
  investment and 89–92
Polity IV data set 4, 8
pooling equilibrium 107, 192 n., 195,
    202, 205, 208, 213, 216, 218, 219,
    220, 221
  condition required for 224
  increasing incentives for 214
  maximal rents 187–8
  political equilibrium shifts towards 200
  possible with yardstick competition
    207
  rent diversion in 201
  retention probability 194
  transfer to special interest 147
posterior probability 186, 187
Poutvarra, P. 42 n.
power:
  agenda setting 164
  authority to limit 94
  coercive 22
  commitment 81
  exercise of 36–7
  intoxication effect from 104
  judicial 232
  proposal 33
  tax 1, 5
Prat, A. 13 n., 107, 131 n., 132,
    133, 134
precedent 94
predation 14, 15
preference aggregation 32, 36
preference restrictions 31
preferences 108
  congruent 139
  distributional 54
  intensity of 72
  leader 59, 61
  linear 51
  making policy makers more responsive
    to 119
  political 38, 95 n.

preferences (*cont.*):
  possibility of deriving social welfare
    from 21
  social 30, 50, 53
  underlying 174
  see also policy preferences; voter
    preferences
Prendergast, C. 100 n., 108 n.
Prescott, E. 35, 78, 80
presidential systems 164
press freedom 13
  and corruption 12
Preston, I. 128
principal–agent problem 2, 17, 100
private goods 4, 39, 40
  transfers to politically favored
    groups 38
private information:
  correlated 167 n.
  difficulties in getting citizens to
    reveal 24
private investment 14, 78, 90, 91
private investment decisions 81, 82, 89
  interdependent 80
privatization policy 87
probabilistic voting model 33, 50 n.
production:
  food 135
  private goods 4
  public goods 4
productivity 89, 90
  unobservable shock to 163
promises 35
property:
  justice in distribution of 53 n.
  systems for protection of 95
property rights 1, 14–17
proportional representation 9, 16, 94
Proposition 13 (1978) 197
protectionism 51
  'green' 147–8
Protestants 11
psychology 40, 41
public choice 2 n., 29, 47, 63, 93, 180,
    195–6, 214
  creation of the field 28
  critique of welfare economics 25–6,
    30, 191
  suspicion about debt as an
    instrument 211
public expenditures 30, 174–227
  approved 52

implications of democratic governance
    for 29
public goods 17, 39, 47, 93, 104, 189, 219
  allocation of resources between political
    rents and 164
  collective reduction being funded 75
  equilibrium level of 174
  explaining individuals' contributions to
    41–2
  geographical targeting of 50
  good NGOs spend all aid resources on
    216
  hopeful undertakings for 36
  incremental level of spending by
    government 220
  incumbents may choose how much to
    spend on 163
  marginal cost of 200
  observable immediately 142
  production of 4
  pure 65 n.
  spending on 175
  taxes to finance 14
public goods provision 46, 49, 215
  assumption that government is the only
    means of delivering 214
  cost of 178, 194, 205, 217, 223, 224
  efficient 24, 99
  higher levels of 71, 143
  retaining the right on behalf of aid
    provider 216
  under-provision 56
public interest 1, 2, 21, 29, 98, 176
  motivations most likely to be in tune
    with 99
public office misuse 42 n.
  see also holding office
public projects 87
  allocation of 75, 76
  financing 55–9, 75
  suboptimal private provision of 67
public resource allocation 4, 26, 59
  Pareto improvement in 46
  short- and long-run effects on
    economy 35
  understanding the political economy
    of 43
public services:
  delivering 3
  efficient provision of 206
  selfishly redistributive 38
  unobservable shock to the productivity
    of providing 163

Publius view 2
pure corruption 61
Putnam, R. 165–6, 169

Qian, Y. 94 n.

Ramsey tax rule 24, 49
random effects model 119
ratchet effects 100
rational choice 106, 172
  behavioral versus 172
rational expectations 80
Rawls, J. 21
Reagan, Ronald 210
reasoning 176
  second-best 70, 206
  structured and scientific 96
recruitment 152, 153
redistribution 8, 53, 55, 56
re-election 40, 78, 87, 100, 101, 108, 137,
    144, 149, 206
  bad politicians 181, 192, 205
  based on relative performance 207
  chances of 107, 115, 127
  comparing politicians who can(not) run
    for 113
  congruent politicians 156
  desire for 104
  dissonant politicians 129–30, 145, 148,
    154, 168
  eligibility for 116, 168
  enhancing the role of 135
  faithful politicians deliver goods in the
    face of 136
  good politicians 181
  higher government spending 143
  incumbents 102, 112, 127, 129–30,
    150, 182, 205, 209
  individuals not subject to 140
  intertemporal distortions created
    by 147
  lower probability of 117, 118
  mechanism imperfect 111
  politicians do something good for 172
  possibilities of 189, 190
  probability of 193, 207
  voters decide 109
  weak 139
re-election rules 164, 170, 179
  incentive-based 182
  voters put in place 110

referenda 74, 198
reforms 48, 73
  constitutional 93, 96
  piece-meal 100
regulation dynamics of 100
regulations 1
  fiscal deficit 95
religion 11
rent extraction 179, 183
  all incumbents desire 163
  bad politicians 180, 182, 194, 199, 201,
    213, 214
  choice between current period or
    future 106
  dissonant politicians 154, 156, 161
  imperfect means of detecting 176
  incumbents cannot control amount
    180
  maximal 106, 192
  multiple agents setting reduces
    possibilities 158
  reduced 158, 164, 177, 193
  re-election a reward for limiting 180
  threat of not being re-elected could
    curtail 37
rent-seeking 1, 29, 43, 48, 127, 176
  costly 61, 64–8
  failures of government due to existence
    of 191
  first term 205
  incumbent can be rewarded for
    reducing 182
  maximal 201
  notion that it will be efficient 146
  providing incentives to reduce 185
  restraining 183, 188, 189
  reward in the future for 170
  short-run advantages in curbing 180
  tax increases likely to enhance
    opportunities for 139
  yardstick competition increases 209
rents 136, 137, 141–2, 144, 145, 153
  capture of 11, 87, 159
  compensating politician for loss of 52
  decision 87
  dissonance 109, 111
  diverted 179, 201
  excessive 52, 176
  expected 160, 161
  fixed pot 159
  forgone 130
  future 169

rents (*cont.*):
  high(er) 148, 188
  incompetents earn 223
  maximal 106, 186, 187, 189, 192, 201,
    208
  permissible 182
  political 88, 164
  politicians have no ability to influence
    amount they take 180
  preserving 42
  private 61, 138
  shared 159, 162
  short-term 161
  survival important in the presence of
    83
  unobservable to voters 175, 184
  see also ego rents
representative democracy 22, 33, 101
  classic critique by thinkers of the left
    170
  importance of elections in 99
  periodic election a cornerstone idea in
    140
  prominent political dynasties 230
  stylized representations of 100, 169
reputation 110, 134
  building 108, 209
  enhancing 148
  poor 208–9
resource allocation 2, 4, 30, 47, 77
  attractiveness of markets for 100 n.
  democratic 46
  fairness in 42
  imperfections in 175
  initially unjust 53
  marginal conditions that must be
    satisfied for 96
  Pareto-efficient, failure to sustain 47
  political rents and public goods 164
  potential imperfection in 63
  private decisions 49
  suboptimal pattern of 46
  see also political resource allocation;
    public resource
responsiveness 101, 134, 135
restraints 106, 150, 175, 176, 190,
  195–210, 213
retention rate 193, 194
retrospective voting 103, 105–6, 110, 164
  relevance of 118
Revelli, F. 168, 206 n.
reverse causality 198 n.
rewards 2, 40, 52, 99, 100

cronies 104, 136
external 41
indexed to behavior while in office 170
relative, public and private life 154
self-interested individuals seek 10–11
right-wing governments 87
rights 95, 96
Rios-Rull, J-V. 88, 92 n.
Robinson, J. 4 n., 8, 35 n., 82, 88, 92
Robinson, J. A. 87
Rodrik, D. 48 n., 72, 73, 88
Roemer, J. 33
Rogoff, K. 35 n., 37, 40, 104, 107, 140,
  142, 143
Roland, G. 94 n.
Romer, T. 33
Rosenthal, H. 33
Roubini, N. 143
Rousseau, Jean-Jacques 229
Rueben, K. 197 n., 198
rules:
  behavioral 172
  campaign 94
  codified ex ante 93
  constitutional 99, 159, 196, 197
  cut-off 155
  decision making 231–2
  formal accountability 101
  good government 24
  legal 95
  necessary to improve or reform 29
  policy 24, 95
  restricting who could hold public office
    94
  see also Bayes; Lindahl–Samuelson;
    Ramsey; re-election rules; voting rules

safeguards 5, 10
Salmon, P. 167 n., 206
sanctions 101, 105
  electoral 39
  legal 102
  trade 147
Sand-Zantman, W. 206
Schaltegger, C. A. 168, 206 n.
Schattschneider, E. E. 98, 128
Schumpeter, J. A. 22, 27
second-best theory 24, 63, 176
second generation models 37
selection 2, 3, 29, 82, 96, 99, 103
  benefits of better information 131
  biased 114

bureaucratic 232
by force 230, 231
countervailing effects on 209
hereditary 229, 230
impact of structural factors on 11
improving 108, 130, 151, 176
incentives and 36–43
leadership 59, 70
long-run disadvantages in reducing 180
worse 162
see also adverse selection; self-selection
selection effect 122, 131, 190, 199, 206, 204, 211, 214
outweighs discipline effect 202
self-enrichment 50
self-esteem 40
self-interest 10–11, 42, 46, 199
desire to win interpreted as 40
importance of constitutions as constraints on 29
markets viewed as perfect outlet for 39
political preferences motivated purely by 38
rational 29
ruthless 38
wasteful spending by officials 201
self-selection 100
Sen, A. K. 21, 22
Senate (US) 120
separating equilibrium 187, 188, 190, 192, 194, 201, 201, 202, 205, 213, 216, 218, 219, 220, 221, 224
transfer to special interest 147
separation of powers 93, 158, 163
dysfunctional 164 n.
settler mortality 15
shareholders 87
Shavell, S. 22
Shepsle, K. 33, 76
Shi, M. 143, 204
shirking politicians 136
shocks 134, 143
competence 142
idiosyncratic 125
popularity 112, 125, 127
productivity 163–4
random 33
unobservable 163
see also cost shocks
short-term policy 85
Siebert, A. 142
signaling issues 107, 108
signaling process 143

signaling theory 35 n.
simplicity 100
single-peakedness 31
Slivinksy, A. 32, 34, 42
Smart, M. 3, 108 n., 131 n., 138, 140, 155 n., 157, 167 n., 168, 171 n., 175, 202, 205, 208, 209
Smith, Adam 25, 38, 39
social capital 17
social surplus 50, 57, 67, 72, 73 n., 76
allows trade-offs 58
corruption increases 63
government caring about 79
maximized 92
optimum 51
reduced 70
social welfare 29, 58, 63, 102
social welfare functions 21, 22, 51, 53, 55, 56, 81
implicit appeal to 50
policy favors granted through corruption have no distributional merit according to 64
specific, invoking 24
socialism 27
limitations on personal freedom under 28
Sonin, K. 42 n.
Sorensen, P. 108 n.
special interests 96, 109, 146
bad incumbent makes transfer to 147
bribery by 159
spending cycle 194–5
Spolaore, E. 87
stagnation 88
standard complete contracts model 205
state capture 10 n.
state failure 35
status quo policy 159, 160
bad 161–2
Stigler, George 20, 30, 146
Stiglitz, J. E. 1 n., 24, 49, 99 n.
Stoker, L. 17 n.
Stole, L. 108 n.
strategic complementarity 91
strategic debt model 214
Stromberg, D. 170 n.
Sturm, D. 108 n., 120, 128, 138, 140, 144, 147, 155 n., 157, 171 n.
Summers, L. H. 176
Sundaram, R. 107
supermajority requirements 197

surplus:
  aggregate 66
  total 67
  see also social surplus
surplus maximization 51, 52, 59, 67, 70,
    74, 81, 87
survival 83, 85, 87
  and turnover 82
Svensson, J. 124 n., 143, 204
Svensson, L. 89, 210
Swedish data 143
Switzerland 94, 168, 198, 206 n.
systemic costs 64

Tabellini, G. 9, 10 n., 32 n., 33, 34 n.,
    35 n., 40 n., 68 n., 89, 95 n., 103, 107,
    125, 210, 232 n.
Takalo, T. 42 n.
talent (mis)allocation 10, 63
targeted policies 144–6
tariff protection 51
taxation 14, 24, 62, 76, 77, 119–20, 183,
    199, 224
  benefit 30, 58
  competition between nations 12
  diverting revenues to private use 51
  expected 195
  implications of democratic governance
    for 29
  increasing the cost of 196, 200–2
  interdependent 168
  justice in 53 n.
  limitations 197
  lump-sum 51, 55, 58, 72, 90, 99
  observable immediately 142
  optimal 55, 56, 91
  Pareto efficient 48
  positive economics of 175 n.
  property 74
  redistributive 91, 92, 99
  reduced 121
  re-election and 116, 194
  setting 196 n., 207
  smoothing 212, 213
  see also head tax; income tax
technological change 7
term-limit effect 113–14, 115, 119–23,
    128, 151, 156, 157, 172, 177, 194, 195
  argument in favor 140
  pure moral hazard model consistent
    with 183
terror suspects 96

Testa, C. 164 n.
theory of justice 21
Tieslau, M. 119
time consistency problem 78, 81
timidity 138, 140, 157, 171
Tirole, J. 40, 41 n., 64 n., 100, 105, 139,
    140 n.
Tocqueville, Alexis de 36
Tollison, R. D. 119
Torvik, R. 87
trade-offs 29, 68
  agency costs of first- and second-term
    incumbents 205
  equity–efficiency 24
  improved selection and reduced
    accountability 216
  payoffs of gainers and losers 58
  voter 158
transactions cost 64, 133
transfers 51, 62, 63, 92
  cash 146, 147
  lump-sum 51, 58–9, 72, 90
  made inefficiently 50
transparency 177, 206, 233
  budgetary, improvements in 197
  fiscal 136, 203–5
  lack of 104
Transparency International 11
Treisman, D. 11 n., 13
trust 9, 10, 36, 41
  and turnout 17–20
  see also fiduciary duty
Tullock, G. 26, 29, 30, 47, 64, 72, 74
turnover 134
  incumbent 132
  policy makers 82
  see also political turnover

unanimity 159
unanimity rule 23, 30, 58
unbalanced growth story 7
uncertainty 84, 103, 104, 143
  electoral, increase in 126
  individual specific 73, 74
  voter, about optimal policy 144
underdevelopment theory 88
unicameral systems 94, 164 n.
uninformed politicians 103
United Kingdom 140, 230
United States 2, 5, 113–23, 144, 196, 229
  Bush dynasty 230

citizens' initiatives 196, 197–8, 200
fiscal transparency 136 n.
large budget deficits 210
presidential elections 36, 106
unobserved types 100, 103
Ursprung, H. 167 n., 206
use of force 46
utilitarianism 21, 51
utility 17, 21, 55, 103, 125, 153, 178
    depends solely on consumption 90
    forgoing an increase in 41
    independent level from holding office
        142–3
    loss of 86
    lower average 24
    maximized 76
    possibility frontier 49
    status quo 23
    transferable 50, 59 n.
    zero 56
utility functions 39

valence issues 101, 124, 125, 144
value judgments 21
values 99
    common 60, 69 n., 101
    democratic 4
    key 165
    self-evident 101
Venice 229
Verdier, T. 67 n., 191
veto power 23, 53
Virginia School 4, 29
virtue 38
voter irrationality 124, 211
voter preferences 32, 41, 165, 180, 185
    incumbents more in tune with 122
    policies skewed towards 102
voter turnout 17–20
voter welfare 112, 113, 130, 149, 162,
    178, 182, 222
    congruent politicians care directly
        about 137
    contrasting with and without election
        140
    discounted value of 150
    dissonant politicians' behavior increases
        166
    enhanced 202
    equilibrium 189–91
    expected 189
    impact on 202, 209

improved 199, 205, 213
increased 190, 200, 201
maximizing 179, 184
non-partisan, reduced 127
partisan, impact on 128
raised 131, 195, 214
reduced 201
selection and incentive effects combine
    to determine 188
strictly higher 185
under pure moral hazard 192
voters/voting 37, 71–4, 90
    accountability of politicians 36, 115,
        158
    controlling 42
    coordination problems 43
    decisive 169
    delivering 'constituency service' 109
    gain from ill-discipline 112
    heterogeneous 125, 128
    homogeneous 103
    ignorant 104, 170
    incumbent performance as basis for 110
    informed 105–6, 133, 167, 204; poorly
        101, 104
    intimidation by politicians 101
    learning from past actions 106
    models unobservable to 103
    no significant change in patterns 113
    pandering to 139
    partisan 125, 126, 128
    probabilistic 33, 50 n., 125
    prospective 106
    randomness in 124
    rational 106, 142, 172
    restrictions on 42
    satisfactory theory of 42 n.
    targeting particular groups 144
    trade-off for 158
    vulnerable 134
    women securing the right 93
    see also non-partisan voters
voting intentions 125
voting rules 93, 181, 186
    voters cannot commit to 193

wages 153, 154
    attractive 104
    from holding office 109
    policies for politicians 170–2
Wagner, R. E. 211

Weberian view 14
Weder, B. 12
Weibull, J. 33 n.
Weingast, B. 33, 75, 76
Weissberg, R. 32 n.
welfare 59, 72
  consequences for 66, 104, 158, 162–4
  corruption will reduce 63
  direct 206
  discounted 112
  enhanced possibilities for 168
  enhancing 73
  equilibrium 189
  no necessary link between
    accountability and 101
  political equilibrium 191
  social decisions that fail specific criteria
    60
  see also social welfare; voter welfare
welfare economics 1, 23, 24, 95, 96
  conflicts with standard framework 30
  making the case for government
    interventionaccording to 45
  public choice critique of 25–6, 30, 191
welfare functions 89
welfare maximization 51, 55, 99

welfarism 21
well-being 25
  indicator of 29
  policies that promote 24
  societal measure of 21
Western Europe 5
Whinston, M. 62
Wicksell, K. 23, 30, 48, 52–3, 54, 55, 56,
    58, 63, 67, 70, 72, 73, 75, 77, 81, 87,
    88, 92, 96
willingness to pay 34
Wilson, J. D. 196 n.
Winer, S. 175 n.
wisdom 38
within-term cycles 141–3
Wittman, D. A. 33 n., 40 n., 47, 72 n., 147
World Bank 11

yardstick comparisons 197

Zaire 50
Zax, J. S. 198
Zimbabwe 102